Red Rosa

VERSO

ROSA
LUXEMBURG
STIFTUNG
NEW YORK OFFICE

The publication of this work was made possible with the support of the Rosa Luxemburg Stiftung—New York Office

**ROSA
LUXEMBURG
STIFTUNG**
NEW YORK OFFICE

First published by Verso 2015

7 9 10 8 6

Verso
UK: 6 Meard Street, London W1F 0EG
US: 20 Jay Street, Suite 1010, Brooklyn, NY 11201
www.versobooks.com

Verso is the imprint of New Left Books

ISBN-13: 978-1-78478-099-9
eISBN-13: 978-1-78478-101-9 (US)
eISBN-13: 978-1-78478-100-2 (UK)

British Library Cataloguing in Publication Data
A catalogue record for this book is available from the British Library

Library of Congress Cataloging-in-Publication Data
A catalog record for this book is available from the Library of Congress

Typeset by Sean Ford
Printed and bound by CPI Group (UK) Ltd, Croydon, CR0 4YY

Red Rosa

A graphic
biography of
Rosa Luxemburg

Written and illustrated by Kate Evans

Edited and with an afterword by Paul Buhle

The following is a fictional representation of factual events. Photographic source material has been used to create the characters and settings. Italicised passages of text are direct quotes from Luxemburg's writings; where these have been edited for brevity the quotations have been reproduced in full in the notes at the end of the book. In addition to this, many of the conversations between the characters have been created using Luxemburg's actual words; once again the original quotes, and context, are included at the end. In order to compress a life as rich as Rosa's into 179 pages, minor events have been omitted, some peripheral characters have been conflated, and in a few places the chronology of events has been reversed for dramatic effect. The notes contain a full explanation of any deviation from the historical record.

Saturday, March 18th, 1871. The people of Paris rise up and seize control of their city.

The ordinary women, men and children of the Paris Commune embark upon an open experiment in *liberté*, *egalité* and *fraternité*.

It will last for two months, until they are brutally massacred by French government forces.

Meanwhile, in the small
city of Zamość, Poland...

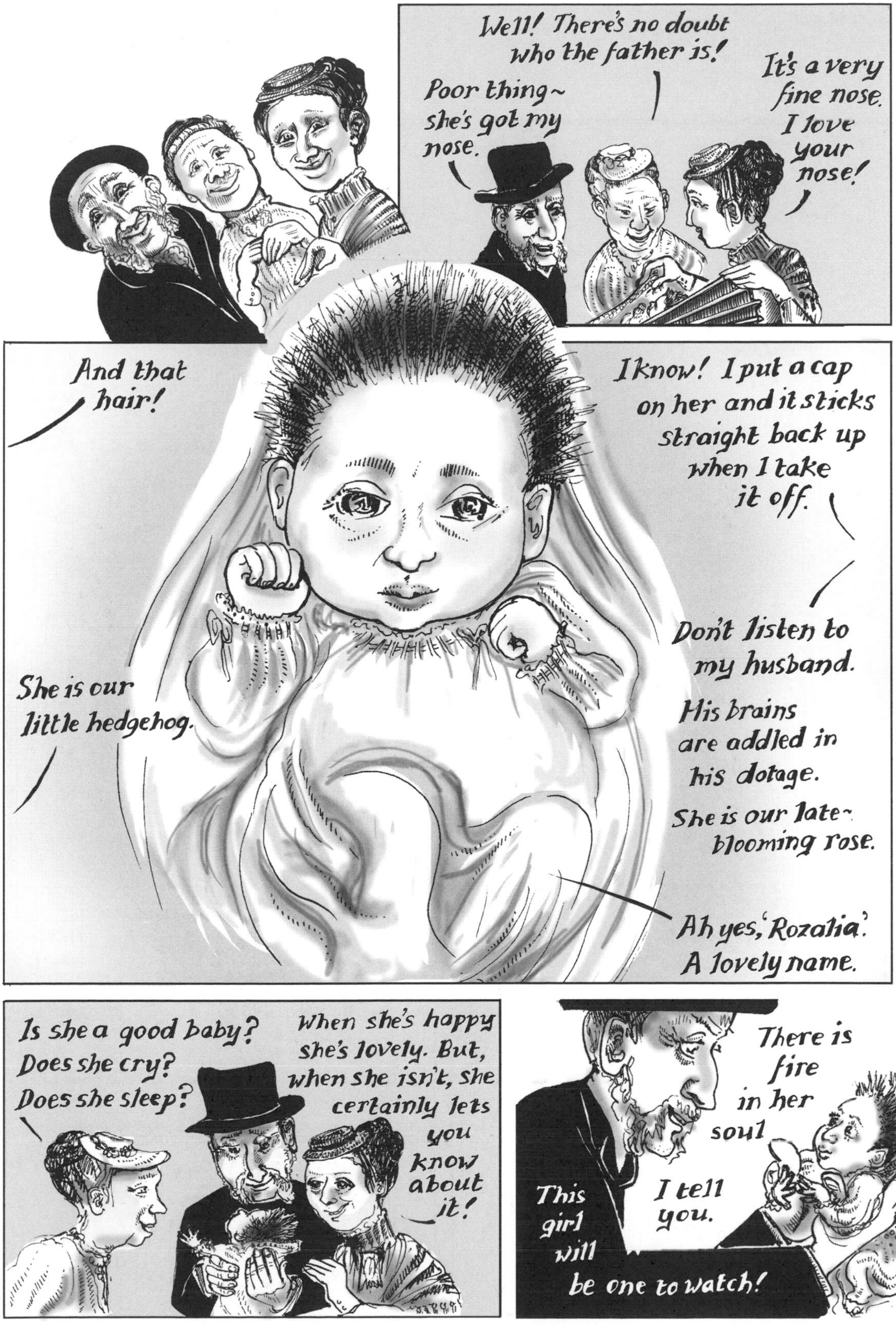
Well! There's no doubt who the father is!
Poor thing~ she's got my nose.
It's a very fine nose. I love your nose!
And that hair!
I know! I put a cap on her and it sticks straight back up when I take it off.
She is our little hedgehog.
Don't listen to my husband.
His brains are addled in his dotage.
She is our late-blooming rose.
Ah yes, 'Rozalia'. A lovely name.
Is she a good baby? Does she cry? Does she sleep?
When she's happy she's lovely. But, when she isn't, she certainly lets you know about it!
There is fire in her soul
I tell you.
This girl will be one to watch!

What do we know of Rosa Luxemburg's childhood?

We can only glean a few crumbs of information.

The family settle in Warsaw when she is three years old.

They rent an apartment on Złota Street, a respectable district, not in the Jewish quarter.

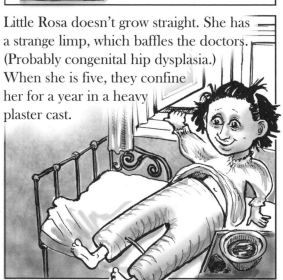

Little Rosa doesn't grow straight. She has a strange limp, which baffles the doctors. (Probably congenital hip dysplasia.) When she is five, they confine her for a year in a heavy plaster cast.

Little Rosa doesn't grow tall.

Her disproportionately small adult frame hints at childhood malnutrition.

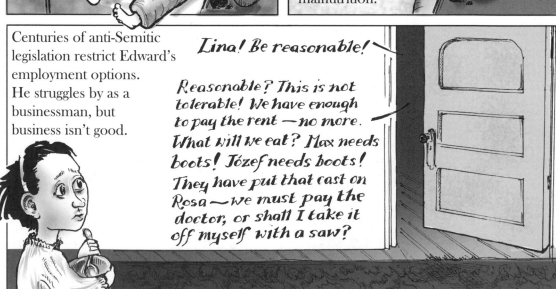

Centuries of anti-Semitic legislation restrict Edward's employment options. He struggles by as a businessman, but business isn't good.

Lina! Be reasonable!

Reasonable? This is not tolerable! We have enough to pay the rent — no more. What will we eat? Max needs boots! Józef needs boots! They have put that cast on Rosa — we must pay the doctor, or shall I take it off myself with a saw?

Little Rosa, everyone's baby, is showered with love and affection...

...encouragement and enthusiasm.

The Luxemburgs are financially poor but culturally rich.

And they are firm believers in betterment through education.

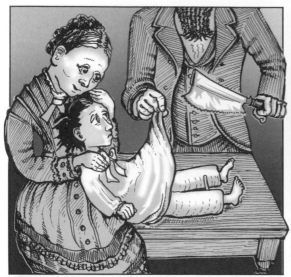

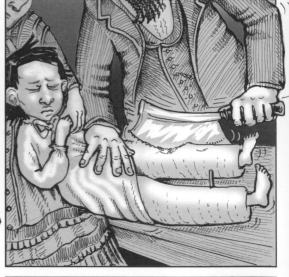

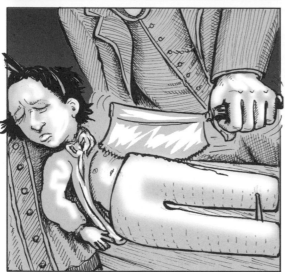

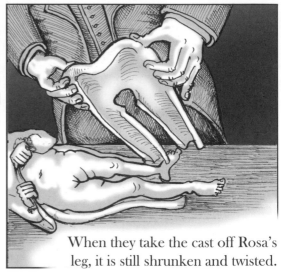

When they take the cast off Rosa's leg, it is still shrunken and twisted.

She will be crippled for life.

Perhaps if you massage the leg it will grow.

And now, good lady, my fee.

At ten, Rosa can write and speak Russian, the language of the occupying rulers; Polish, the language of her country; Hebrew, the language of her religion; and German too, for good measure.

The best school is reserved for Russian children...

...but she wins a scholarship to the Second Gymnasium.

Only a few places are allocated to Jews. They set the bar higher for them.

Little Rosa studies hard.

She can't afford to trip up.

Mama! My poetry assignment was to write a poem for the visit of the German Kaiser. So listen.

Yes, dear.

'So we see you at last, mighty man of the West.'

'Don't go pretending I'm coming to pay tribute Because I don't give a fig about getting honours from people like you.'

'As to politics, I'm wet behind the ears so I won't waste time on a long speech. But there's one thing you shouldn't forget, my dear Wilhelm.'

'Tell that creeping toad Von Bismarck that he shouldn't wear a hole in the trousers of peace, and thereby shame them.

'You do that for Europe, oh Kaiser of the West!'

Your school assignment.

Dear oh dear oh dear.

Edward, when you said this girl would go far, I disagree. There's only a short drop on the hangman's noose.

Rosa's parents' concerns are real. There is no political freedom in Tsarist Poland. Dissent will not be tolerated.

When Rosa is fourteen, four socialists are hanged on the slopes of the Warsaw Citadel.

Intended to deter new recruits to the socialist cause, this simply piques Rosa's interest.

I wish I had my own pony. Papa says I can ride my sister's, but it's not the same.

I know.

Warsaw is the centre of industry for the Russian empire.

Absolute wealth and utter destitution jostle in uneasy juxtaposition.

Once Rosa's eyes have opened, how can she fail to see?

Of course, the poor don't feel things the same way that we do. We should suffer dreadfully if we had to live like that, but they really don't mind!

Quite so!

I WANT TO BURDEN THE CONSCIENCE OF THE AFFLUENT WITH ALL THE SUFFERING AND ALL THE HIDDEN BITTER TEARS

When Rosa graduates from school, the gold medal that her stellar academic performance merits is withheld from her 'on account of her rebellious attitude'.

All avenues for further education are barred to women. What will she do?

This little fifteen-year-old slip of a girl must have caused quite a stir.

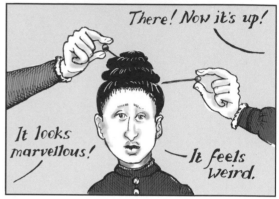

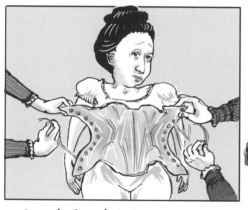

Rosa faces so many restrictions.

As a woman, she is the legal property firstly of her father, and then of her husband.

Women are commodities, and, to trade well on the marriage market, Rosa must have...

...a fine dowry...

...or, failing that, graceful deportment, feminine charm, submissiveness and eagerness to please...

...or, as a last resort, strength, stamina for menial manual labour, and good childbearing hips.

A prodigious intellect, Rosa's main asset, doesn't enter into the balance sheet when calculating female worth.

She is Jewish. Anti-Semitism is everywhere. The Tsarist authorities operate an apartheid state, with Poles 'of the Mosaic faith' confined to ghettos and shtetls.

PEOPLE OF THE JEWISH FAITH ARE RESTRICTED TO THE PALE OF JEWISH SETTLEMENT

ALL JEWS ARE EXPELLED FROM MOSCOW AND ST PETERSBURG

MORTGAGES MAY NOT BE ISSUED TO JEWS

THE RIGHT OF JEWS TO SELL ALCOHOL IS HEREBY REVOKED

JEWS MAY NOT OPERATE IN BUSINESS ON SUNDAYS OR CHRISTIAN HOLIDAYS

THE QUOTA OF JEWS IN EDUCATION IS RESTRICTED TO 10%

JEWS MAY NOT PARTICIPATE IN LOCAL ELECTIONS

The secret police provoke pogroms — a racist mob rages down Złota Street. Women in Warsaw are raped and men are murdered for being Jewish.

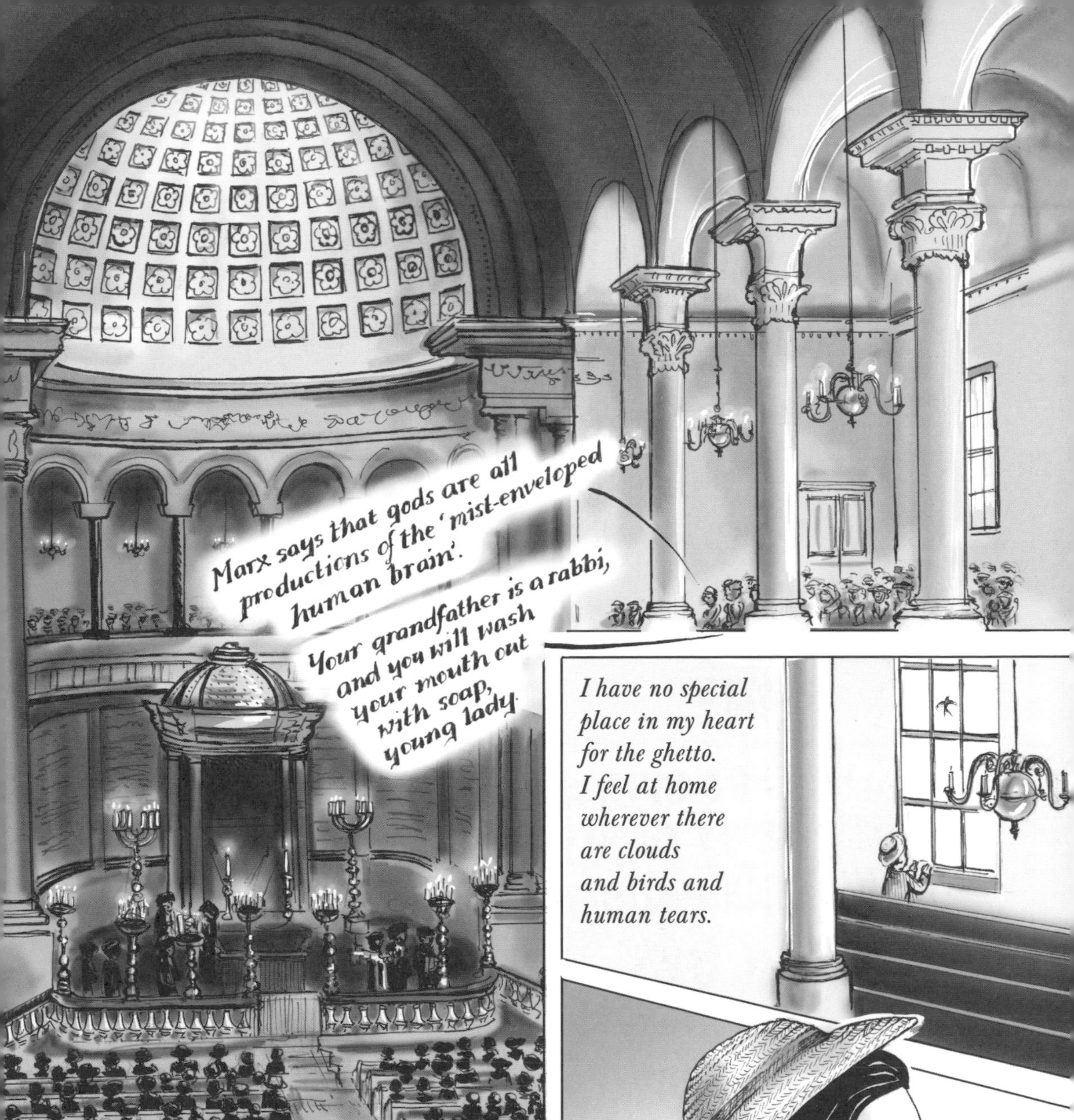
Marx says that gods are all productions of the 'mist-enveloped human brain'.
Your grandfather is a rabbi, and you will wash your mouth out with soap, young lady.
I have no special place in my heart for the ghetto. I feel at home wherever there are clouds and birds and human tears.
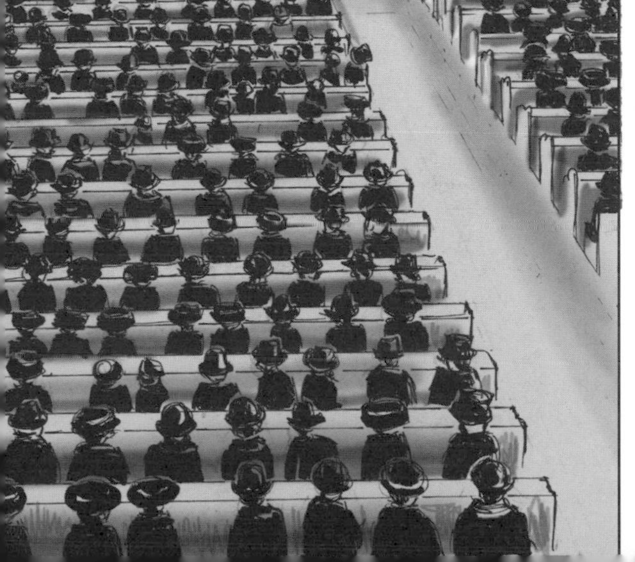

Rosa's lack of religious faith cannot buy her freedom. Her cultural identity is written on the features of her face. She will always be seen as a Jew.

We can see how Rosa's life is mapped out: duty, subservience, religion and obedience.

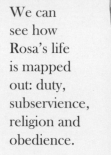

Rosa doesn't see that. She escapes into a whole new world. Revolutionary literature.

What are you reading, Rosa?

Hirsch's Commentary on the Torah.

Very good.

Hey little sister. What are you really reading?

The Communist Manifesto!

What are you reading now, Rosa?

Poetry, Mama.

That's not what you're really reading, is it?

Nope. Wage Labour and Capital.

I'm reading A Young Lady's Companion, Mama.

Marvellous.

Do you want to know what I'm really reading?

KARL MARX Das Kapital

Rosa, what's the book about?

Das Kapital? Mm, interesting question.

It's about things ~ about everything we have. Take this salt, for example. It has two properties. It has a use-value. I can use it. I can sprinkle it on my food...

...and it also has an exchange-value. Say I've had enough salt — I don't want my food too salty — I could take my salt and swap it with you for some pepper.

Everything has a use-value and an exchange-value, but these intrinsic properties are mutually incompatible.

She's so clever.

It's wasted on a—

BOOF!

If I want to use my salt by eating it, then I can't exchange it with you. And if I want to exchange it, then I can't eat it.

Two sides of the same coin?

We're coming to coins in a minute.

Different use-values have different qualities. We use salt for its saltiness and pepper for its pepperiness.

ACHOO!

Different exchange-values have different quantities. It doesn't matter what it is, only how much you have.

If I had enough salt I could swap it for your pocket watch.

I'm not sure I want that much salt, Rosa.

PARP

Aha! That's where money comes in.

Once money is involved, anything can be exchanged for anything and everything becomes a commodity.

Let's look at simple exchange. Pretend this is you...

...and this is me...

...and you have a watch...

...and I have some salt...

I want a watch. Do you want a massive pile of salt?

No.

Oh.

Now let's introduce money. Give me a coin, Max.

It's an expensive business, being your brother.

I'll sell my salt to someone else.

Would you like to buy some salt?

Yes. I'll give you one gold coin for it.

How much for the watch?

One gold coin.

Here it is.

The dazzling money form. It seems like a good idea. It seems as if it works for us...

...but instead we work for it.

This book isn't just about things —it's really about people. What makes a thing 'worth something'? It's the human labour that goes into creating it.

When we buy a watch we pay for the work done, first by the gold-miner and then the jeweller. But we can't see it. We say that the thing itself has 'worth' when really we mean 'work'.

Before we had money, people related to each other directly. They recognised the efforts, the needs, the desires of other people as just as valid as their own.

How are you?

Do you need anything?

Money changed that.

I don't know if I like you. How much money do you have?

Here's Marx's phrase: We have 'material relations between persons and social relations between things'.

We treat objects like people. We desire them. We fetishise them. We treat them as valuable.

We expect them to make us happy.

I love the shiny watch!

I do love the shiny watch, Rosa. I'm taking it back before you pour salt in it.

We treat people like objects. A person isn't a person anymore.

He's a jeweller... or a miner...

a beggar... or a boss.

It's money that makes inequality possible.

... In fact, it makes it inevitable.

I have a lovely bowl of soup. Look! There's a starving person — that's their fault for not having money — they should work harder.

When I sold that salt to buy the watch I made that transaction to satisfy human needs. I needed a watch, and my brother needed money.

I don't actually need any money, Rosa.

Yes, you do. I've still got your coin!

Once money is involved people can exchange goods in order to make more money.

This guy bought my salt not because he wanted salt, but so he could sell it again...

...at a profit.

Money is power ~ it really is. It's the embodiment of all the effort that all the people put into making all those things.

And now one person owns it. And he wants more.

He can't really make money by buying and selling things — sometimes he'd win and sometimes he'd lose.

There's only one commodity he can buy that always creates a profit.

Human labour power.

I sold my watch to buy food. Now it's all gone and I'm hungry.

Behold! I have built a factory!

That's a loaf of bread, Rosa.

It's symbolic, OK?

I'll give it a chimney.

That's celery.

Oh do be quiet.

How much do you need, little worker, to pay your rent and feed your family?

Six kopecks a day.

Come work for me! I'll pay you six kopecks a day. Your troubles are over.

Now you work in the factory, turning stuff into things. In just six hours you create six kopecks' profit for the factory owner. This is the money he pays you in wages. But the day isn't over yet. No, you labour for eight hours more. Now you're making 'Surplus value', not for you but for the factory owner.

This is capital.

I have more money. I'll buy more machinery for my factory. But I need more workers. I'll employ your sister. Women are cheaper. I'll pay her just two kopecks a day.

It's the way of the world, Rosa. It's human nature.

Really?

'Nature does not produce on the one side owners of money, and on the other men possessing nothing but their labour power. This relation has no natural basis, neither is its social basis one that is common to all historical periods.'

21

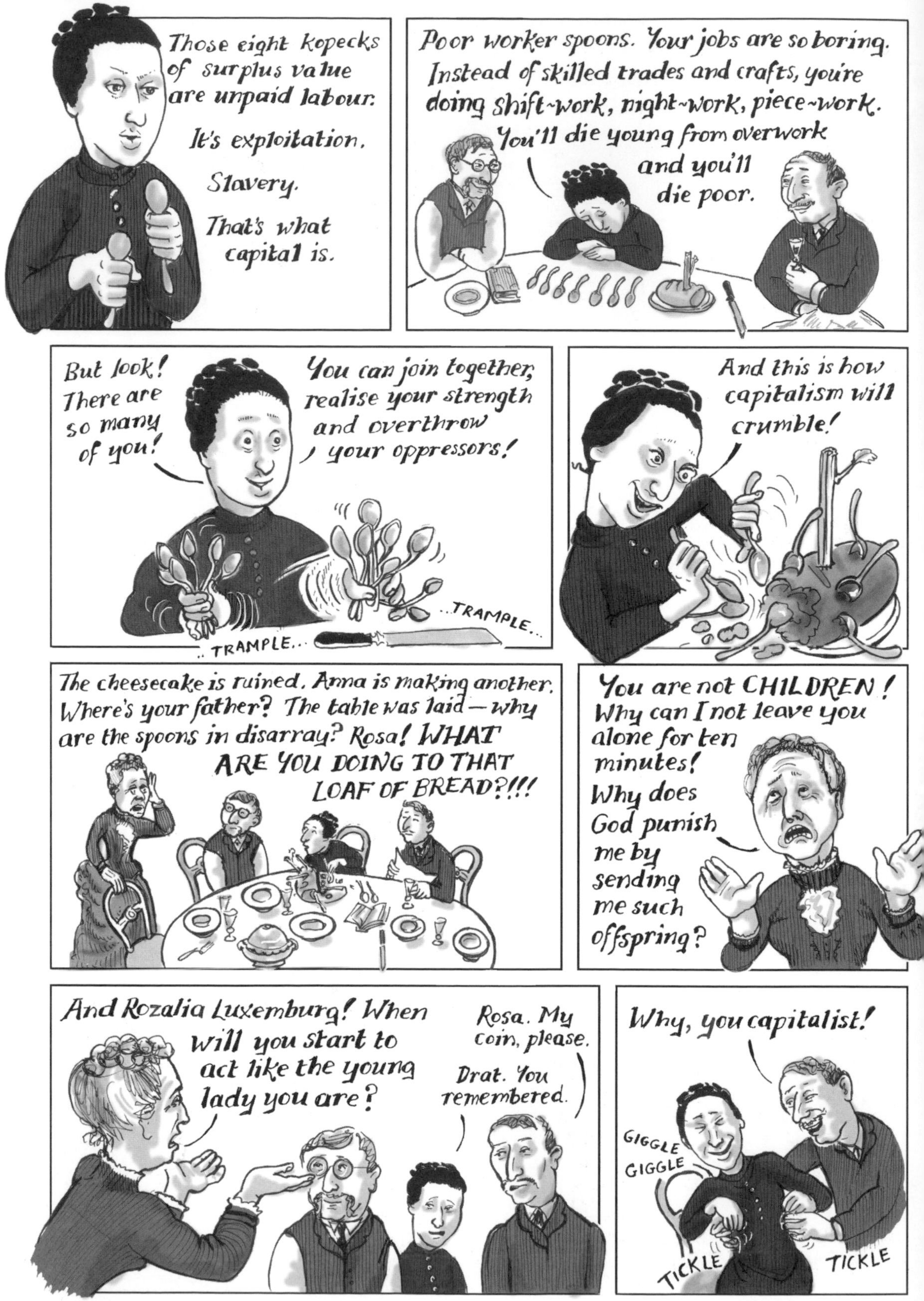
Those eight kopecks of surplus value are unpaid labour.
It's exploitation.
Slavery.
That's what capital is.
Poor worker spoons. Your jobs are so boring. Instead of skilled trades and crafts, you're doing shift-work, night-work, piece-work.
You'll die young from overwork and you'll die poor.
But look! There are so many of you!
You can join together, realise your strength and overthrow your oppressors!
..TRAMPLE...
..TRAMPLE..
And this is how capitalism will crumble!
The cheesecake is ruined. Anna is making another. Where's your father? The table was laid — why are the spoons in disarray? Rosa! WHAT ARE YOU DOING TO THAT LOAF OF BREAD?!!!
You are not CHILDREN! Why can I not leave you alone for ten minutes!
Why does God punish me by sending me such offspring?
And Rozalia Luxemburg! When will you start to act like the young lady you are?
Rosa. My coin, please.
Drat. You remembered.
Why, you capitalist!
GIGGLE
GIGGLE
TICKLE
TICKLE

After two short years, Rosa's political activities are curtailed.

Rosa. I'm so sorry. You can't come here again.

We've had a tip~off. The police are becoming interested in you.

To survive here, we have to keep changing our identities. We're continuously moving.
We have to be anonymous, subtle — and, Rosa, you're not.

You're very obvious. There's only one tiny, limping, Jewish girl spreading the socialist word.
It's only a matter of time before they cart you off to Siberia...
Or worse...

Mama! Papa! You must send me to Switzerland!

It's the only way!

What?

Why?

I can study there! The University of Zurich admits women ~ it's the only one that does!

Come! I must! I simply must!

23

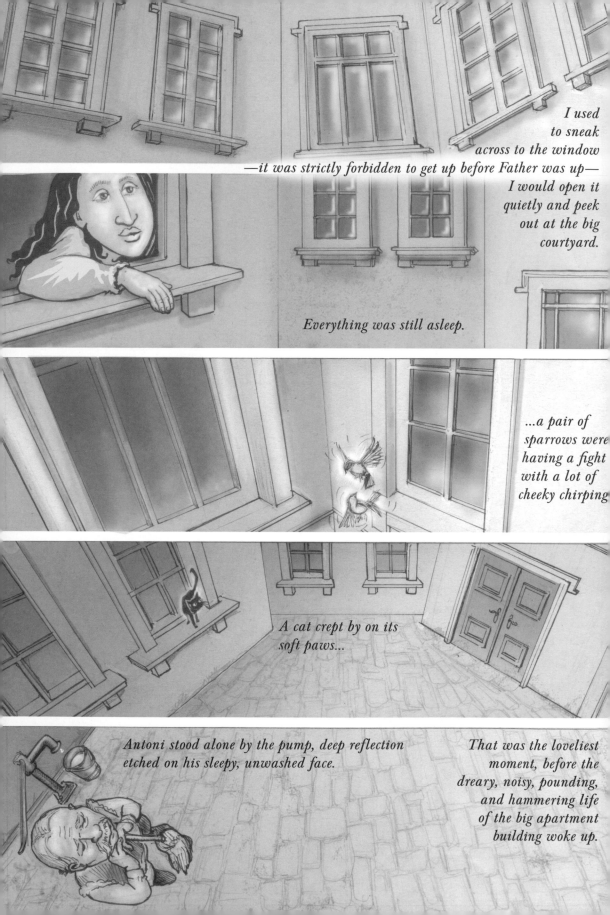

I used to sneak across to the window —it was strictly forbidden to get up before Father was up— I would open it quietly and peek out at the big courtyard.

Everything was still asleep.

...a pair of sparrows were having a fight with a lot of cheeky chirping

A cat crept by on its soft paws...

Antoni stood alone by the pump, deep reflection etched on his sleepy, unwashed face.

That was the loveliest moment, before the dreary, noisy, pounding, and hammering life of the big apartment building woke up.

I firmly believed that 'life', that is, 'real life', was somewhere far away, off beyond the rooftops...

...and way up high swam sweet-smelling clouds with a touch of pink, before dissolving into the grey sky over the metropolis.

...the window panes glittered with the early morning gold of the young sun...

The solemn stillness of the morning hour spread above the triviality of the courtyard's paved surface...

You alone will make our family's name famous.

Rosa Luxemburg alone.

We can admire her audacity, but we should also commend her courage.

To head off to a new country for a new life
requires a tremendous leap of faith.

27

Switzerland
Winter
1889

VERSITÄT
ZÜRICH

UNIVERSITÄT
ZÜRICH

Rosa's first loves are botany and zoology.

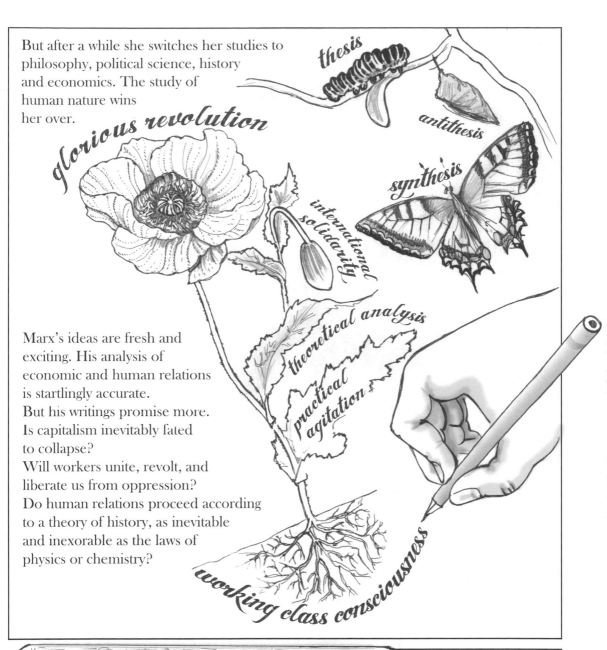

But after a while she switches her studies to philosophy, political science, history and economics. The study of human nature wins her over.

glorious revolution

thesis

antithesis

synthesis

international solidarity

theoretical analysis

practical agitation

Marx's ideas are fresh and exciting. His analysis of economic and human relations is startlingly accurate.
But his writings promise more.
Is capitalism inevitably fated to collapse?
Will workers unite, revolt, and liberate us from oppression?
Do human relations proceed according to a theory of history, as inevitable and inexorable as the laws of physics or chemistry?

working class consciousness

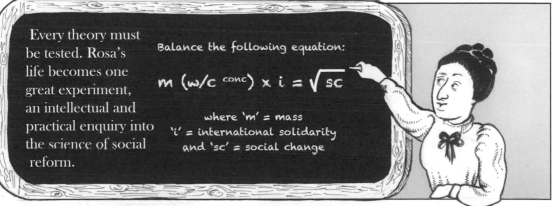

Every theory must be tested. Rosa's life becomes one great experiment, an intellectual and practical enquiry into the science of social reform.

Balance the following equation:

$$m\,(w/c^{\,conc}) \times i = \sqrt{sc}$$

where 'm' = mass
'i' = international solidarity
and 'sc' = social change

On the personal as well as the political level, Rosa proves herself ready for radical change.

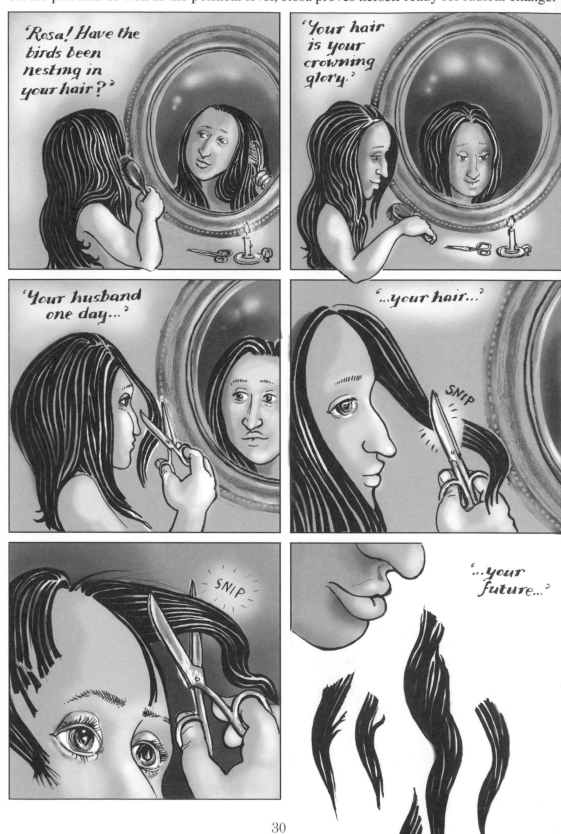

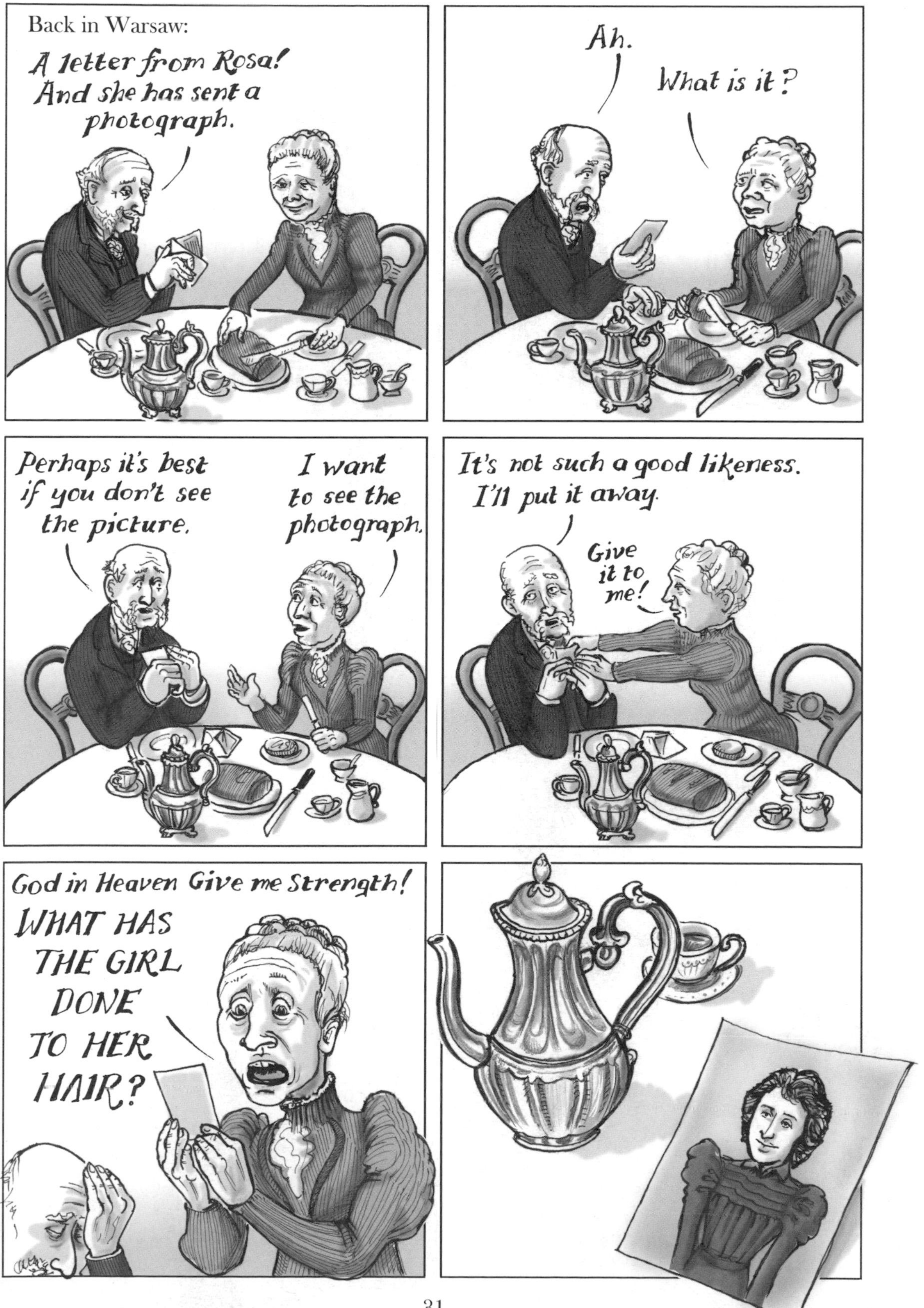

Back in Warsaw:
A letter from Rosa! And she has sent a photograph.
Ah.
What is it?
Perhaps it's best if you don't see the picture.
I want to see the photograph.
It's not such a good likeness. I'll put it away.
Give it to me!
God in Heaven Give me Strength!
WHAT HAS THE GIRL DONE TO HER HAIR?

The cream of the Russian socialist movement is in exile in Zurich, and Rosa undertakes some extra-curricular activities.

The revolutionary intelligentsia must spread scientific socialism among the workers and, together, storm the stronghold of autocracy!

Mr Plekanhov? Rosa Luxemburg.

Enchanted, I'm sure.

I wanted to speak with you about the founding of the Russian Social Democracy Movement.

Another time.

He doesn't want to share his precious pearls of wisdom with the youth.

I tried to set up a publishing venture with him, but he wasn't up for it.

Oh.

Rosa Luxemburg.

Enchanted, I'm sure.

What's your name?

Er... Jan Tyska.

Morning, Mr Grosovski.

Morning.

What's your real name?

You can tell me. I'm not the secret police.

Leonie

Really?

No, really Leo.

Leo what?

Jogiches.

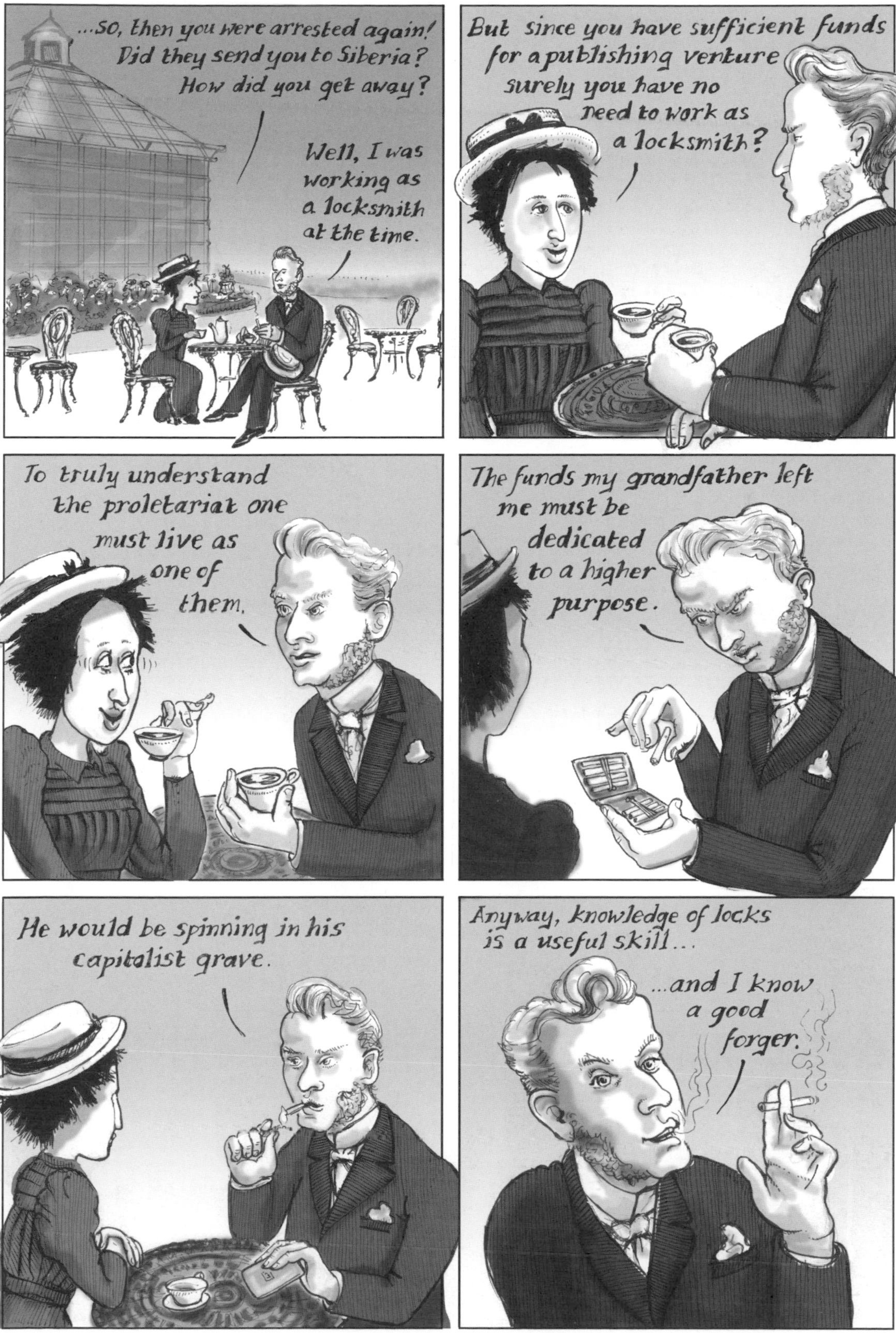
...so, then you were arrested again! Did they send you to Siberia? How did you get away?
Well, I was working as a locksmith at the time.
But since you have sufficient funds for a publishing venture surely you have no need to work as a locksmith?
To truly understand the proletariat one must live as one of them.
The funds my grandfather left me must be dedicated to a higher purpose.
He would be spinning in his capitalist grave.
Anyway, knowledge of locks is a useful skill...
...and I know a good forger.

The situation in Lithuania, where I am from, is closely allied to that of Poland. Should socialists struggle for national independence?

Poland can never achieve a classless state with powerful capitalist neigbours Prussia and Russia waiting to crush socialist aspirations.

Achieving independence under capitalism will simply hand power to the Polish bourgeoisie!

Far better to work for international working-class solidarity!

The need for revolution breaks through national boundaries!

Yet the Communist Manifesto itself calls for Polish national emancipation.

The First International declared that Polish independence would strike a blow against capitalism.

But it would do no such thing!

Resisting capitalist annexation and imperialist war is not the same thing as dismantling capitalism!

One does not flow from the other...

And why this slavish adherence to Marx's dictates?

We are not his disciples!

Question everything!

Rosa Luxemburg and Leo Jogiches. Together they are ready to conquer the world (in the name of the proletariat, of course).

She has never met anyone like him. Knowledgeable, dedicated, driven, meticulous, mysterious, a gold mine of information.

Beautiful.

And he's a nice Jewish boy.

In their life together Rosa will value Leo's thoroughness and intellectual rigour. And he will need her too...

You arrived in the evening with groceries...

...I ran downstairs with the lamp...

Careful, Rosa.

I'll drop the eggs.

...and we struggled together dragging the heavy packages upstairs...

We unloaded them on the table...

...oranges, cheese, salami and a little cake in a paper wrapper...

We never had a more fabulous supper than on that little table in an empty room with the balcony door open and the sweet aroma coming up from the garden.

You were cooking eggs in the frying pan with great skill...

CHUGGACHUGGACHUGGACHUGGACHUGGACHU

...from the distance in the darkness we could hear the train to Milan going over the bridge with a tremendous clatter

Pick me up and carry me to bed

— But you're too heavy

The extent of Rosa's knowledge is startling. How did she learn to control her own fertility? How was this secret women's wisdom transmitted from prostitutes to university graduates? We will never know. But she knew what or when or how to avoid pregnancy, and she used that knowledge for her own private pleasure.

Little bird

My precious gold

She couldn't marry Leo. How can one marry a man who has six different names?

But she secretly became, on her own terms, his wife.

How to be a Revolutionary Socialist

Study The secrets of historical development can be unlocked through rigorous intellectual analysis.

Quite.

Rosa's speciality is economics. She embarks upon a dissertation on Polish industrialisation.

...the average monthly wage for men is 20 rubles, 15.3 for women... and for children, 8.8 rubles... ...and annual coal production is... ...express that as a percentage...

...but those figures are in English pounds. What is the rate of exchange?

(It is still used today as the main reference book on the topic.)

The capitalist method strives to materially bind together the most distant places, little by little, to make them economically dependent on each other and eventually transform the entire world into one productive mechanism.

Very good.

I am clever! Give me a kiss!

One cannot let oneself become distracted. There can be no let-up in the pace.

Jo-jo I'm so poorly.

But you **must** complete the article 'Step by Step Towards a History of the Bourgeois Classes in Poland'!

Darling, don't worry. It's OK. You can do it.

Travel

The Polish library in Paris is a valuable resource.

My only one, my Bobo, when will I see you? I miss you so much my soul is simply thirsting!

Today I saw the Arc de Triomphe, the Eiffel Tower and the Grand Opera. I'm deafened by the noise...

...and how many beautiful women there are here! Really all of them are beautiful, or at least they seem to be...

No! Under no circumstance will you come here! You stay in Zurich!

But always ***keep one step ahead of the police***

Write back to me with caution. If necessary, use a code. There's a police agent here who regularly visits the concierge.

Travel broadens the mind. It can also expand the waistline.

Form a party

The Association of Polish Socialists insists upon chasing a pipe dream of national independence.

Theoretical inconsistency. — Oi vavoy!

The time has come to campaign under our own banner!

How about 'Social Democracy of the Kingdom of Poland'!

and Lithuania!

Very well 'Poland and Lithuania'. How does it sound?

Very grand! Very good!

Speak at the Socialist International

Why speak of 'national self-determination'? Under capitalism the nation does not exist! Instead we have classes with antagonistic interests and rights. The ruling class and the enlightened proletariat can never form one undifferentiated national whole.

Strong words.

Such magnetism!

Who is she?

I don't know, but she's got my vote!

(These conferences promote international solidarity and foment world revolution.)

41

Build the membership

That's Leo's job.

Write the propaganda

That's Rosa's. *...With all these articles plus one by Krichevsky, that still leaves seven columns unfilled. Let's have one on women and one and a half on wages. I'll have to write another lead article, a political one. My head feels quite empty — but I'll write it anyhow.*

Although Leo will find fault with it.

I checked the proofs. You didn't make any improvements to the article on social patriots.

I rewrote that article six times! If I ask for changes at this stage, the typesetter has to break open the whole issue.

It is a laborious process, writing, editing...

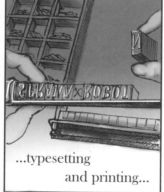

...typesetting and printing...

...but the power of these flimsy, smuggled newssheets is enormous. It is the only way to spread the socialist message among the people back home.

Warsaw, May 1897.

Parcel, sir

Thank you, young man. Is it a book? It is! It is!

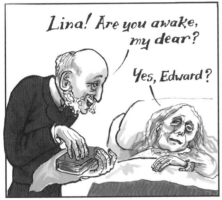

Lina! Are you awake, my dear?

Yes, Edward?

Here it is! Her doctoral thesis! 'The Industrial Development of Poland'. Published by Dunker and Humblot!

Oh! It's marvellous!

And there's a note: 'from your loving daughter Rosa, Doctor of Public Law and Economic Affairs.'

Dr Rosa Luxemburg!

Aaaagh!

More morphine, mama?

Please, Anna.

Oh, I am so glad to have lived to see this day.

43

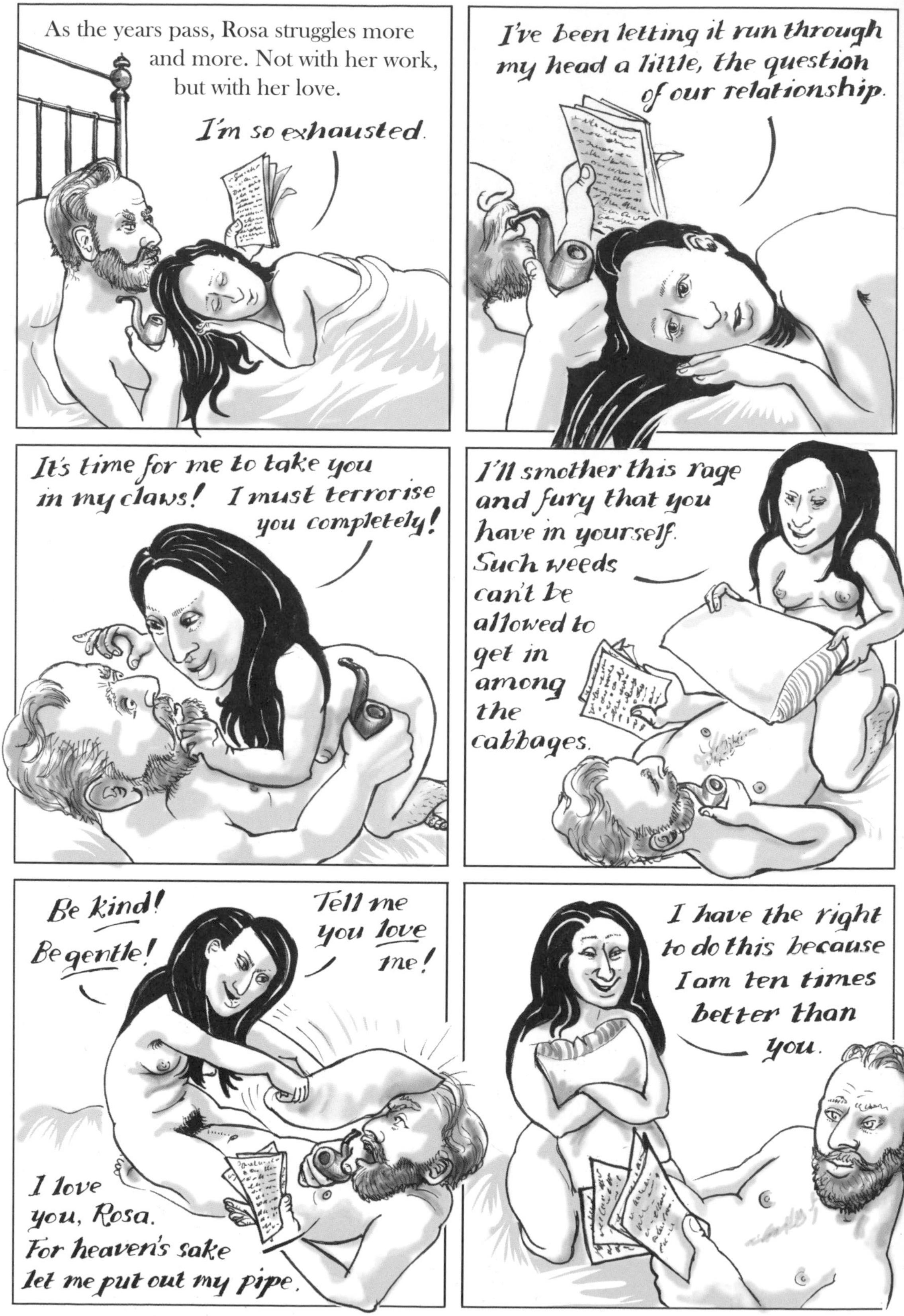
As the years pass, Rosa struggles more and more. Not with her work, but with her love.
I'm so exhausted.
I've been letting it run through my head a little, the question of our relationship.
It's time for me to take you in my claws! I must terrorise you completely!
I'll smother this rage and fury that you have in yourself. Such weeds can't be allowed to get in among the cabbages.
Be kind! Be gentle!
Tell me you love me!
I love you, Rosa. For heaven's sake let me put out my pipe.
I have the right to do this because I am ten times better than you.

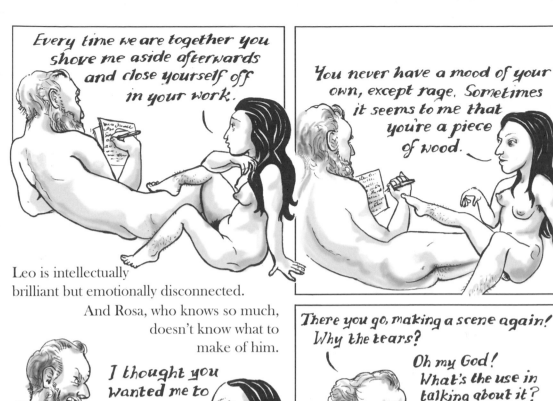

Leo is intellectually
brilliant but emotionally disconnected.
   And Rosa, who knows so much,
        doesn't know what to
             make of him.

Berlin
1898

New beginnings.

I have arrived here as a complete stranger and all alone, to 'conquer Berlin'.

And having laid eyes on it, I now feel anxious in the face of its cold power.

The city makes a most unfavourable impression on me: tasteless, massive, a proper barracks. And the Prussians with their arrogant demeanour, as if each one had swallowed the stick used for beating him.

But a Johnny-without-a-country, such as I am, must make do, even with a German Fatherland.

A revolution is made of a million tiny moments. Once again Rosa turns her life around...

...and in Germany she finds herself a home.

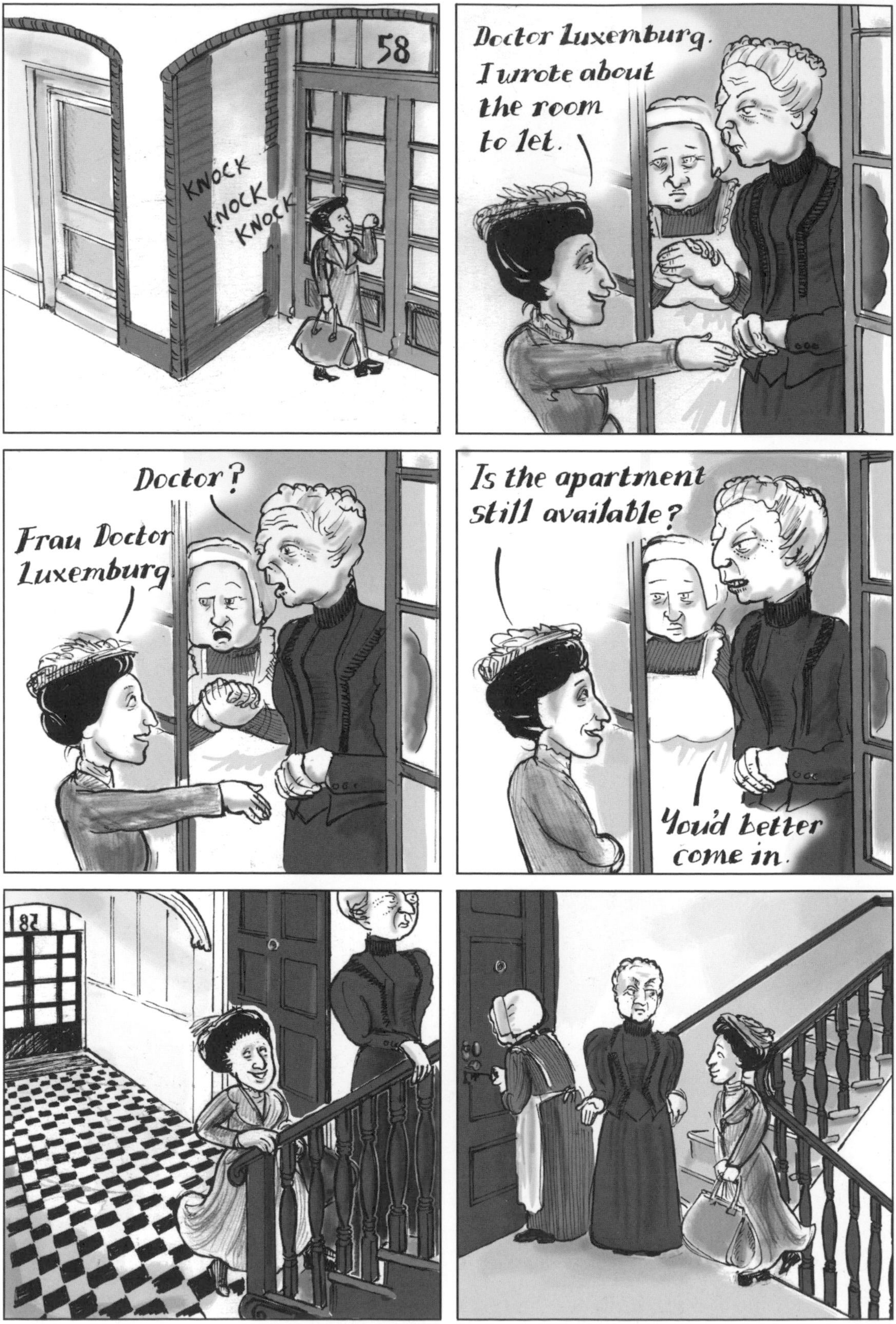
58
KNOCK
KNOCK
KNOCK
Doctor Luxemburg. I wrote about the room to let.
Doctor?
Frau Doctor Luxemburg.
Is the apartment still available?
You'd better come in.

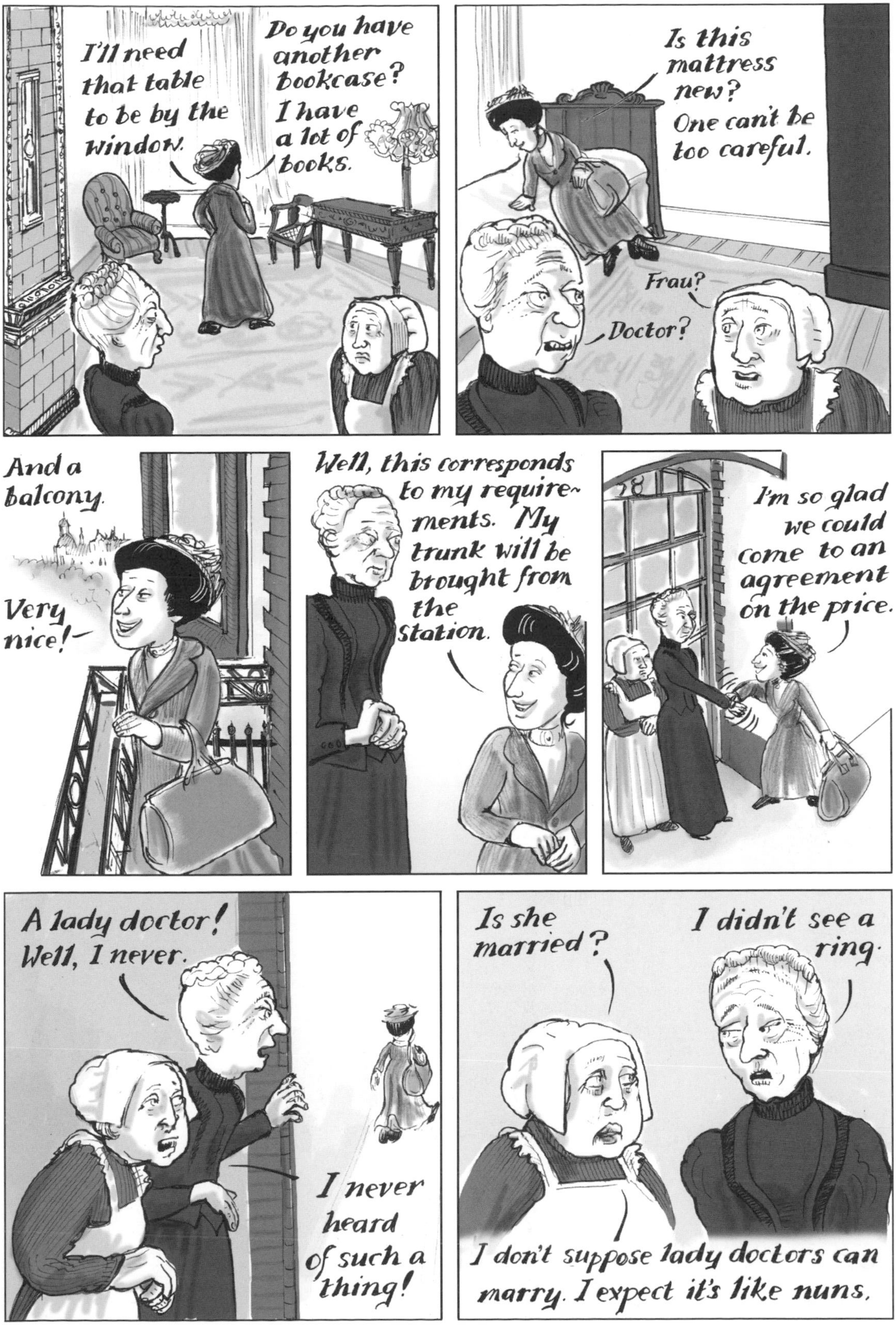

I'll need that table to be by the window.
Do you have another bookcase? I have a lot of books.
Is this mattress new? One can't be too careful.
Frau?
Doctor?
And a balcony.
Very nice!
Well, this corresponds to my requirements. My trunk will be brought from the station.
I'm so glad we could come to an agreement on the price.
A lady doctor! Well, I never.
I never heard of such a thing!
Is she married?
I didn't see a ring.
I don't suppose lady doctors can marry. I expect it's like nuns.

But no! Here we see the young bride-to-be on the morning of her wedding.

Oh where is he? He can't be late for this!

Nervously, the young couple enter their names into the civil register.

Rosa gazes into the eyes of the man who has granted her everything her heart desires...

Do you Rozalia Luxemburg...

...take this man, Gustav Lübeck, as your lawful wedded husband?

I do.

German citizenship!

Your papers.

Germany! Now the world's most industrialised country! With the fastest-growing socialist movement! The newly legalised Social Democratic Party (SPD) has more than 100,000 members. Ninety different socialist daily newspapers provide plenty of opportunities for Rosa to make a living as a journalist and theoretician. To work to spark world revolution here in Germany? That's worth marrying a complete stranger for.

I'll pay the photographer.

Do thank your mother for arranging this.

Of course.

Goodbye then.

Good bye.

The SPD is committed to the collapse of capitalism. Nearly 1.8 million men voted SPD in the last Reichstag elections, almost a quarter of the electorate. And 1898 is an election year...

Herr Auer? Doctor Luxemburg.

I remember you from the International.

I am here to take an active part in the work of the SPD, and to this end I have obtained German nationality.

Really? That is marvellous!

Now where will my talents be of the most use? I should address the Polish coal miners of Upper Silesia. A word spoken in Polish has quite a different effect from the 'foreign' German tongue.

Upper Silesia? Are you sure?

Educating conservative Catholic mine workers about socialism won't be easy.

I won't know I can do it unless I try. I'll have to take a chance and step out on the ice.

I want to affect people like a clap of thunder...

...to inflame their minds with the breadth of my vision, the strength of my conviction and the power of my expression.

Upper Silesia, June 9th, 1898.

May I present Frau Doctor Luxemburg!

51

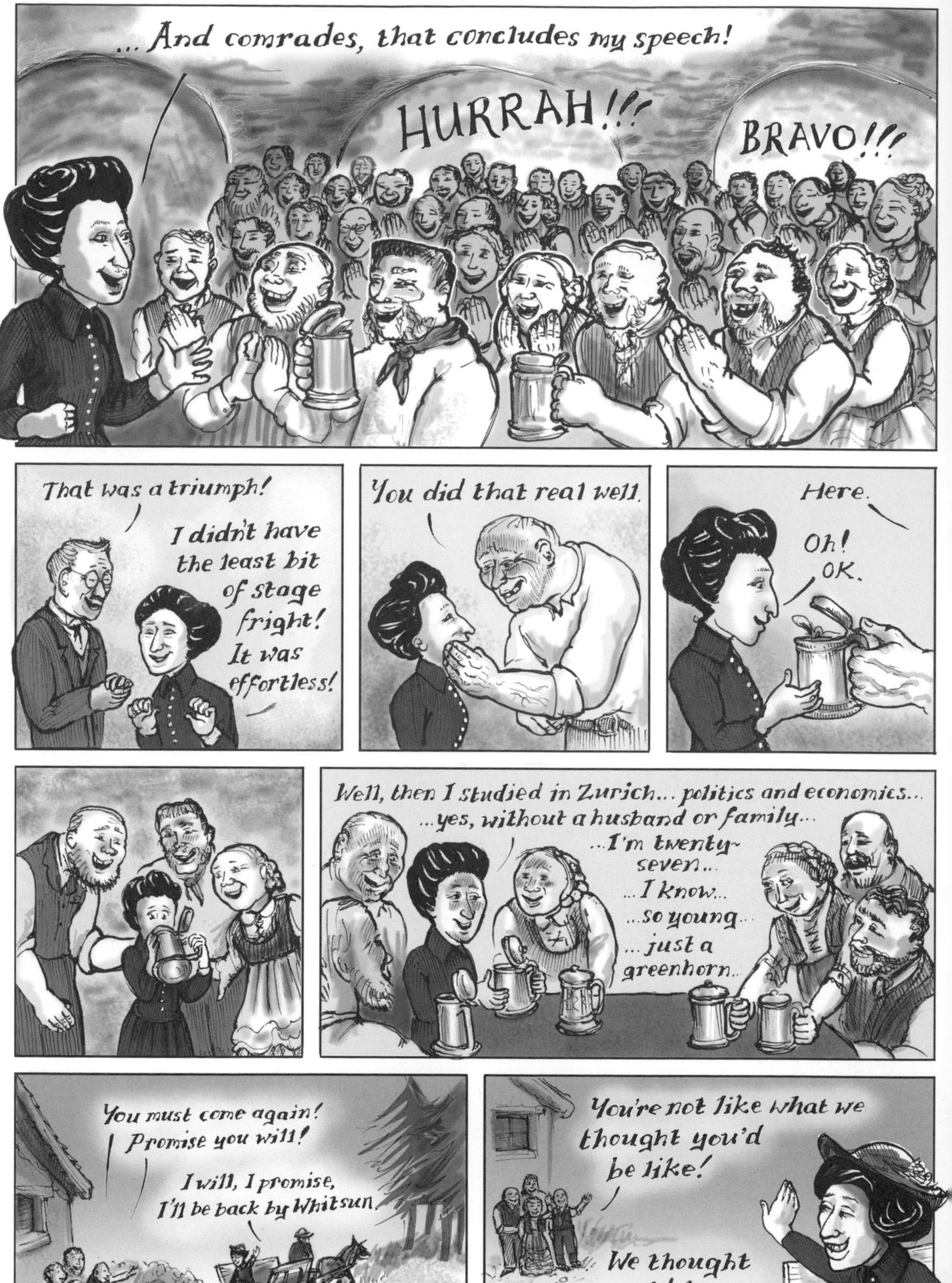
...And comrades, that concludes my speech!
HURRAH!!!
BRAVO!!!
That was a triumph!
I didn't have the least bit of stage fright! It was effortless!
You did that real well.
Here.
Oh! OK.
Well, then I studied in Zurich... politics and economics...
...yes, without a husband or family...
...I'm twenty-seven...
...I know...
...so young...
...just a greenhorn...
You must come again! Promise you will!
I will, I promise, I'll be back by Whitsun.
You're not like what we thought you'd be like!
We thought you'd be old and fat!

June 16th, 1898.
27% of the electorate vote SPD!
More than two million votes!
But the class bias in the German
suffrage system sees
this translated
into just 14%
of the seats in
the Reichstag.

In any case, the Reichstag doesn't run
the country. The king, Kaiser Wilhelm,
holds absolute power — the Reichstag
just ratifies the budget. All the SPD
delegation can do
is make a solemn
annual show of
refusing to
do that.

Rosa was more interested in the election
campaign than the result. She can't even
vote, let alone hold political office.
She has other
fish to fry.

PFFFFT

SMASH

'The Problems with Socialism' by
Eduard Bernstein? I'll tell you what
the problem is with socialism! The
problem is this attempt by a petit-
bourgeois
idiot to
redefine
the direction
of our party.

How **dare**
he call
himself a
socialist?

Reform or Revolution? Either? Or?
These methods cannot be picked
from the counter of history as
    one chooses hot or
    cold sausages!
    They are different
    moments in the
    same class struggle!

Bernstein's article is
crucially important.
It marks a potential
new direction for the
socialist movement.

I'm going to pull this
article to pieces.
Let me get my pen.

And in posing the question
'What is this socialism that
we are fighting for?'
Rosa helps us see
exactly what this
capitalism is
that we are
fighting
against.

One of the strengths of Marxist analysis is that it recognises the contradictions inherent in complex systems.

Marx took Hegel's theory of dialectics — the idea that everything contains its opposite — and applied it to the world around us.

Ma'am? Shall I take your plate?

Yes, yes.

One cannot have light...

...without dark.

There cannot be a bourgeoisie...

...without a proletariat to break its back.

And most importantly, and fundamentally, capitalism creates the forces that tend towards its own destruction.

As a result of its own inner contradictions, capitalism moves towards a point when it will be unbalanced, when it will simply become impossible.

(History has not yet proven the validity of this theory. That doesn't mean it isn't true.)

This isn't just because building factories brings the workers together...

Fuelled by the progressive socialisation of the process of production...

...so that they recognise their common class interest and start to resist their exploitation.

...the growing class consciousness of the proletariat...

It is inherent within capitalist economics. The continual pursuit of profit is, by definition, unsustainable. The quest for surplus value runs away with itself, and the system swings from boom...

...and the ungovernable chaos of the capitalist economy...

...to bust.

...the market outlet will begin to shrink because the world market has been extended to its limit and has been exhausted by the competition of the capitalist countries...

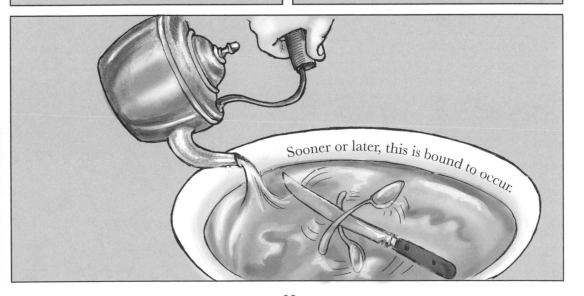

Sooner or later, this is bound to occur.

Bernstein preferred to believe that, as capitalism matures, it develops complex mechanisms, such as credit, which iron out the instabilities in the system. And, if unlimited economic growth is possible, there will be no sudden crisis. So evolution, not revolution, is the key to social change.

It's a seductive philosophy for those with the most invested in the status quo.

...the final goal, whatever it may be, is nothing to me: the movement is everything...

The genius of Luxemburg's response is that it is soundly grounded in economic theory. Far from taming capitalism's excesses, she explains how credit fuels its flames:

When the tendency of capitalist production to expand limitlessly strikes against the limited size of private capital, credit steps in to surmount those limits... Credit aggravates the inevitable crisis... It accelerates the exchange of commodities... it provokes overproduction... and then, at the first symptom of stagnation, credit melts away. It abandons the exchange process just when it is still indispensable. Credit stimulates bold and unscrupulous utilisation of the property of others... it leads to reckless speculation... It helps to bring on and extend the crisis by transforming all exchange into an extremely complex and artificial mechanism which, having a minimum of metallic money as a real base, is easily disarranged at the slightest occasion.

...the struggle for reforms is the means; revolution is the goal...

The resonance of her words rings down through the centuries, predicting the credit default swaps and other complex, artificial financial mechanisms that in 2008 will bring the global economy to its knees.

Rosa's riposte is a resounding success. It establishes her as an intellectual force to be reckoned with and is instrumental in keeping the Party on a revolutionary track.

Dr Luxemburg!

Herr Kautsky!

Having won her spurs in the movement, she forges lasting friendships with leading members of the SPD.

We were discussing your excellent critique of Bernstein.

It had to be written. When Bernstein asks 'Reform or Revolution?' he really poses the question 'To be, or not to be?'

Luise Kautsky, mother, and Mathilde Wurm, social worker...

Do tell us more.

Revolution is the only factor distinguishing Social Democracy from bourgeois radicalism.

...their husbands, Dr Emanuel Wurm and Karl Kautsky, who edit *Neue Zeit*, the journal of Marxist critical thought...

Without it, we're no longer struggling against the existing order, but vainly attempting to repair it.

Indeed!

...Franz Mehring, a stalwart of the SPD...

Without revolution, Social Democracy ceases to exist!

Well said!

...and Clara Zetkin, editor of the feminist paper *Die Gleichheit*, and single parent.

Really, I was surprised. Bernstein's arguments have no theoretical base. Not one single original idea. It was sufficient for opportunism to speak to prove it has nothing to say.

I couldn't agree more.

Kostya, don't do that.

Rosa is not intellectually intimidated by her new peers and is keen to retain her individual voice.

Her relationship with Leo is limping along.

The future looks bright.

Dr Luxemburg does indeed breathe new life into the socialist propaganda.

The secret is to live the subject-matter fully in one's heart. Then one finds words that are fresh, rather than the old familiar phrases.

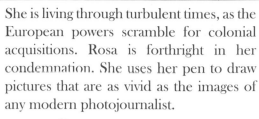

She is living through turbulent times, as the European powers scramble for colonial acquisitions. Rosa is forthright in her condemnation. She uses her pen to draw pictures that are as vivid as the images of any modern photojournalist.

In Madagascar, French artillery fire swept thousands of flowering human lives from the face of the earth... a free people lay prostrate on the ground... the brown queen of the 'savages' was dragged off as a trophy.

The sugar cartel American Senate sent cannon upon cannon, warship upon warship, golden dollars millions upon millions to Cuba, to sow death and devastation...

Far off in the African south, where a tranquil people lived by their labour and in peace, there we saw how the English wreak havoc...

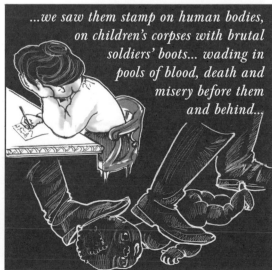

...we saw them stamp on human bodies, on children's corpses with brutal soldiers' boots... wading in pools of blood, death and misery before them and behind...

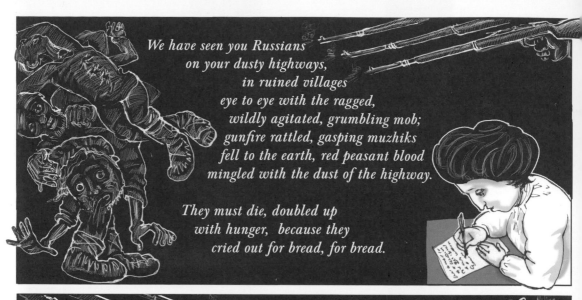

We have seen you Russians
on your dusty highways,
in ruined villages
eye to eye with the ragged,
wildly agitated, grumbling mob;
gunfire rattled, gasping muzhiks
fell to the earth, red peasant blood
mingled with the dust of the highway.

They must die, doubled up
with hunger, because they
cried out for bread, for bread.

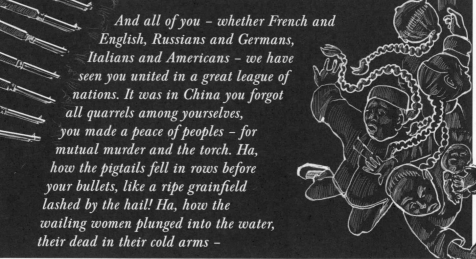

And all of you – whether French and
English, Russians and Germans,
Italians and Americans – we have
seen you united in a great league of
nations. It was in China you forgot
all quarrels among yourselves,
you made a peace of peoples – for
mutual murder and the torch. Ha,
how the pigtails fell in rows before
your bullets, like a ripe grainfield
lashed by the hail! Ha, how the
wailing women plunged into the water,
their dead in their cold arms –

Oh! A wasp!

ZOOOOM

Rosa ~ have you read the latest in the bourgeois press? You're certainly getting noticed.

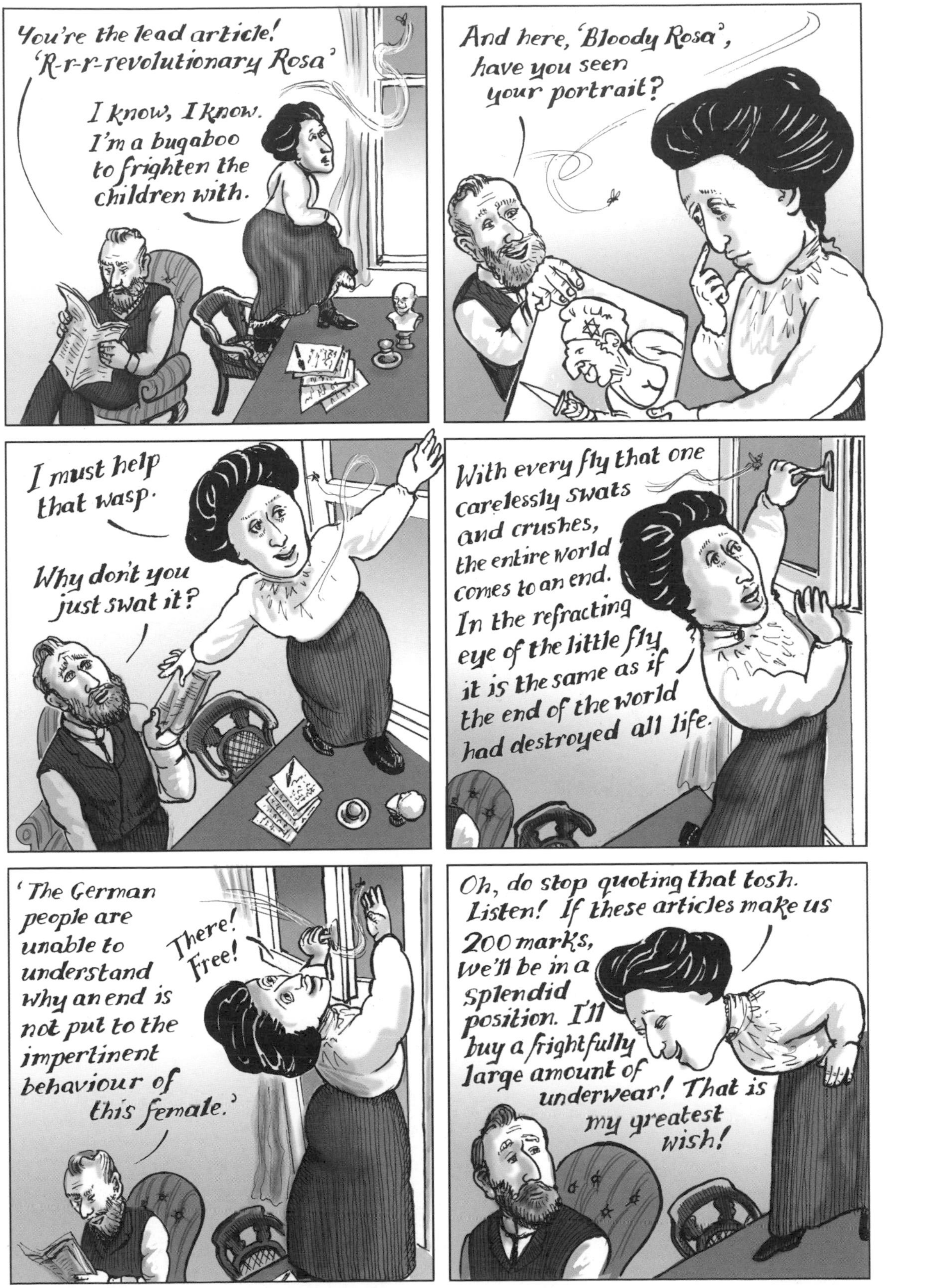
You're the lead article! 'R-r-r-revolutionary Rosa'
I know, I know. I'm a bugaboo to frighten the children with.
And here, 'Bloody Rosa', have you seen your portrait?
I must help that wasp.
Why don't you just swat it?
With every fly that one carelessly swats and crushes, the entire world comes to an end. In the refracting eye of the little fly it is the same as if the end of the world had destroyed all life.
'The German people are unable to understand why an end is not put to the impertinent behaviour of this female.'
There! Free!
Oh, do stop quoting that tosh. Listen! If these articles make us 200 marks, we'll be in a splendid position. I'll buy a frightfully large amount of underwear! That is my greatest wish!

Is that really her greatest wish? What about motherhood? Isn't that what *every* woman desires?

Rosa is nearly thirty. She isn't getting any younger.

Oh!

Isn't she enchanting? Don't you wish we could bundle her up and take her home with us?

Oh, Jo-jo. Will I never have a baby?

A w-w-what?

Rosa chooses not to have a child. If she hadn't, we might never have heard of her. An obscure volume on the industrial history of Poland could have been her only contribution to posterity.

Married to one unsuitable father...

...and in a relationship with another...

Never mind.

...however it is that Rosa avoids motherhood, she keeps on doing it.

When I think of my own mother, I have to shudder. I mean ~ what was the point of a life like that?

We were like the Chaffinch family here...

...See Mama, careworn, emaciated, unkempt...

...while the Little Darling waits for her to stuff her beak.

It was an unbreakable law of nature. Mother existed exclusively to fill our little beaks, which were forever opened wide in every possible way. Above all, the beak of the paterfamilias.

It is one thing to dedicate one's life to the service of others as a revolutionary socialist. It is quite another to do that in the domestic sphere. And, while Rosa calmly contemplates the risk of death on the gallows or the barricades, a lingering death in childbirth doesn't appeal.

Did you say something?

You should go back to the other room. The maid will be here soon.

Rosa does what any sensible, childfree, independent, broody soul should do.

MIMI!

NO!

SPRING!

Oh, you naughty Meu~meu. Those birds were much too quick for you!

She gets herself a cat.

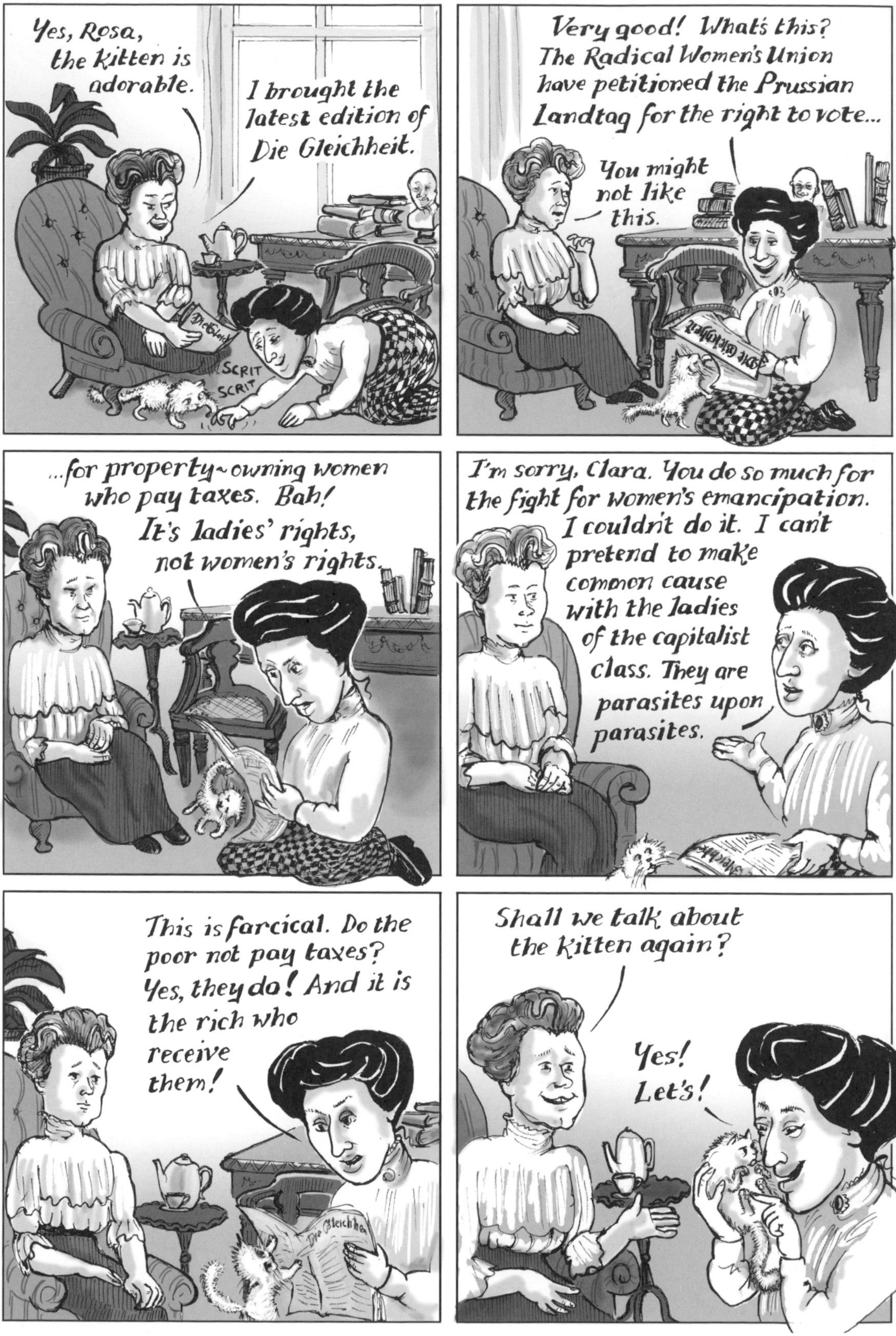
Yes, Rosa, the kitten is adorable.
I brought the latest edition of Die Gleichheit.
SCRIT SCRIT
Very good! What's this? The Radical Women's Union have petitioned the Prussian Landtag for the right to vote...
You might not like this.
...for property-owning women who pay taxes. Bah!
It's ladies' rights, not women's rights.
I'm sorry, Clara. You do so much for the fight for women's emancipation. I couldn't do it. I can't pretend to make common cause with the ladies of the capitalist class. They are parasites upon parasites.
This is farcical. Do the poor not pay taxes? Yes, they do! And it is the rich who receive them!
Shall we talk about the kitten again?
Yes! Let's!

Late August, 1904.

Oh, Mimi! How will you manage without me?

I have left money for eggs, she likes eggs, and sprats, but get fresh ones, not the stinking ones from the Thursday market, and you must pick her some fresh grass every day because she likes that too, and a little cream, not milk...

Thank you, thank you, Gertrude. You must pet her lots!

Mimi, how can I bear to leave you?

Kisses for you!

Don't forget me!

Eventually, inevitably, the authorities decide to clip Dr Luxemburg's wings. She is sentenced to three months in prison for insulting the Kaiser.

Why're yew in 'ere then? Whatchew done?

Specifically, I spoke the words 'a man who talks about the security and good living of the German workers has no idea of the real facts'.

What? They banged you up fer that?

Why are you in here?

Arson.

Oh, my goodness.

Rosa utilises her remarkable ability to make the best of a bad situation and takes the opportunity to catch up on some correspondence.

Dearest Luise,
Many thanks for the photo of Karl. It's the first really good picture of him that I've seen. The eyes, the expression, it's superb!

Only the neck-tie, teeming with little white bean shapes, which really catch the eye...

...such a tie is grounds for divorce.

Just six weeks into her sentence, something unexpected happens.

BLAM!

LUXEMBURG! You're free to go. Early release.

What? Why?

General amnesty due to the coronation of King Friedrich of Saxony Gawd-Bless-His-Soul-Long-Live-The-King!

I am in here for insulting the monarchy. I will NOT be released early for some idiotic coronation.

I won't go!

I REFUSE TO LEAVE!!!

I PROTEST!!!

The international socialist movement is growing. Trade unions consolidate their membership fees and structures. Party bureaucracies proliferate. Socialist deputies take their seats in national parliaments. In France, they even participate in a bourgeois government: a socialist politician in a ministerial role.

This creates a pressure to scale back the aims of the movement — to aspire to what seems achievable, rather than what is desirable.

Opportunism.
Rosa is determined to stamp it out.

It's not enough to keep repeating our criticisms of opportunism, like parrots.

You do so much more than that, Rosa.

Remember your amendment at the last Conference of the International? 'Socialist tactics must only be based on total class struggle.'

You didn't tell me about that, Karl.

It was a work of genius. And when Jean Jaurès spoke to defend the French and oppose the motion, after he finished there was no one to translate for him, so what did our Rosa do?

She stood up and translated his speech to German for him! Passionately repeating all the words he'd used against her.

I didn't know about that! He never tells me anything, Rosa.

She won the motion of course.

You are kind, Karl, but back to my point. What is to be done about this opportunist trend? With this purely negative activity we are not making any steps forward, and, for a revolutionary movement, not to move forward means to fall back.

Opportunism is a plant that grows in swamps, spreading quickly and luxuriantly in the stagnant water of the movement. Where the current flows swiftly and strongly it dies away by itself.

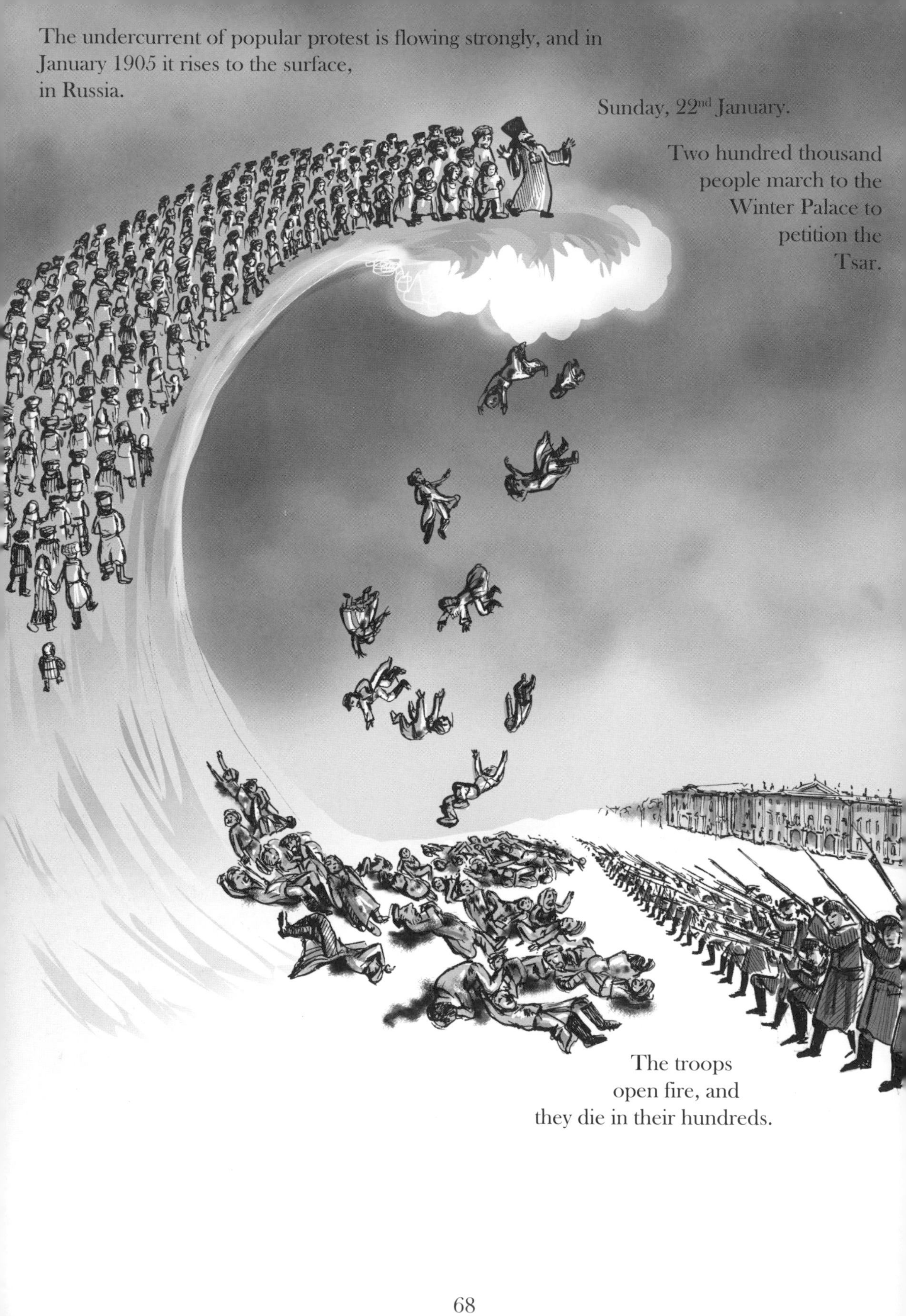
The undercurrent of popular protest is flowing strongly, and in January 1905 it rises to the surface, in Russia.
Sunday, 22nd January.
Two hundred thousand people march to the Winter Palace to petition the Tsar.
The troops open fire, and they die in their hundreds.

As news of the massacre spreads, a wave of anger sweeps across the Russian empire.

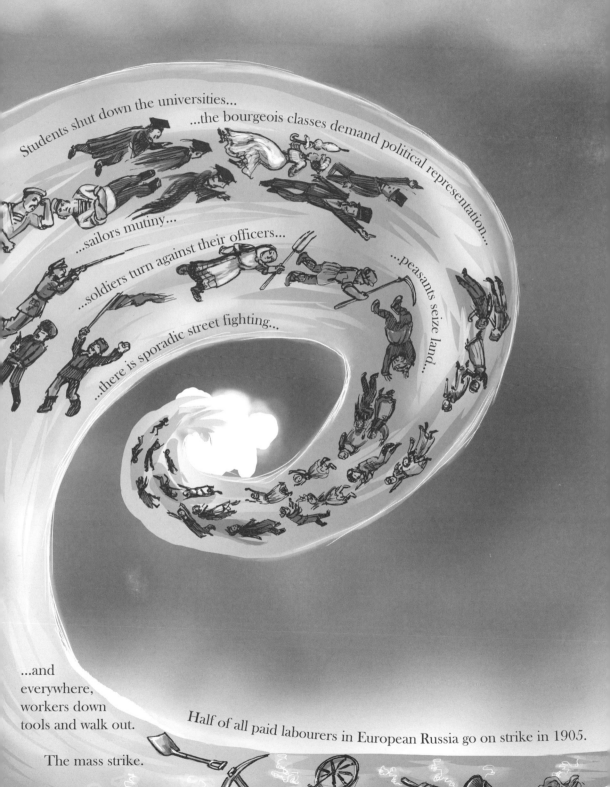

Students shut down the universities...

...the bourgeois classes demand political representation...

...sailors mutiny...

...soldiers turn against their officers...

...peasants seize land...

...there is sporadic street fighting...

...and everywhere, workers down tools and walk out.

The mass strike.

Half of all paid labourers in European Russia go on strike in 1905.

By October, the Tsar is forced to concede major reforms, legalising political parties and creating the Duma, a constituent assembly.

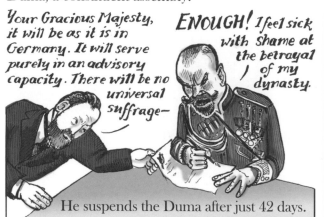

Your Gracious Majesty, it will be as it is in Germany. It will serve purely in an advisory capacity. There will be no universal suffrage—

ENOUGH! I feel sick with shame at the betrayal of my dynasty.

He suspends the Duma after just 42 days.

Rosa is sick too. She is incapacitated with stomach trouble for much of the year...

...and she is sickened by the lukewarm response of her fellow socialists to events across the border.

SPD Congress, Jena, 17th September 1905.

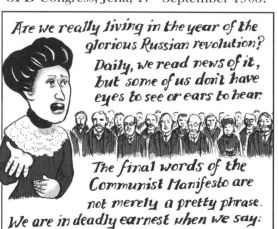

Are we really living in the year of the glorious Russian revolution?

Daily, we read news of it, but some of us don't have eyes to see or ears to hear.

The final words of the Communist Manifesto are not merely a pretty phrase. We are in deadly earnest when we say: Workers! We have a world to win!

August Bebel, the SPD leader, mocks her concerns. The debate has taken an unusual turn. I have never heard so much talk of revolution. I can't help glancing at my boots to see if we are not already wading in blood!

HA HA HA HA

When the revolution comes in Germany, Rosa will no doubt be on the Left, and I will be on the Right...

...but we will hang her. We won't allow her to spit in our soup!

It is too early to tell who will hang whom!

Throughout 1905, when Leo is agitating in Warsaw, Rosa is itching to get to the action.

Don't go! It's so dangerous! So cold! And you have been so ill!

Be careful, Rosa.

Luise, I'll be fine.

I have this lovely blanket you gave me.

Finally, on December 28th, she slips away.

A blanket cannot deflect bullets.

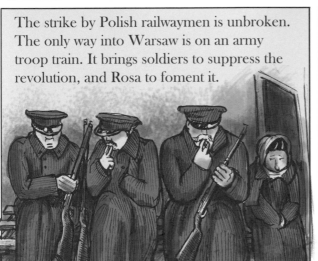

The strike by Polish railwaymen is unbroken. The only way into Warsaw is on an army troop train. It brings soldiers to suppress the revolution, and Rosa to foment it.

It creeps along at a snail's pace, unheated and unlit, fearing ambush and derailment.

Your passport... 'Anna Matschke'.

Yes, that's me.

'Occupation: Journalist'. You'll find plenty to write about.

Hopefully, in Warsaw I won't be met with machine guns.

The city is like a place of the dead. The strike is absolute. Soldiers are everywhere. Tomorrow I start the work.

I'm home!

Rosa has arrived at the end of the revolution, and the Russian state is successfully reasserting control. But nobody knows that yet.

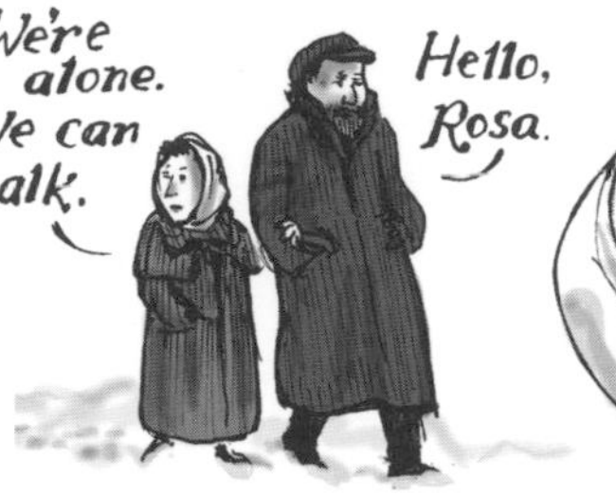
We're alone. We can talk.
Hello, Rosa.

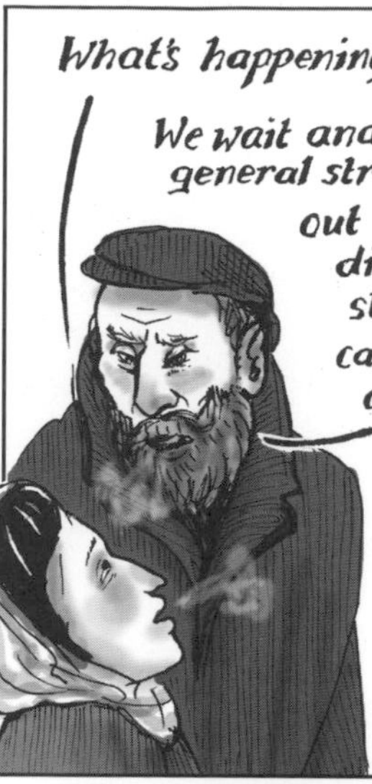
What's happening, Leo?
We wait and see. The general strike has played out its role. Only direct, universal street-fighting can bring about a resolution.
But, for that, there must be preparation for the right moment.

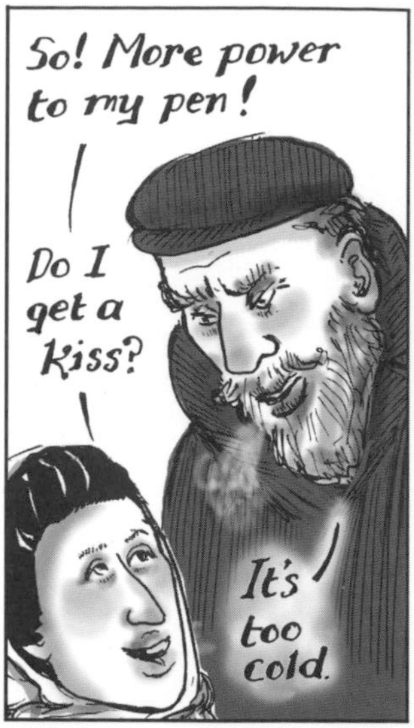
So! More power to my pen!
Do I get a kiss?
It's too cold.

With Warsaw locked down under martial law, she throws herself into the production of illegal newspapers, printed at gunpoint.

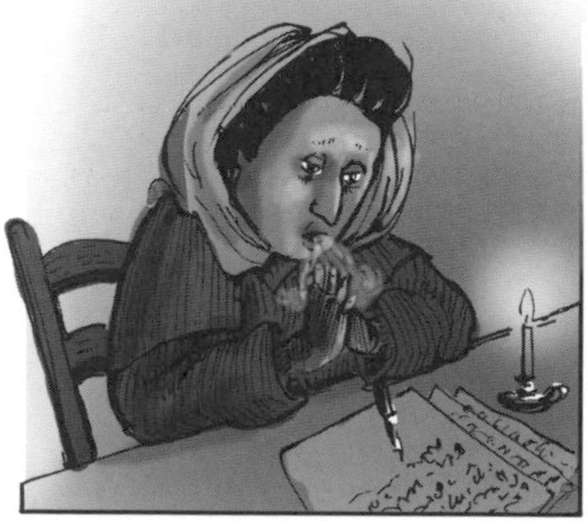

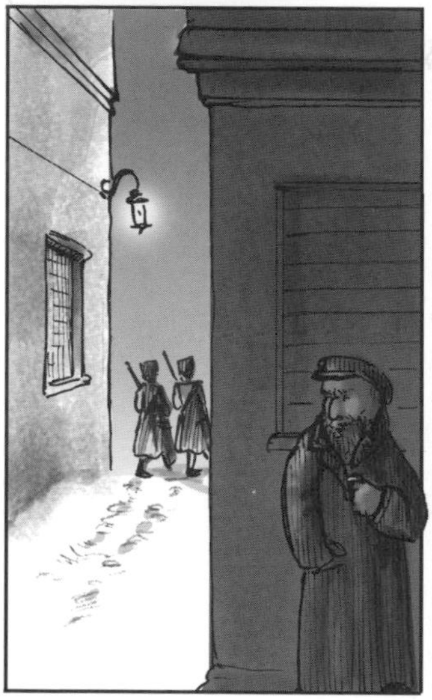

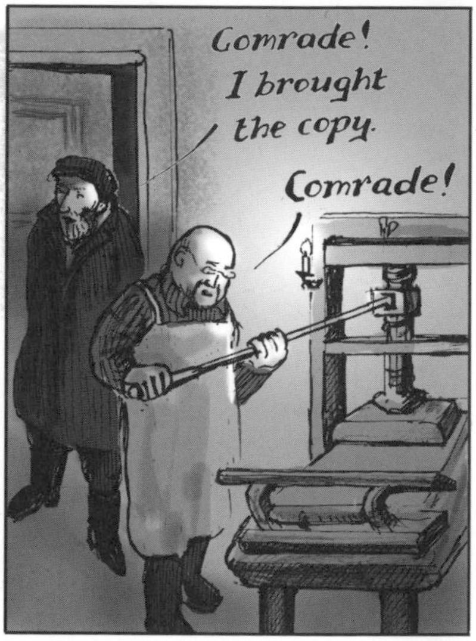
Comrade! I brought the copy.
Comrade!

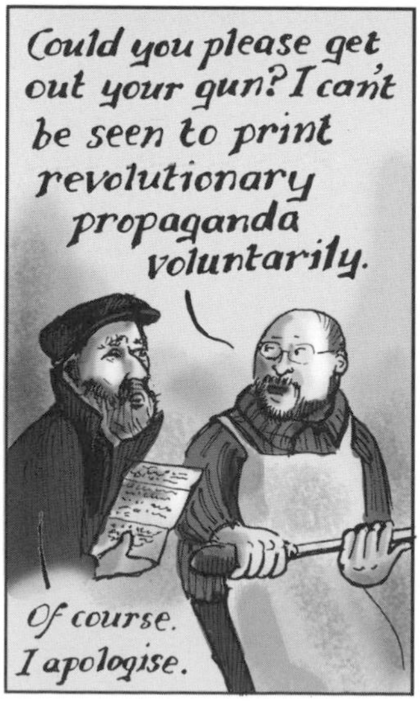
Could you please get out your gun? I can't be seen to print revolutionary propaganda voluntarily.
Of course. I apologise.

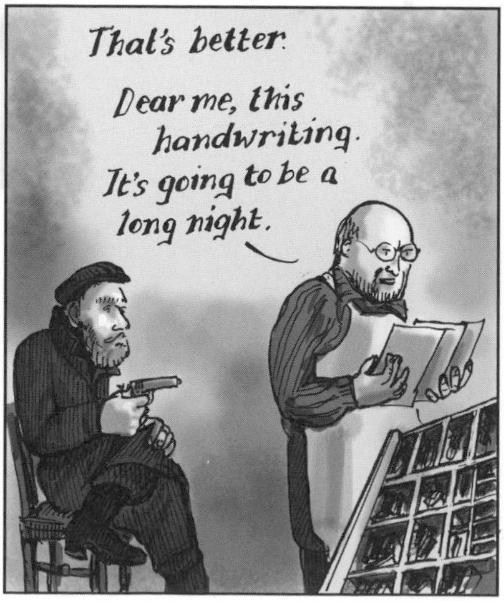
That's better.
Dear me, this handwriting. It's going to be a long night.

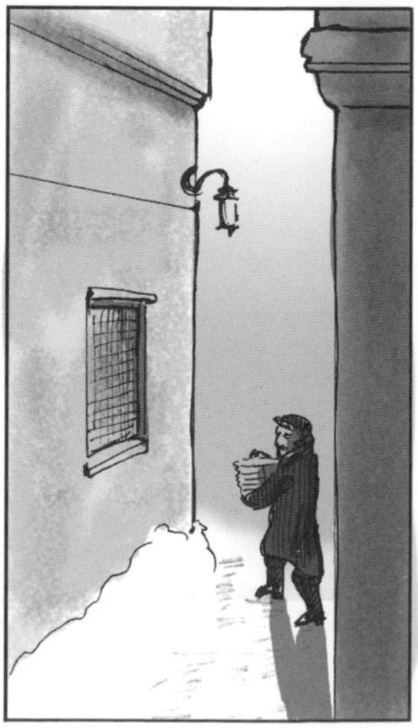

Rosa isn't here to preach. She wants to learn. She researches the particular circumstances of the 1905 uprising.

I've been elected to the worker's council. We do all the hiring and firing.

We have a weekly collection for the unemployed. Share the wages, and no one goes hungry.

And were there general strikes before this year?

Oh, yes. Let me tell you about them.

November 1902. 20,000 strikers in Rostov take to the streets.

January 1897. Petersburg textile workers strike for an eleven-hour working day.

July 1903. Shop workers in Tiflis refuse to continue to work seventeen-hour days.

March 1902. Unemployed petroleum workers in Batum resist their forced removal.

July 1903. 50,000 striking workers bring Odessa to a standstill.

July 1903. Railwaymen, women and children in Kiev sit down on the train tracks and are shot dead.

March 1905. Warsaw workers win 15% pay rise.

May 1905. Workers across Russia achieve a working day of ten hours or less.

September 1905. Mass strike in Warsaw in protest at the execution of socialist Martin Kasprzak.

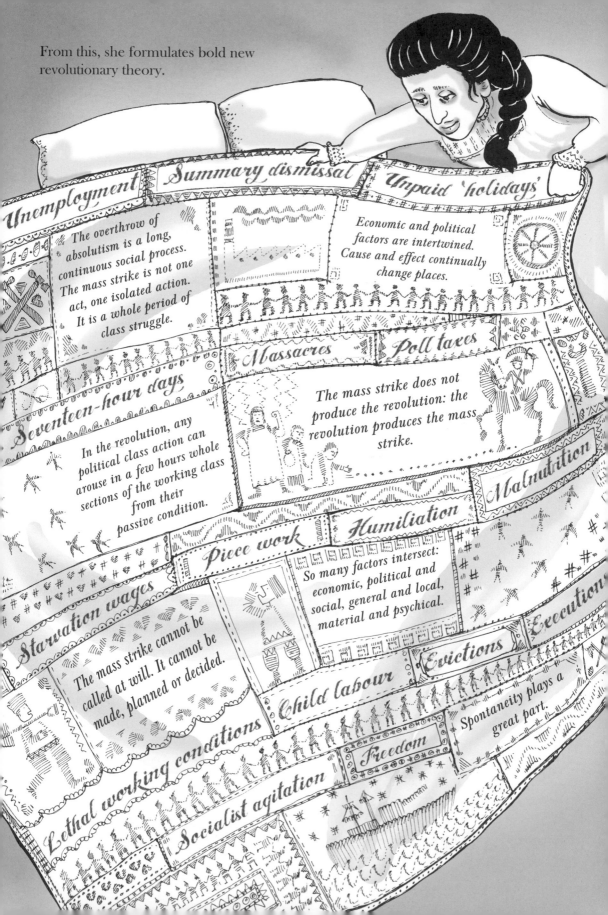

From this, she formulates bold new revolutionary theory.

Unemployment

Summary dismissal

Unpaid 'holidays'

The overthrow of absolutism is a long, continuous social process. The mass strike is not one act, one isolated action. It is a whole period of class struggle.

Economic and political factors are intertwined. Cause and effect continually change places.

Massacres

Poll taxes

The mass strike does not produce the revolution: the revolution produces the mass strike.

Seventeen-hour days

In the revolution, any political class action can arouse in a few hours whole sections of the working class from their passive condition.

Malnutrition

Piece work

Humiliation

So many factors intersect: economic, political and social, general and local, material and psychical.

Starvation wages

The mass strike cannot be called at will. It cannot be made, planned or decided.

Executions

Evictions

Child labour

Spontaneity plays a great part.

Lethal working conditions

Freedom

Socialist agitation

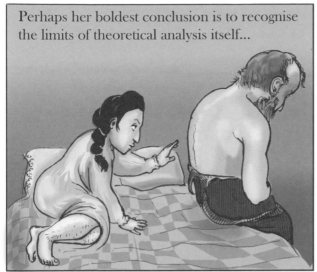

Perhaps her boldest conclusion is to recognise the limits of theoretical analysis itself...

The mass strike. A bit of pulsating life of flesh and blood...

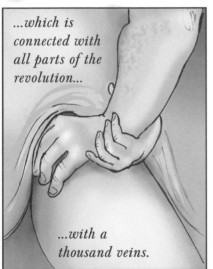

...which is connected with all parts of the revolution...

...with a thousand veins.

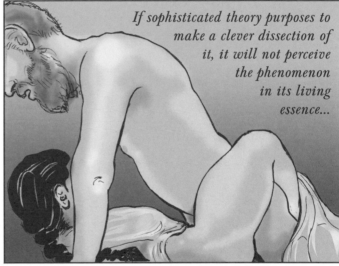

If sophisticated theory purposes to make a clever dissection of it, it will not perceive the phenomenon in its living essence...

...but kill it altogether.

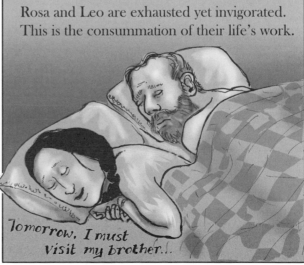

Rosa and Leo are exhausted yet invigorated. This is the consummation of their life's work.

Tomorrow, I must visit my brother...

She is taken in chains to the Warsaw Citadel.

Her brother visits. Weakened from hunger strike, she is carried from her cell.

In July, the authorities (lavishly bribed) agree to a release on the grounds of ill health.

Rosa is bailed first to Warsaw, then to Finland, where she works up her revolutionary booklet *The Mass Strike*.
It is autumn before she returns home to Germany.

Nobody sets bail for Leo Jogiches.

September 13th, 1906.

77

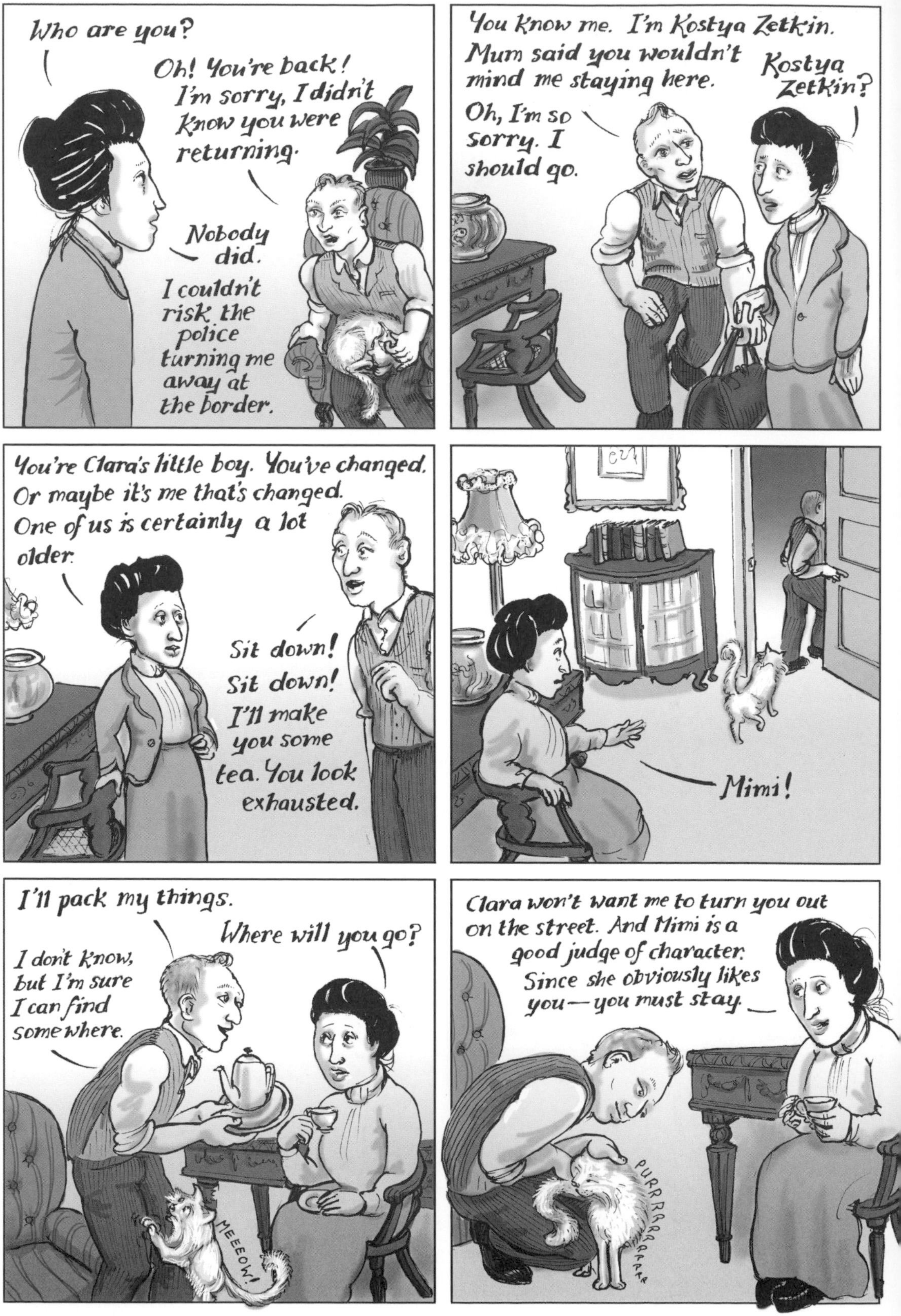
Who are you?
Oh! You're back! I'm sorry, I didn't know you were returning.
Nobody did.
I couldn't risk the police turning me away at the border.
You know me. I'm Kostya Zetkin. Mum said you wouldn't mind me staying here.
Kostya Zetkin?
Oh, I'm so sorry. I should go.
You're Clara's little boy. You've changed. Or maybe it's me that's changed. One of us is certainly a lot older.
Sit down! Sit down! I'll make you some tea. You look exhausted.
Mimi!
I'll pack my things.
Where will you go?
I don't know, but I'm sure I can find somewhere.
MEEEOW!
Clara won't want me to turn you out on the street. And Mimi is a good judge of character. Since she obviously likes you—you must stay.
PURRRRRRRRRR

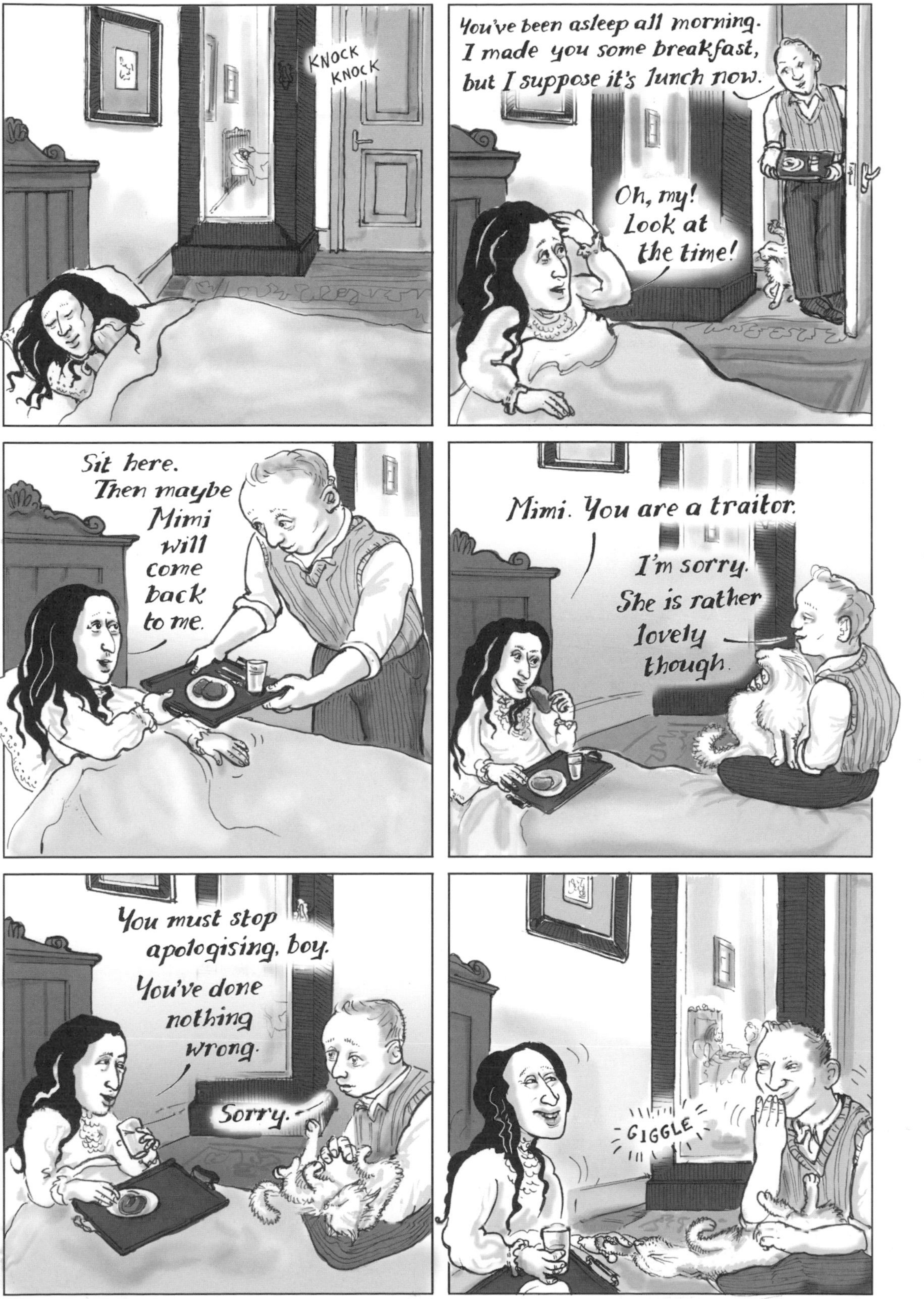
KNOCK KNOCK
You've been asleep all morning. I made you some breakfast, but I suppose it's lunch now.
Oh, my! Look at the time!
Sit here. Then maybe Mimi will come back to me.
Mimi. You are a traitor.
I'm sorry. She is rather lovely though.
You must stop apologising, boy.
You've done nothing wrong.
Sorry.
GIGGLE

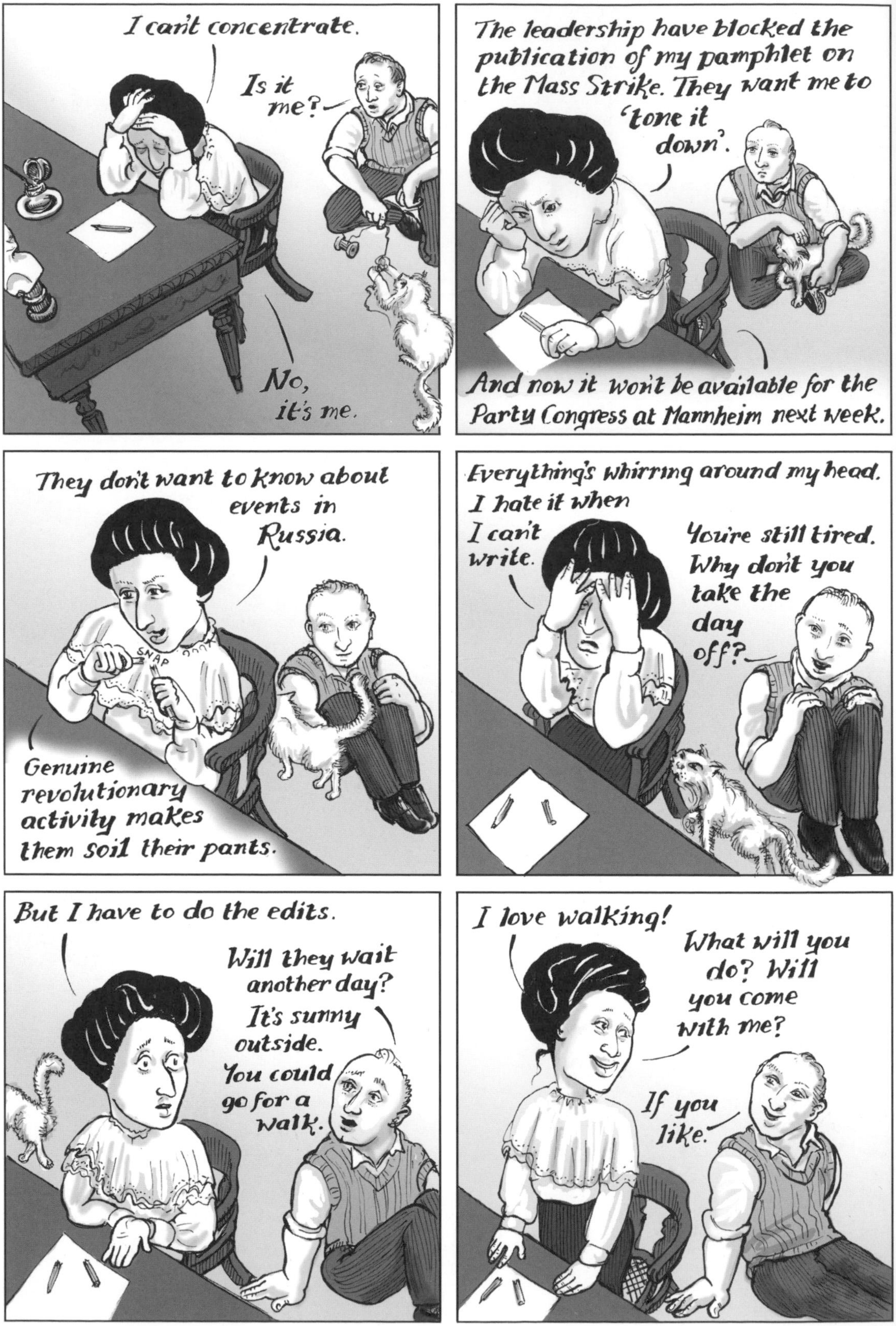
I can't concentrate.
Is it me?
No, it's me.
The leadership have blocked the publication of my pamphlet on the Mass Strike. They want me to 'tone it down'.
And now it won't be available for the Party Congress at Mannheim next week.
They don't want to know about events in Russia.
SNAP
Genuine revolutionary activity makes them soil their pants.
Everything's whirring around my head. I hate it when I can't write.
You're still tired. Why don't you take the day off?
But I have to do the edits.
Will they wait another day? It's sunny outside. You could go for a walk.
I love walking!
What will you do? Will you come with me?
If you like.

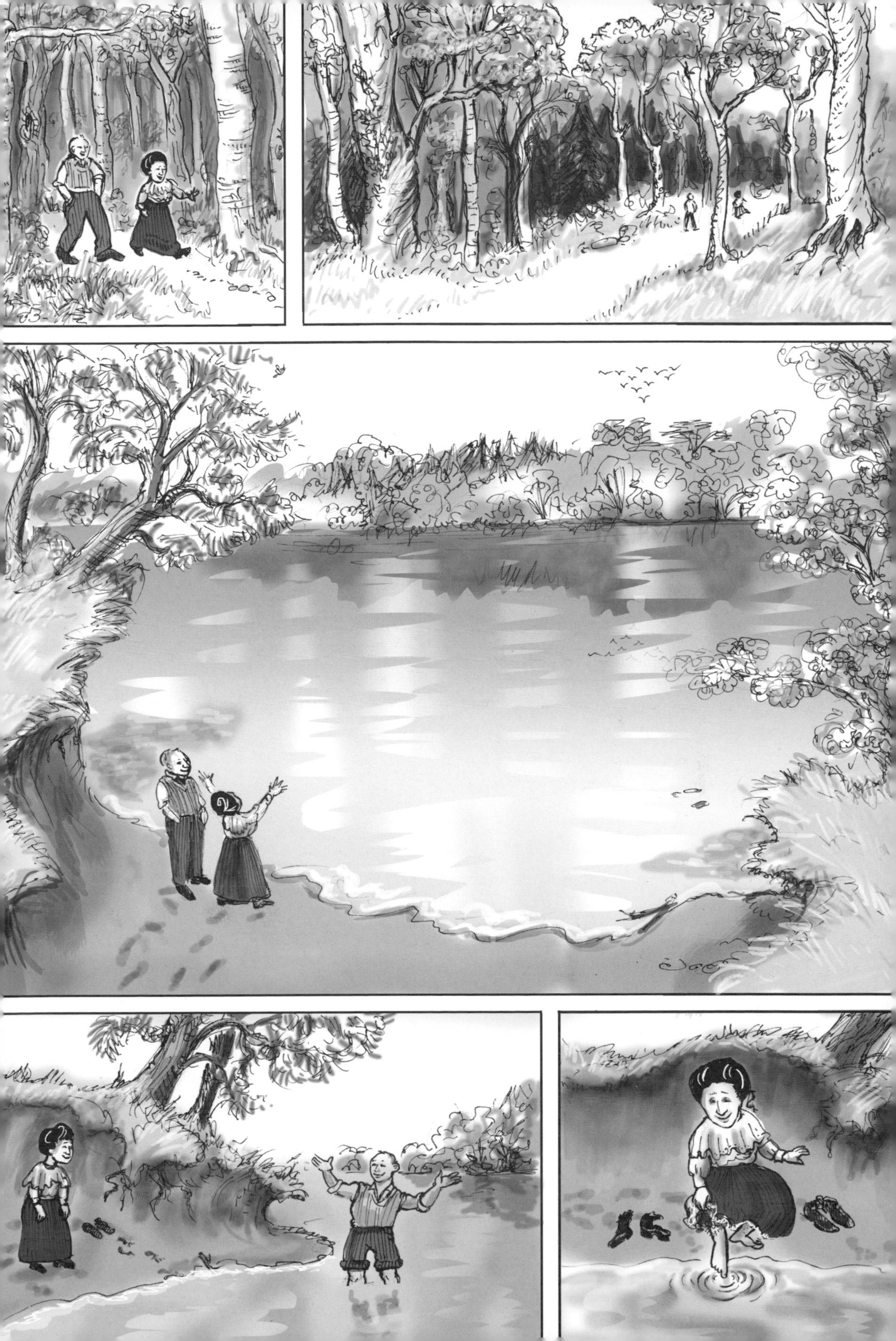

I'll take the tray.

January 1907.

Thank you, Son.

He's so well brought-up!

It's very good of you to let Kostya stay.

I'm glad of the company, Clara. I don't know when I'll ever see Leo again.

I know all mothers fret, but I do wish Kostya would do something with his life.

Give him time. I'm sure he'll find his feet.

He's doing better than our glorious Party leaders.

Far better to be a dreamer than to aim to shoot down the dreams of others.

The Party Congress was a joke. The leadership is dedicated to parliamentary politics. They seek to twist and turn everything to that. Yet, meanwhile, the masses, and the great mass of comrades, have had their fill of parliaments and politicians....

...They would joyously welcome any breath of fresh air in Party tactics.

Kostya, we'll be back later.

The crowds at Mannheim were shouting 'Tell us about Russia!'

I can honestly say that the months I spent in Russia were the happiest of my life.

The revolution is everything!

All else is bilge.

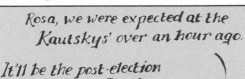

Rosa, we were expected at the Kautskys' over an hour ago.

It'll be the post-election post-mortem. I confess I'm not in a hurry to attend.

No doubt Bebel will be there. Let's see if I can put on a happy face.

Doctor Luxemburg! Frau Zetkin! It is late. We feared you were lost!

Herr Bebel! Alas — the tragedy! You can write our epitaph:

'Here lie the last two men of German Social Democracy.'

Terrible news, Rosa! We must rethink the entire SPD strategy. You have heard the election results?

What of them?

How can you say that?

The number of SPD seats in the Reichstag fell from 81 to 43!

And we polled 50,000 more votes overall! Nearly 3,600,000 men voted SPD!

And just think how m[a]... more women would h[ave]... if they could.

If the bourgeois parties collude with their electoral tricks to keep us out of office, what concern is that of ours?

The concern is... the point is... God, woman! Do you not see what the point is? I have spent a lifetime building this party. I was the only Socialist deputy in the Reichstag back in 1871. Do you want us to go back to those days?

Why is it that the largest party in the Reichstag polls only the fourth largest number of seats? The shoddy electoral system that makes one Prussian landowner's vote worth seventeen times that of a working man.

Let us fight for equal suffrage!

Dammit! Let's call for a republic! Let us have a Reichstag with genuine power! That would be a parliament worth voting for!

She's an electoral liability, Kautsky. For God's sake, don't let any of those wild ideas make it into the paper.

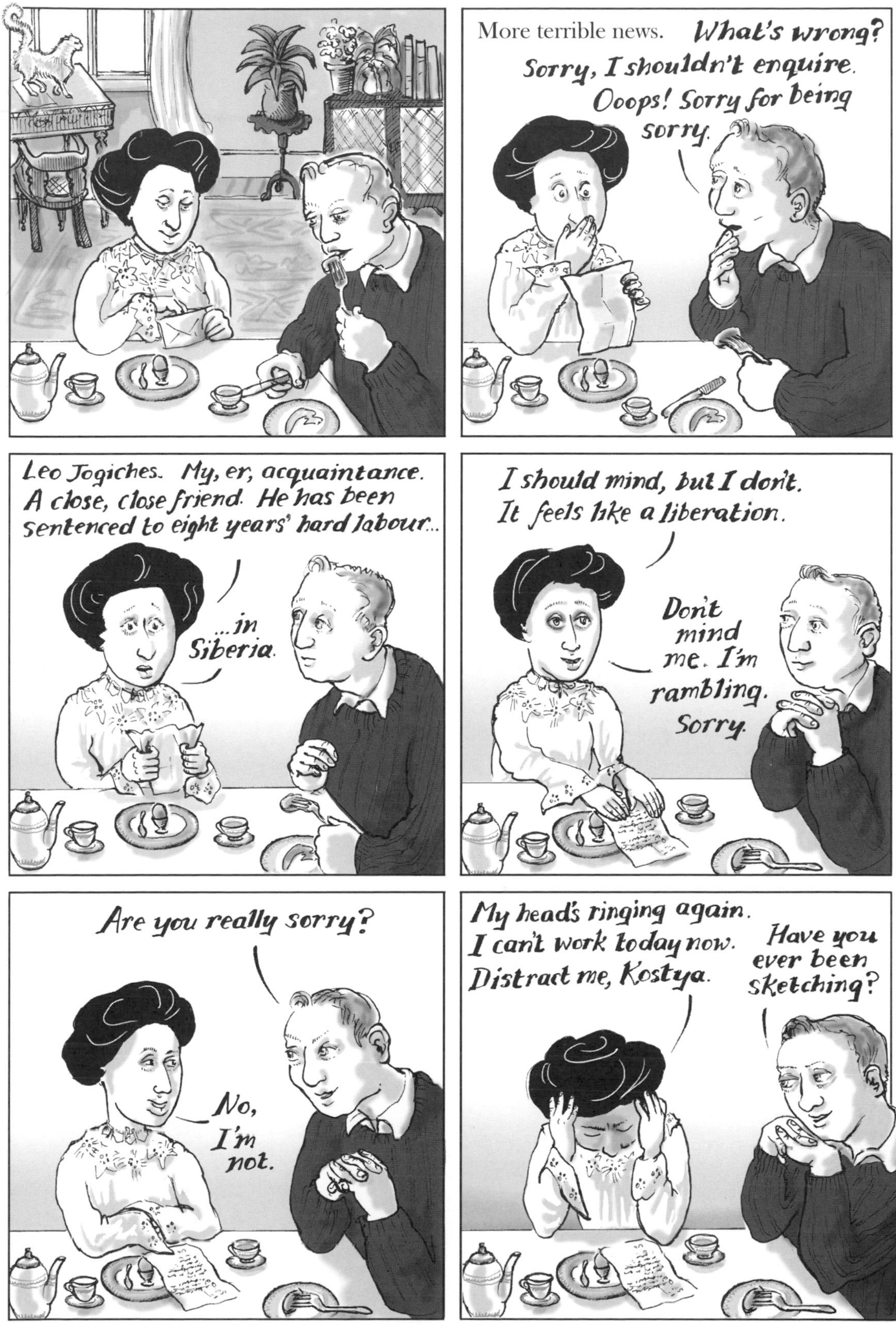
More terrible news.
What's wrong?
Sorry, I shouldn't enquire.
Ooops! Sorry for being sorry.
Leo Jogiches. My, er, acquaintance. A close, close friend. He has been sentenced to eight years' hard labour...
...in Siberia.
I should mind, but I don't. It feels like a liberation.
Don't mind me. I'm rambling. Sorry.
Are you really sorry?
No, I'm not.
My head's ringing again. I can't work today now. Distract me, Kostya.
Have you ever been sketching?

You're very good at this!

Oh, if only I had nothing to do but paint — it would absorb me completely.

Crazy dreams!

"HOOOWEEET"

Listen! A willow warbler.

I know.

There he is.

You know about birds?

I'm not just a pretty face.

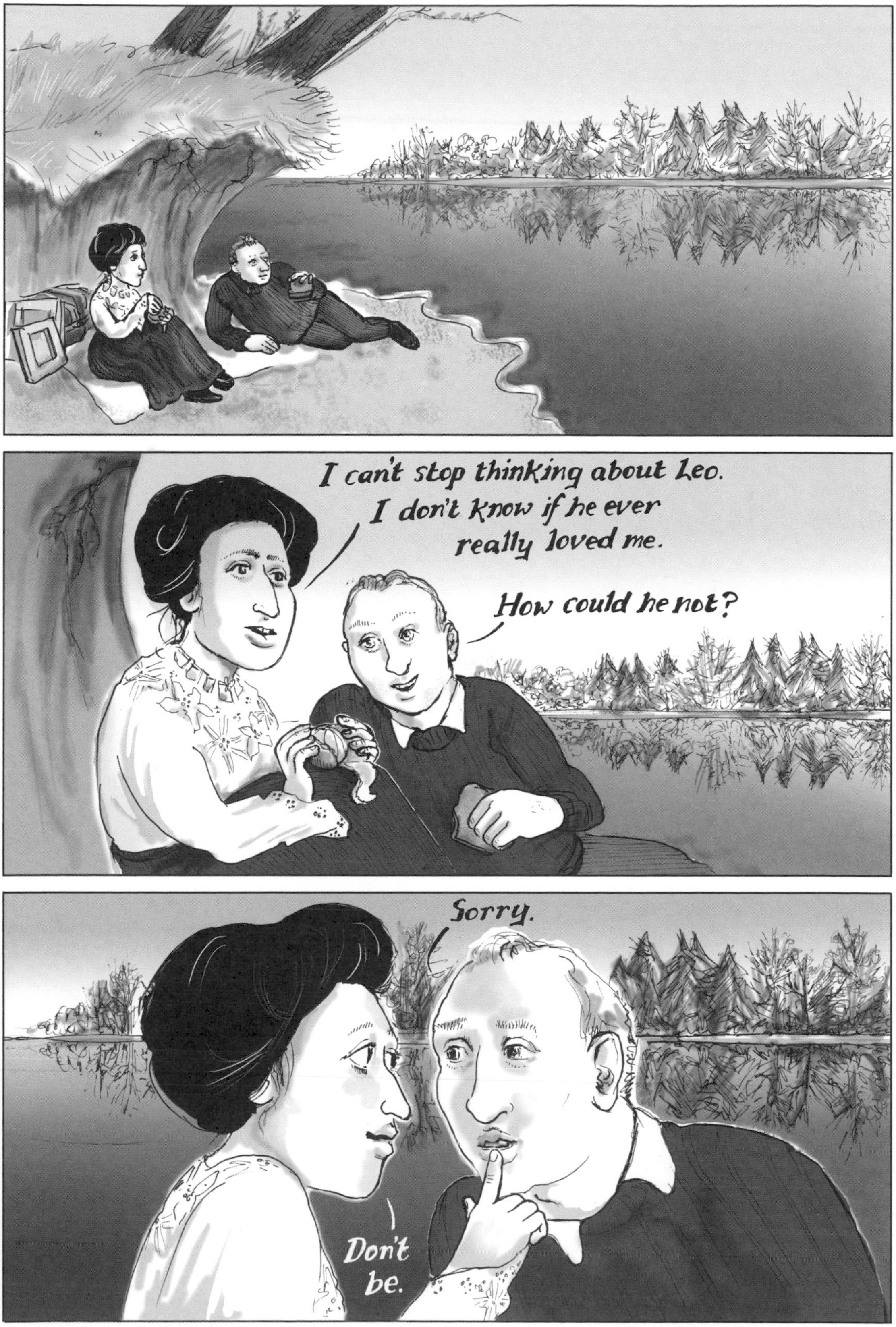
I can't stop thinking about Leo. I don't know if he ever really loved me.
How could he not?
Sorry.
Don't be.

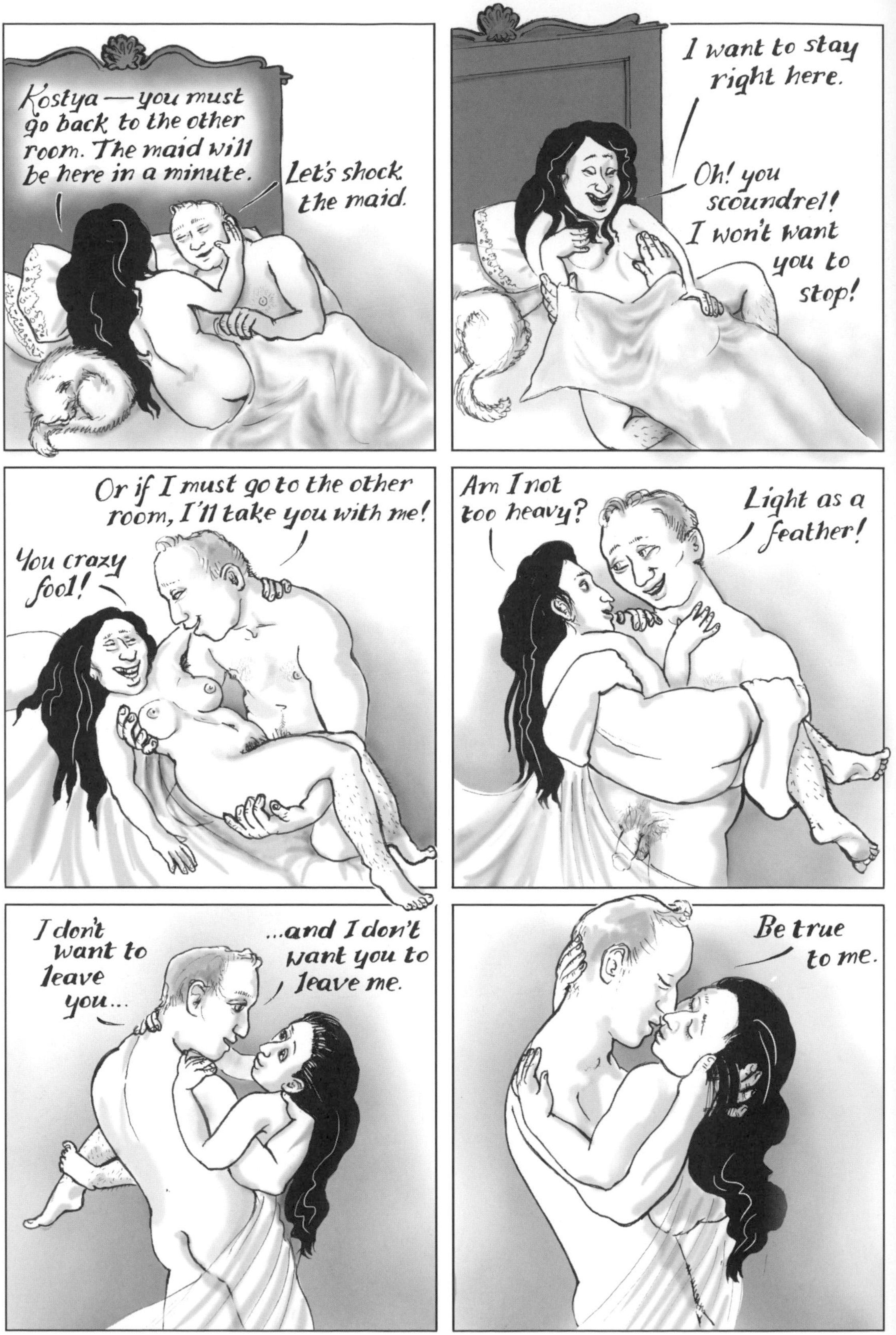
Kostya — you must go back to the other room. The maid will be here in a minute.
Let's shock the maid.
I want to stay right here.
Oh! you scoundrel! I won't want you to stop!
Or if I must go to the other room, I'll take you with me!
You crazy fool!
Am I not too heavy?
Light as a feather!
I don't want to leave you...
...and I don't want you to leave me.
Be true to me.

May 13th, 1907. London's East End.

The Russian Social Democrat Congress gets under way tomorrow. I'm sitting alone in a restaurant in the infamous Whitechapel district, and it's after ten o'clock at night.

Dear Kostya

In a foul mood I travelled through the endless stations of the dark Underground...

...and emerged, lost, in this strange and wild part of the city.

It's dirty here.

A dim street-light is flickering.

Drunken people stagger, shouting, down the middle of the street, newspaper boys are yelling, flower girls are screeching, omnibuses creak past and crack their whips...

Flahrs for the luvverly laydey!

...It is chaos.

Finally, I found the hotel...

Why, the very name is suspicious as hell.

A brightly lit dining room, but empty.

I breathed a sigh of relief when I saw two women sitting at a little table.

But I then saw that all the guests were familiar with these women...

*...and were sitting down at the table to join them **still wearing their hats.***

On the other side of the wall I can hear a variety show of an unambiguous sort. As the couplets are recited...

"We saw 'er daughter!"

"Should'a warned 'er!"

...after each one comes raucous applause, with stamping feet, as though a wild horde was loose.

'Oi! Oi! Oi! The hoi polloi!'

But suddenly inside me now some gypsy blood has been awakened.

The shrill chords of night in the big city, with its demonic magic, have touched certain strings in my soul.

Somewhere in the depths an indistinct desire is coming to light...

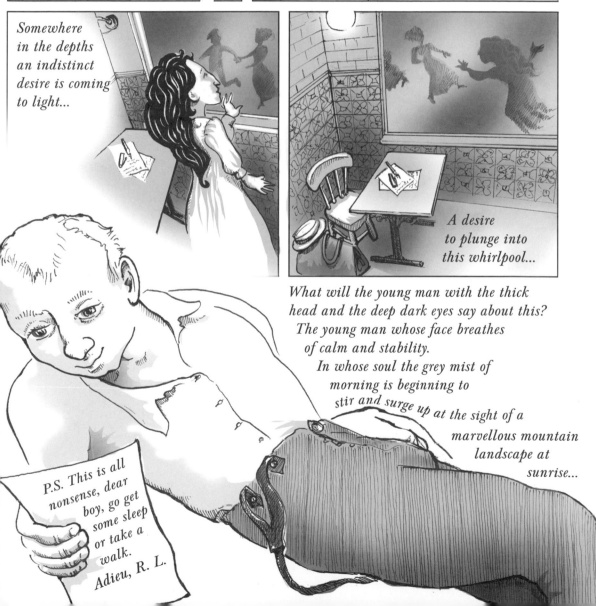

A desire to plunge into this whirlpool...

What will the young man with the thick head and the deep dark eyes say about this? The young man whose face breathes of calm and stability. In whose soul the grey mist of morning is beginning to stir and surge up at the sight of a marvellous mountain landscape at sunrise...

P.S. This is all nonsense, dear boy, go get some sleep or take a walk. Adieu, R. L.

Rosa has reckoned without Leo Jogiches, the man whom prison cannot hold.

May 22nd 1907. London.

You must have known I would come here.

What are you doing?

Leo, you know I'm no longer your wife.

I'm leaving.

I won't let you go.

Leo, please. I'm meeting my brother.

You'll be staying here in London, even if in a hospital.

You're not going back to him.

I would sooner strike you dead!

Ah! Max! How's life in London?

Leo! What a surprise! I see you survived your Siberian adventures.

Are you taking good care of that sister of mine?

Oh, yes. I'll take care of her.

Rosa is utterly unprotected. No woman of her generation can turn to the police for assistance with domestic abuse. Certainly not an unmarried woman, whose illicit ex-lover has six different names. Back in Berlin, she is in a perilous position.

You can't come back to my apartment. It's not safe. Leo burst in on me yesterday. The state of mind he's in — it's no joke — his inner self is shattered — he's become abnormal.

He said I must promise not to see you, or he would kill me right there and then.

Oh, my love.

And he took hold of something in his pocket.

I made no promise. I said nothing. I felt an icy calm. I didn't even turn my head. I couldn't sleep there after that, so I went to the Kautskys'. He was back this morning. He read your letters.

Rosa, the man's a wanted felon...

...surely, if it came to it?

I can't believe you would suggest such a thing. With everything he does for socialism? I can't! The revolution is too important for this. Our work must continue.

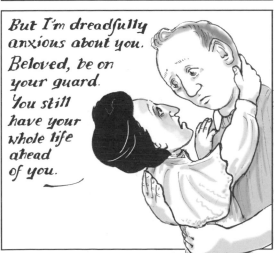

But I'm dreadfully anxious about you. Beloved, be on your guard. You still have your whole life ahead of you.

What about you? How will you keep yourself safe?

I bought this.

I sleep with it under my pillow.

93

Stop day-dreaming about the plot of some romantic **love drama!** We are not in the **cinema!** This is the **Party School!** We are here to learn about **Capitalism!**

THWACK!

Who can define 'historical materialism' for me...? Nobody...? If I want you to learn one thing, it's the importance of history. Only by analysing the <u>past</u>, and comparing it with the <u>present</u>, can we hope to forge a better <u>future</u>.

Historical

Materialism

What is material? Er, things?

Yes. Stuff... ...things... matter... By studying the material things in society—the objects we produce and the way we produce them—the social relations between people are revealed.

Historical Materialism The study of the productive forces in society

Social history, like physics or chemistry, is simply a study of matter-in-motion.

Urkommunism

Let us examine the ancient German village commune. For whom does this labourer work?

Himself.

Yes. This corn, these geese, these shoes —are they commodities?

No, they are neither bought nor sold.

Exactly. They are made for the people, by the people.

One cannot imagine anything simpler and more harmonious than this, the life of the so-called primitive.

The immediate needs of everyday life and the equal fulfilment of everyone—this is the starting point and endpoint of the economic system.

Everyone works for everyone else and collectively decides on everything.

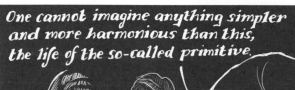

Why?

Because we have communism of the land and the soil.

The common possession of the means of production on the part of those who work.

Urkommunism truly is a global form of production. One can find examples of it on every inhabited continent.

So, an essay please on the agricultural village commune of a society of your choice. 2,000 words, please, for Monday.

Class is dismissed.

Autumn 1907. Rosa is employed to lecture in political economy at a new institution: the SPD Party School.

How did it go?

Very well!

Entirely by chance I'm quite prepared to teach this course. The ideas I have drafted for my book on economics* fit perfectly.

And think! 3,000 marks a year — I am rich!

Niuniu, we have the whole weekend to ourselves. Where shall we go?

Let's make the most of the last of the sunshine.

Oh, let's! I love to be roasted by the sun.

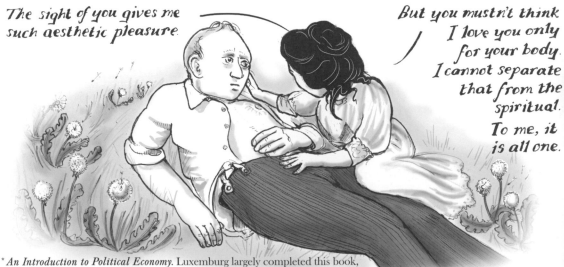

The sight of you gives me such aesthetic pleasure.

But you mustn't think I love you only for your body. I cannot separate that from the spiritual. To me, it is all one.

*An Introduction to Political Economy. Luxemburg largely completed this book, but the manuscript of this and other major works were destroyed by looting soldiers after her death.

The same village, but now we see it in modern times. Common property ceases to exist, and, along with it, the common labour and common will that regulates this.

We have the money economy.

All interactions are based upon exchange.

What does this mean?

Each person is now on his own: the farmer, the shoemaker, the gooseherd, etc.

The community no longer has anything to say to him, no-one can order him to work for the whole, nor does any-one bother about his needs.

Each person's share of the social labour is dictated by the market. Whatever he can sell, he labours at. Whether he can sell it determines whether he is rewarded.

If he is lucky he can buy dinner. If not, he can go and hang himself, for all society cares.

Social wealth is no longer distributed according to need. It matters not to the market whether our labourer has two mouths to feed, or ten.

The community that was previously a whole has been broken up into individual little particles.

Each person now floats like a piece of dust in the air and wonders how he will manage.

Perhaps you will ask, is not submission to the vagaries of the market a small price to pay for individual freedom?

Alas, how unfree is this worker here.

The distinctive feature of capitalism is the precariousness of the worker.

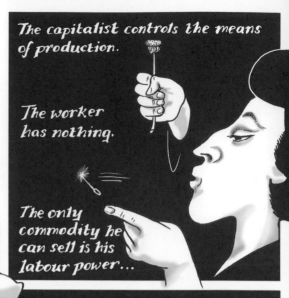

The capitalist controls the means of production.

The worker has nothing.

The only commodity he can sell is his labour power...

...and the entire process revolves around the exploitation of that labour.

The worker may think himself free. But what choice does he have other than to sell his labour?

Jobs are scarce and insecure, for the capitalist keeps a reserve army of the unemployed ready at his bidding.

The capitalist certainly considers himself free. But what choice does he have but to press his workforce ever harder, driving up his profit? For if he doesn't swim ahead of the competition he will sink...

All humanity groans with frightful suffering under the yoke of a blind social power, capital, that it has itself unconsciously created.

The underlying purpose of every social form of production, the satisfaction of society's needs, is turned completely on its head.

Production is no longer for the sake of people.

Production for the sake of profit becomes the law all over the earth.

98

Herr Ebert, a word please.

You struggled with the assignment.

I did. Is it obvious?

Your use of obscure, high-flown terms suggests that you're unclear about the subject matter.

And here, the concept of the dialectic confuses you.

How can something contain its opposite? It makes my head hurt. I like things to be straight-forward, either black or white.

Ah, but in this tension between the opposing forces in society we find the possibility for transformation. As the great philosopher Hegel said: 'Contradiction is the very moving principle of the world.'

What use is abstract philosophy to the working man? Will it feed him? Clothe him?

Transformation, Herr Ebert. Revolution.

Oh, that old theme again!

Dear me, Kautsky tells me that man is tipped for the top in the Party. What kind of socialists are we breeding here?

Never mind. I can but do my best to inspire them.

Rosa is an inspirational teacher because she never stops learning. The continual repetition of the basic tenets of Marxism throws up an interesting problem for her.

Imagine a world where capitalism is complete. This is what Marx envisaged when writing Kapital: 'treat the whole world as one nation and assume that capitalism is everywhere established'. So, everyone is a worker or a boss.

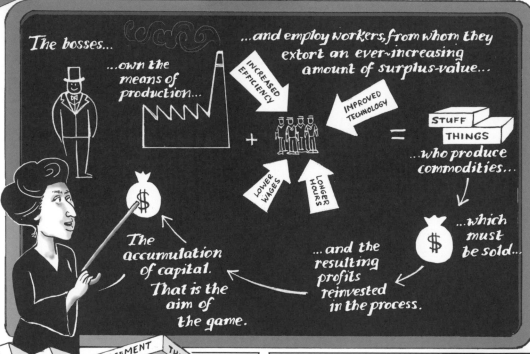

The bosses...

...own the means of production...

...and employ workers, from whom they extort an ever-increasing amount of surplus-value...

INCREASED EFFICIENCY

IMPROVED TECHNOLOGY

LOWER WAGES

LONGER HOURS

STUFF

THINGS

...who produce commodities...

...which must be sold...

...and the resulting profits reinvested in the process.

The accumulation of capital. That is the aim of the game.

THINGS · ITEMS · REPLACEMENT · THINGS · SPARE PARTS · GIFTS · MORE THINGS · NECESSITIES · FASHION · FRIVOLITIES · OTHER STUFF

But, in order for this to take place, an ever-increasing supply of products must be sold to an ever-expanding market of consumers. There must be a demand for the product. But from whom? Who buys these goods?

It is not the workers who consume the commodities, for they earn barely enough to keep body and soul together.

The capitalist class, when viewed as a single entity, cannot buy up all the surplus produce, for to do so would be to squander the profit.

'Aha!' You may reply, 'In our society, not everyone is a worker or a boss. We have other occupations: poet, parson, prostitute. These people buy the products.' But from whence do they obtain their income? From tending to the workers and the bosses. They are parasitic upon the capitalist process. They have no income that is independent from it.

This is not the answer.

How is the unending expansion of capitalism possible?

How does the continual accumulation of capital occur?

We will return to this question later.

Please forgive this authorial intrusion into the narrative, but is any of this still relevant today?

I mean, we know who the consumers are these days — it's us!

Surely things are different now?

The rich nations have spawned a vast, indebted middle-class, indoctrinated into continuous, conspicuous consumption.

We greedily gobble up the products of the exploited workers overseas.

Also, capitalists no longer wear top hats.

But hang on, no, it's still the same. That consumer-class wealth (however we got it) is still derived from capitalism, from economic 'growth'. So Luxemburg's basic proposition remains valid. And if capitalism is mathematically impossible, how come I'm standing here wearing clothes made in China? And how were you able to buy this book?

We don't need to take Rosa's declaration of chastity too seriously; Kostya is not her last lover. But, to pay her due credit as a woman grown to maturity, we could cease constructing her identity solely through the tired old trope of romance.

There are bigger things in her life.

The question of the right to vote in Prussia is on everybody's lips. And we have seen, we cannot reform this law by parliamentary means.

Now only direct mass action can bring about change!

CHEER!

HOORAH! BRAVO!

April 1910. The defeat of a bill to reform the unfair Prussian suffrage system sparks protests and strikes around the country. Luxemburg leaps up to fan the revolutionary flames.

You were very persuasive. I think I'm convinced.

That's what I like to hear, Dr Diefenbach.

Eight public meetings down, six more to go...

Another momentous split.

Rosa publicly falls out with Karl Kautsky, the most respected Marxist theoretician of the SPD.

I have nothing more to say to you.

Then stand aside, because I am here to visit your wife.

What's going on? Karl never tells me anything.

He has refused to publish my call for a republic.

It's 'not the Party line'~ the very idea is banned! Pfui! To quote Marx: our government is 'nothing but military despotism embellished with parliamentary forms'. Yet it has the support of Karl Kautsky! Who needs the police to call us into line? Herr Kautsky will police us himself!

All Germany is ready for industrial action yet Karl is not! He says a mass strike is 'unthinkable'. Here! We have the strongest socialist movement in the world yet our proletariat is apparently the most powerless.

Do you think you can make it up with him?

Lulu, he has stabbed me in the back.

You will still visit me?

That invertebrate cannot keep me from your door.

Come! Let's visit Clara.

♪ ♪ ♪ ♪
La la la la la la la

FIGARO! FIGARO!

Hush, Rosa! You'll wake the neighbourhood.

You always put me in a champagne mood, Rosa.

Oh! Life is making my fingers tingle.

With you two I'm ready for any foolishness!

When shall we three meet again? In thunder, lightning or in rain?

HA HA HA HA HA HA HA HA HA

Dear Rosa must not be allowed to spoil our plans.

105

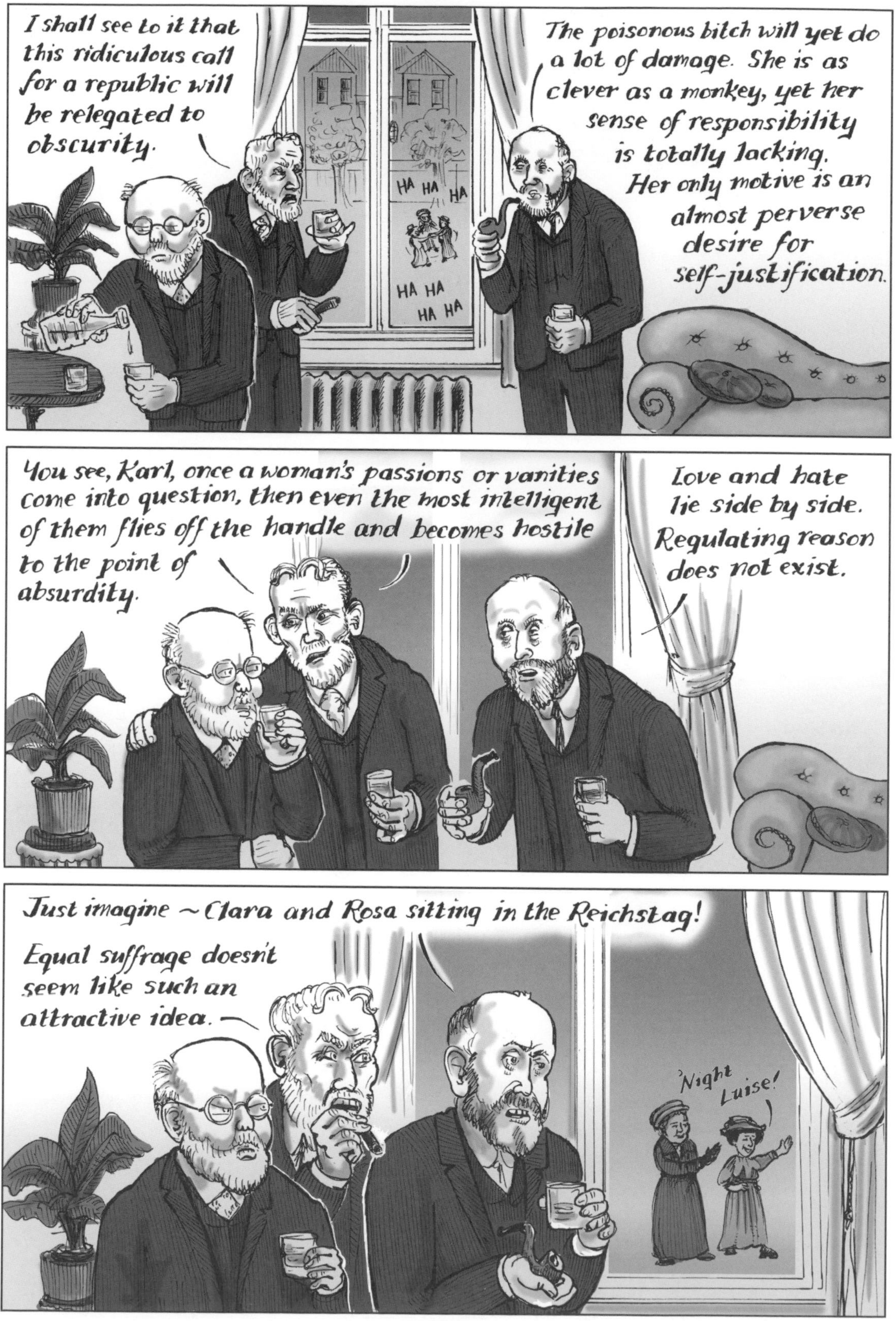
I shall see to it that this ridiculous call for a republic will be relegated to obscurity.
The poisonous bitch will yet do a lot of damage. She is as clever as a monkey, yet her sense of responsibility is totally lacking. Her only motive is an almost perverse desire for self-justification.
HA HA HA
HA HA HA HA
You see, Karl, once a woman's passions or vanities come into question, then even the most intelligent of them flies off the handle and becomes hostile to the point of absurdity.
Love and hate lie side by side. Regulating reason does not exist.
Just imagine ~ Clara and Rosa sitting in the Reichstag!
Equal suffrage doesn't seem like such an attractive idea.
'Night Luise!

September 1912.

Mimi! I am as clever as a monkey! There is a hole in Marx's work on capital accumulation, and I am determined to track it down.

Oh, Mimi, you ask who am I to question the works of the great thinker Marx? That is precisely the attitude I detest. So many slavishly follow the principles of socialism, and so few question them.

Marx never finished the second volume of Das Kapital. The manuscript stops halfway through. The problem of accumulation is touched upon, but never explored.

We are led to believe that the market simply grows bigger because the market grows bigger.

The logic is circular. Yes, Mimi ~ like a cat chasing its tail.

Perhaps the capitalist class absorbs the expanded market for consumer goods by purchasing technology to produce more goods? But the next year, even more products come to market. That just pushes the problem from one year to the next. Round and round the logic goes.

Stop it, Mimi, You're making me dizzy.

In a world formed purely of capitalists and workers there is just no way that the capitalists, viewed in their entirety, can get rid of the surplus goods, change the surplus value into money, and accumulate capital.

Dr Diefenbach! What a surprise!

I was in the area. I dropped by. May I distract you?

Not now, Hans ~ the problem of the accumulation of capital has me by the throat.

Oh.

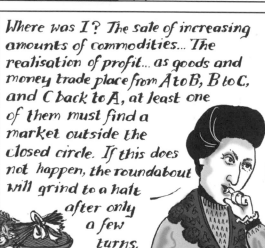

Where was I? The sale of increasing amounts of commodities... The realisation of profit... as goods and money trade place from A to B, B to C, and C back to A, at least one of them must find a market outside the closed circle. If this does not happen, the roundabout will grind to a halt after only a few turns.

The solution to the problem ties together all the strands of Luxemburg's life's work into a neat theoretical whole.

Imperialism, Mimi. Capitalism expands by forcing its way into non-capitalist markets. It must in order to exist.

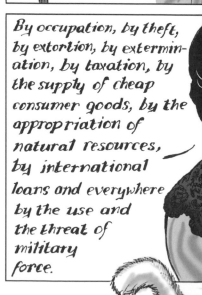

By occupation, by theft, by extortion, by extermination, by taxation, by the supply of cheap consumer goods, by the appropriation of natural resources, by international loans and everywhere by the use and the threat of military force.

Capitalism can never peacefully co-exist with other forms of existence. It is a rampaging tiger committed to the destruction or absorption of all other ways of life except its own.

It is fifty years before the word 'globalisation' will be coined. Luxemburg formulates its mathematical proof. She uncovers the engine that drives the process inexorably onward.

Capitalism is a creeping cancer, a strangling vine.

Capitalism tends to engulf the entire globe and to stamp out all other economies, tolerating no rival at its side. Yet it is unable to exist by itself; it needs other economic mediums as its soil.

But there's more: it truly does sow the seeds of its own destruction. Once it achieves its endpoint, the domination of all forms of industry, it must collapse in upon itself.

Torn apart by its internal contradictions, it can no longer exist.

It strives to become universal, yet it is immanently incapable of this, and must break down. In its living history it is a contradiction in itself.

It is the ultimate dialectic. The torsion in the forces that tear the world apart.

It will also be half a century before we hear the term 'military-industrial complex', yet Luxemburg makes explicit the inextricable tie between capitalism and militarism.

Force is the only solution available to capitalism; the accumulation of capital employs force as a permanent weapon.

Her words are timely. Europe resonates with the marching feet of troops about to engage in the deadliest conflict the world has ever known.

ALL EUROPE WILL BE CALLED TO ARMS, AND SIXTEEN TO EIGHTEEN MILLION MEN, THE FLOWER OF THE NATIONS, ARMED WITH THE BEST INSTRUMENTS OF MURDER, WILL MAKE WAR UPON EACH OTHER.
THEY ARE LEADING US STRAIGHT INTO A CATASTROPHE.
THEY WILL REAP WHAT THEY HAVE SOWN.

World war.

Rosa has proved its logical inevitability.

Capitalism is prepared to set the world on fire.

110

The German Social Democratic movement has never been more important. While Rosa writes, they poll their greatest ever election victory, taking more than 4.25 million votes. With 110 deputies, they are, at last, the largest party in the Reichstag.

And they are bound by the resolution of the 1907 Stuttgart meeting of the International (which Rosa helped to draft): 'It is the duty of the working classes and their parliamentary representatives to do everything to prevent the outbreak of war.'

OPPOSE THIS CRIME OF WAR! ARE THE WORKING PEOPLE OF TODAY REALLY NOTHING BUT SHEEP TO BE LED MUTELY TO THE SLAUGHTER?

WILL NOT A CRY OF HORROR, OF FURY AND OF INDIGNATION FILL THE COUNTRY AND LEAD THE PEOPLE TO PUT AN END TO THIS MURDER?

WE ARE FIGHTING WITH ALL OUR MIGHT AGAINST CAPITALISM THAT IS PREPARING TO CHANGE EUROPE INTO A SMOKING BATTLEFIELD.

Well, at least Rosa is.

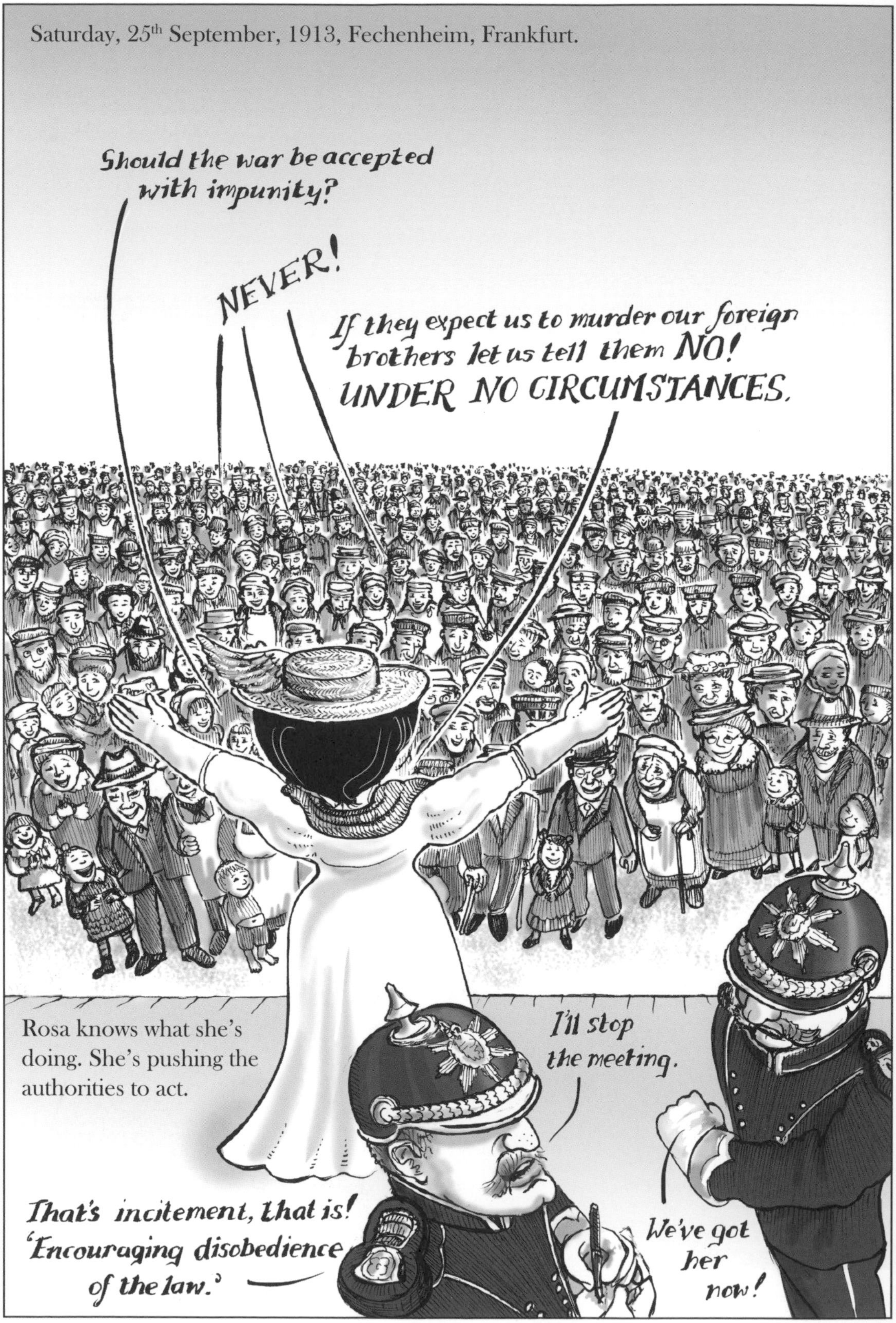
Saturday, 25th September, 1913, Fechenheim, Frankfurt.
Should the war be accepted with impunity?
NEVER!
If they expect us to murder our foreign brothers let us tell them NO! UNDER NO CIRCUMSTANCES.
Rosa knows what she's doing. She's pushing the authorities to act.
I'll stop the meeting.
That's incitement, that is! 'Encouraging disobedience of the law.'
We've got her now!

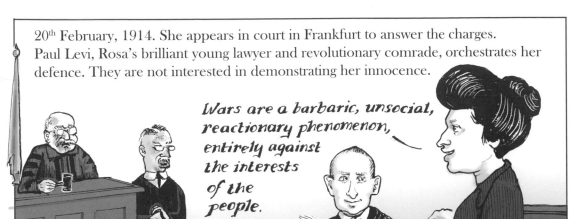

20th February, 1914. She appears in court in Frankfurt to answer the charges. Paul Levi, Rosa's brilliant young lawyer and revolutionary comrade, orchestrates her defence. They are not interested in demonstrating her innocence.

Wars are a barbaric, unsocial, reactionary phenomenon, entirely against the interests of the people.

When the majority of people come to this conclusion, then wars will become impossible.

And it is precisely the task of Social Democracy to arouse this consciousness.

Imprisonment is inevitable, but Rosa lodges an appeal. The prosecution argues against granting her bail...

There is a substantial risk that the defendant will flee.

Sir, I believe that you would flee. A Social Democrat does not. She stands by her actions and laughs at your judgements.

And now~ sentence me!

One year in prison!

BLAM!

Commencement of the prison term is delayed pending appeal. Dr Luxemburg is free to leave.

There are comrades who assume that you will leave Germany to escape this prison sentence.

Leo Jogiches. I could be amused by that if it were not really rather sad.

I would not flee even if I were threatened by the gallows.

Sacrifices are part of a socialist's work.

They are simply a matter of course.

Long live the struggle.

CHINK

We must build on the publicity this trial has afforded. We have been invited to speak all over Germany.

We? Myself and Herr Levi.

Mm, your attorney. How do you like him?

Yes, he's very good.

Rosa likes her attorney rather a lot.

Are you ready Herr Levi?

Indeed, I am, Dr Luxemburg.

They 'like' each other all summer, until their relationship mellows into friendship.

You're very good, you know.

Yes, I know.

But you're a playboy. You break a lot of hearts, but you won't break mine.

114

Luxemburg and Levi attend rallies, they give speeches...

...and once again the authorities take note.

June 1914

The old guard of SPD lawyers are alarmed and confused by Levi's willingness to subvert the judicial process for political ends.

A call for witnesses? In a newspaper?

What are you playing at, man? Fräulein Luxemburg~

~Doctor Luxemburg.

~she already has one prison sentence hanging over her head. Surely the best course of action is to apologise, plead innocence, delay the proceedings.

Oh, no, we're pressing for the earliest trial date. The Minister of War wants to drag the issue of military abuse into obscurity. We want it in the open.

We go to court, we attract the press. Through the press, we reach the public.

It's a court of law! Not a circus!

Think of your defendant. What if your stratagem backfires?

Dr Luxemburg agrees, the propagandist effect of a harsh punishment would be absolutely extraordinary!

Good God! Are you even trying to get her acquitted?

Wait and see, old boy!

116

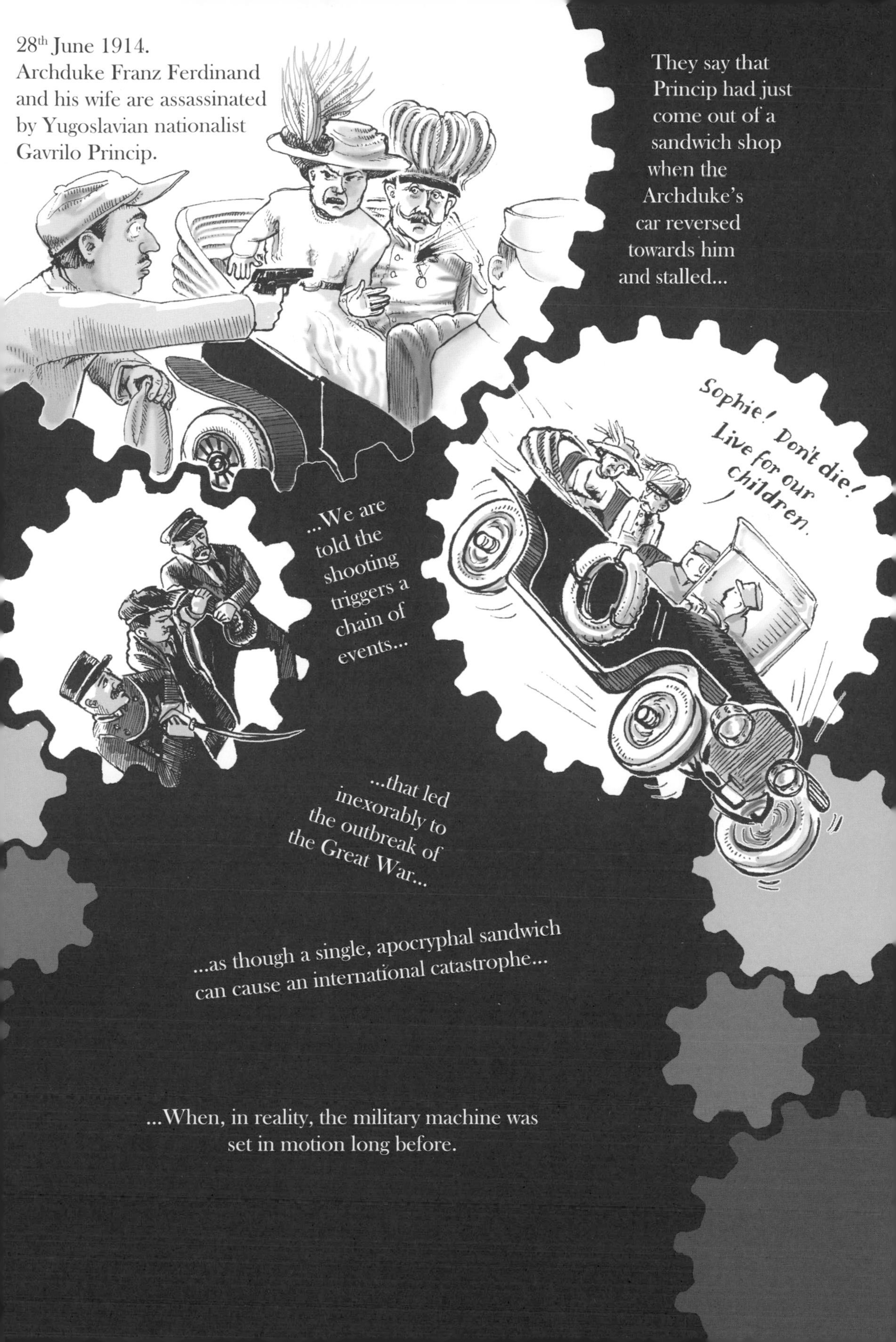
28th June 1914.
Archduke Franz Ferdinand and his wife are assassinated by Yugoslavian nationalist Gavrilo Princip.
They say that Princip had just come out of a sandwich shop when the Archduke's car reversed towards him and stalled...
Sophie! Don't die! Live for our children.
...We are told the shooting triggers a chain of events...
...that led inexorably to the outbreak of the Great War...
...as though a single, apocryphal sandwich can cause an international catastrophe...
...When, in reality, the military machine was set in motion long before.

The very next day, Rosa's trial begins. Levi turns the tables to put the military establishment in the dock.

I note that the Minister of War has initiated these charges. Why has the Minister not presented himself for cross-examination? How can this trial proceed without him?

Judge Seligman, you are a former army officer, yes? Assistant Judge Schultze, you were an officer too? What impartiality can you bring to this case?

The defence humbly requests that the judges retire to consider their own fitness to rule.

Gentlemen of the Jury. Here are one hundred and six witnesses, common soldiers all, to testify to the inhumanity and cruelty of German army officers. But these are just a sample. We can testify to thirty thousand instances of abuse ~ one can easily document half a million.

The officer corps is the guilty party.

Faced with the prospect of a stream of witness reports of army brutality reported daily in the national press, the Minister of War quietly shelves the proceedings.

Sir? The Luxemburg case?

DON'T TALK TO ME ABOUT THAT WOMAN!

4th August 1914.

You have your freedom.

For the moment, but who cares? For once, I wish I'd dedicated my life to getting women the right to vote. Dammit, Clara. I wish we were in there right now.

The Reichstag is assembled for the crucial vote to approve the Kaiser's plans for war. The SPD have never approved a capitalist budget before.

But now they do. Unanimously. One hundred and ten Socialist deputies vote for World War.

In the hour of danger we will stand by the Fatherland.

I wasn't happy with the decision, but we can't break protocol.

It'll all be over by Christmas.

My God! What have you done?

Will none of you look me in the eye?

The Socialist International, Brussels, July 30th, 1914.

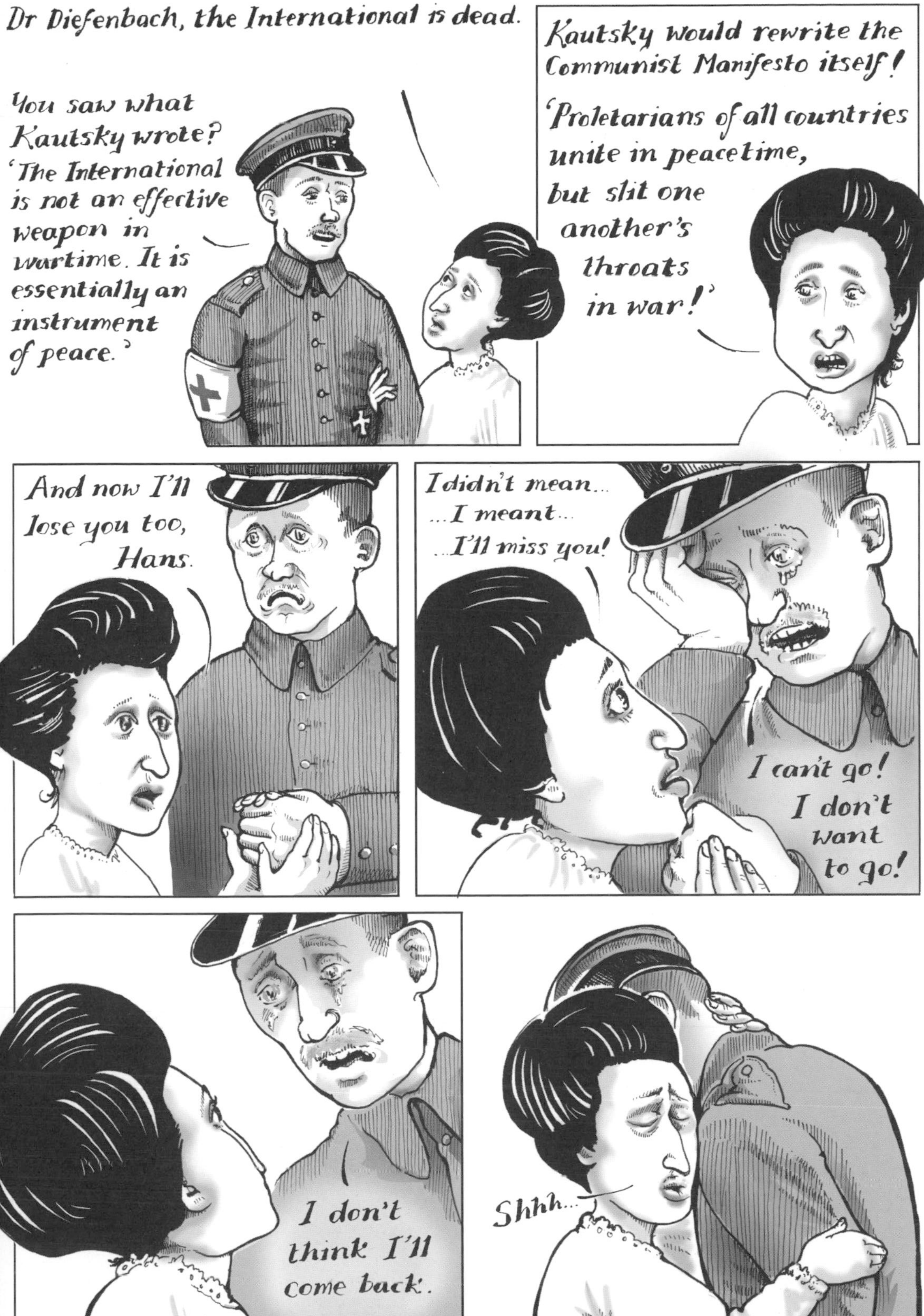

Dr Diefenbach, the International is dead.
You saw what Kautsky wrote? 'The International is not an effective weapon in wartime. It is essentially an instrument of peace.'
Kautsky would rewrite the Communist Manifesto itself!
'Proletarians of all countries unite in peacetime, but slit one another's throats in war!'
And now I'll lose you too, Hans.
I didn't mean... ...I meant... ...I'll miss you!
I can't go! I don't want to go!
I don't think I'll come back.
Shhh...

The constraints of censorship are severe. Rosa knows she is destined for imprisonment, but fights on while she can.

'We find it necessary to assure foreign comrades that we regard the war from an entirely different standpoint. Martial law makes it impossible for us to enlarge upon our point of view.'

It's a letter to the international press. I don't think they can hang us for it.

~ Herr Liebknecht? Clara?

I'll sign it.

Pass it here.

December 2nd, 1914. The Reichstag considers another request for war credits.

A single man stands in opposition: SPD deputy Karl Liebknecht.

He is prevented from making any more political statements...

...and arrested on May 1st, 1916.

DOWN WITH THE WAR!

THE ENEMY IS HERE! IN YOUR OWN COUNTRY!

Let him go, you brutes!

July 10th, 1916.　　　Rosa is taken into 'military protective custody'.　　　Indefinitely.

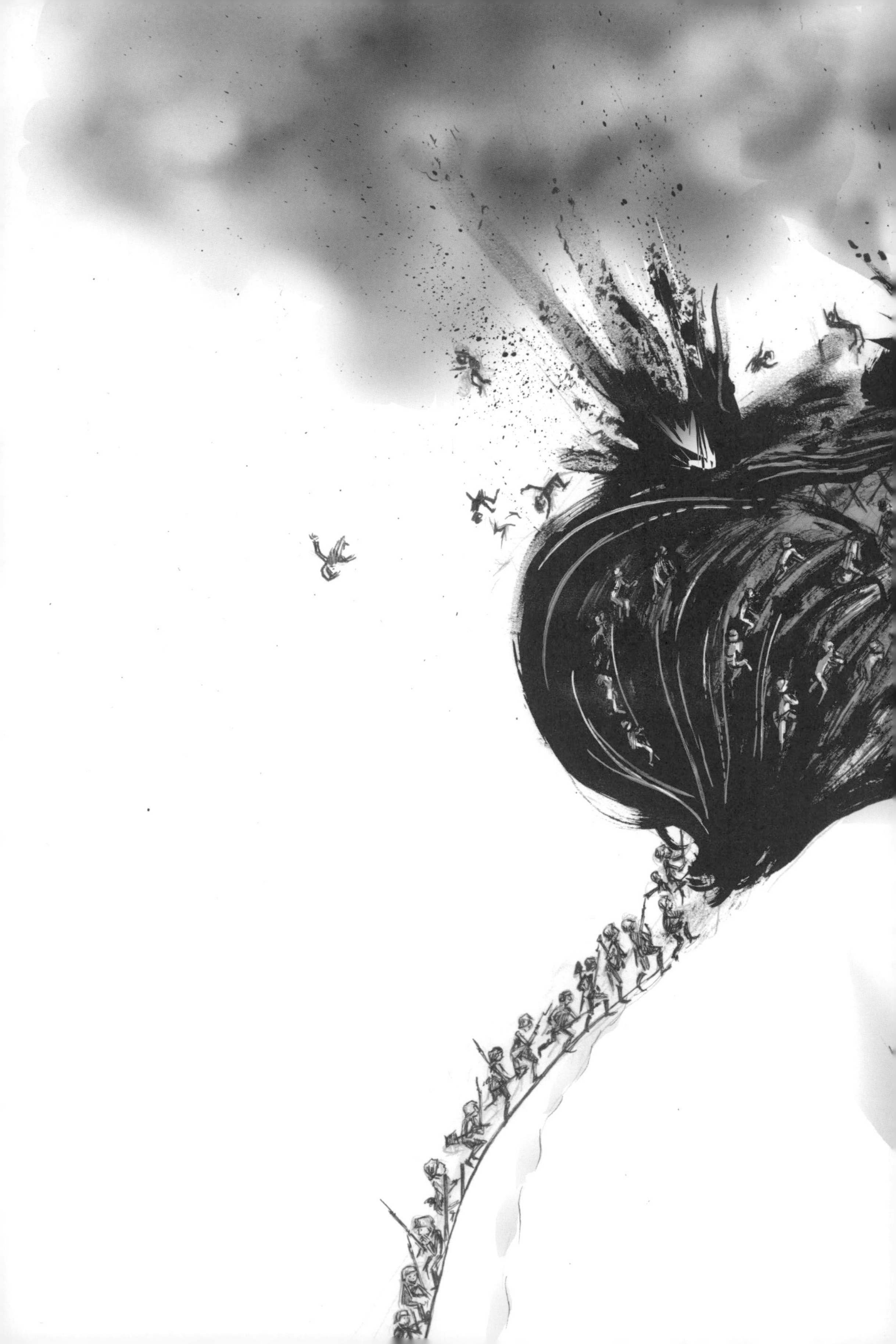

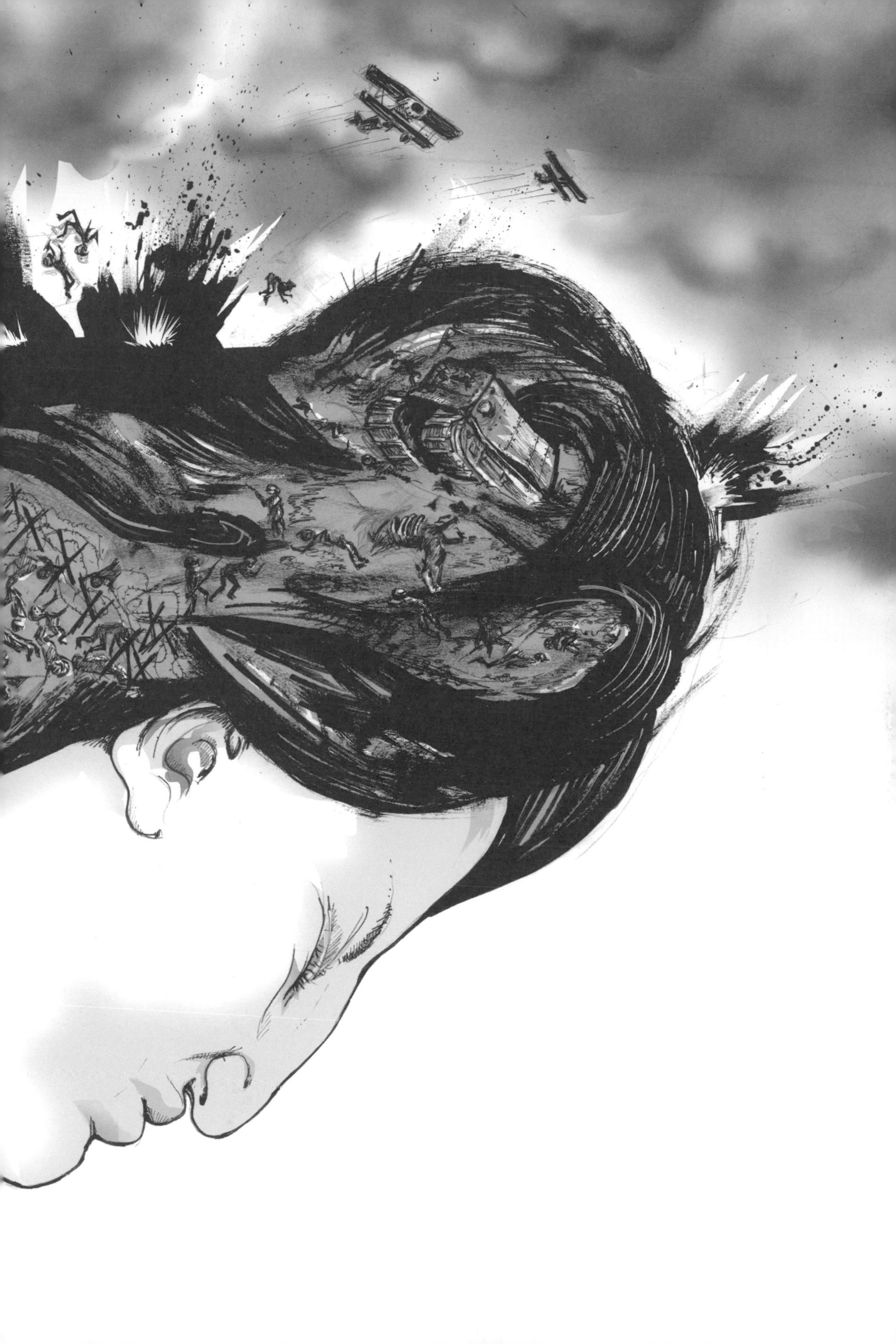

Mass murder has become a monotonous task, and yet the final solution is not one step nearer. Capitalist rule is caught in its own trap, and cannot ban the spirit it has invoked.

Gone is the first mad delirium. Gone are the patriotic street demonstrations, the singing throngs, the violent mobs. The show is over. The curtain has fallen on trains filled with reservists, as they pull out amid the joyous cries of enthusiastic maidens. We no longer see their laughing faces, smiling cheerily from the train windows upon a war-mad population. Quietly they trot through the streets, with their sacks upon their shoulders. And the public, with a fretful face, goes about its daily task.

Into the disillusioned atmosphere of pale daylight there rings a different chorus; the hoarse croak of the hawks and hyenas of the battlefield. Ten thousand tents, guaranteed according to specifications, 100,000 kilos of bacon, cocoa powder, coffee substitute — cash on immediate delivery. Shrapnel, drills, ammunition bags, marriage bureaus for war widows, leather belts — only serious propositions considered. And the cannon fodder that was loaded onto the trains in August and September is rotting on the battlefields of Belgium and the Vosges, while profits are springing, like weeds, from the fields of the dead.

Business is flourishing upon the ruins. Cities are turned into shambles, whole countries into deserts, villages into cemeteries, nations into beggars, churches into stables; popular rights, treaties, alliances, the holiest words and the highest authorities have been torn into scraps. Hunger revolts in Venetia, in Lisbon, in Moscow, in Singapore; pestilence in Russia; misery and desperation is everywhere.

Shamed, dishonoured, wading in blood and dripping with filth, thus capitalist society stands. Not as we usually see it, playing the roles of righteousness, of order, of ethics—but as a roaring beast, as an orgy of chaos, as a pestilential breath, devastating culture and humanity—so it appears in all its hideous nakedness.

The Junius Pamphlet.   Rosa Luxemburg.   Published 1916.

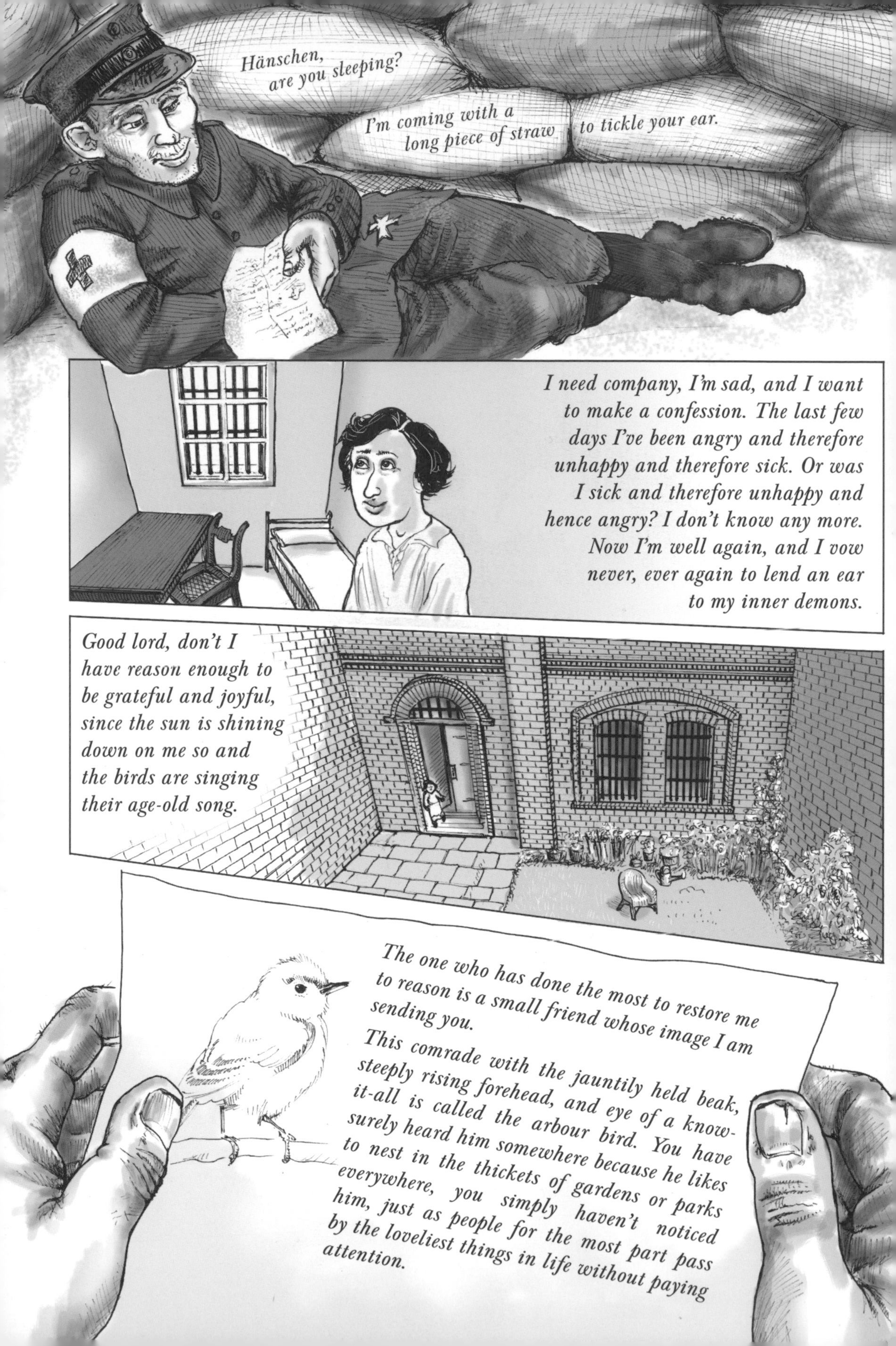

Hänschen, are you sleeping?
I'm coming with a long piece of straw
to tickle your ear.
I need company, I'm sad, and I want to make a confession. The last few days I've been angry and therefore unhappy and therefore sick. Or was I sick and therefore unhappy and hence angry? I don't know any more. Now I'm well again, and I vow never, ever again to lend an ear to my inner demons.
Good lord, don't I have reason enough to be grateful and joyful, since the sun is shining down on me so and the birds are singing their age-old song.
The one who has done the most to restore me to reason is a small friend whose image I am sending you.
This comrade with the jauntily held beak, steeply rising forehead, and eye of a know-it-all is called the arbour bird. You have surely heard him somewhere because he likes to nest in the thickets of gardens or parks everywhere, you simply haven't noticed him, just as people for the most part pass by the loveliest things in life without paying attention.

This bird is quite an oddball. He doesn't sing just one song or one melody, like other birds, but he is a public speaker, he holds forth, making his speeches to the garden, and does so with a very loud voice full of dramatic excitement, leaping transitions, and passages of heightened pathos.

He brings up the most impossible questions, then hurries to answer them himself, with nonsense, makes the most daring assertions, heatedly refuting views that no one has stated, charges through wide open doors, then suddenly exclaims in triumph: *Didn't I say so? Didn't I say so?*

Immediately after that he solemnly warns everyone who's willing or not willing to listen: *You'll see! You'll see!* (He has the clever habit of repeating each witty remark twice.)

He never grows tired of filling the garden with the most blatant nonsense, and during the stillness that reigns while he's giving his speeches, one can almost see the other birds exchanging glances and shrugging their shoulders.

Sweet dumbhead!

I don't shrug mine; instead, I laugh every time with joy. You see, I know that his foolish chatter is actually the deepest wisdom and that he's right about everything.

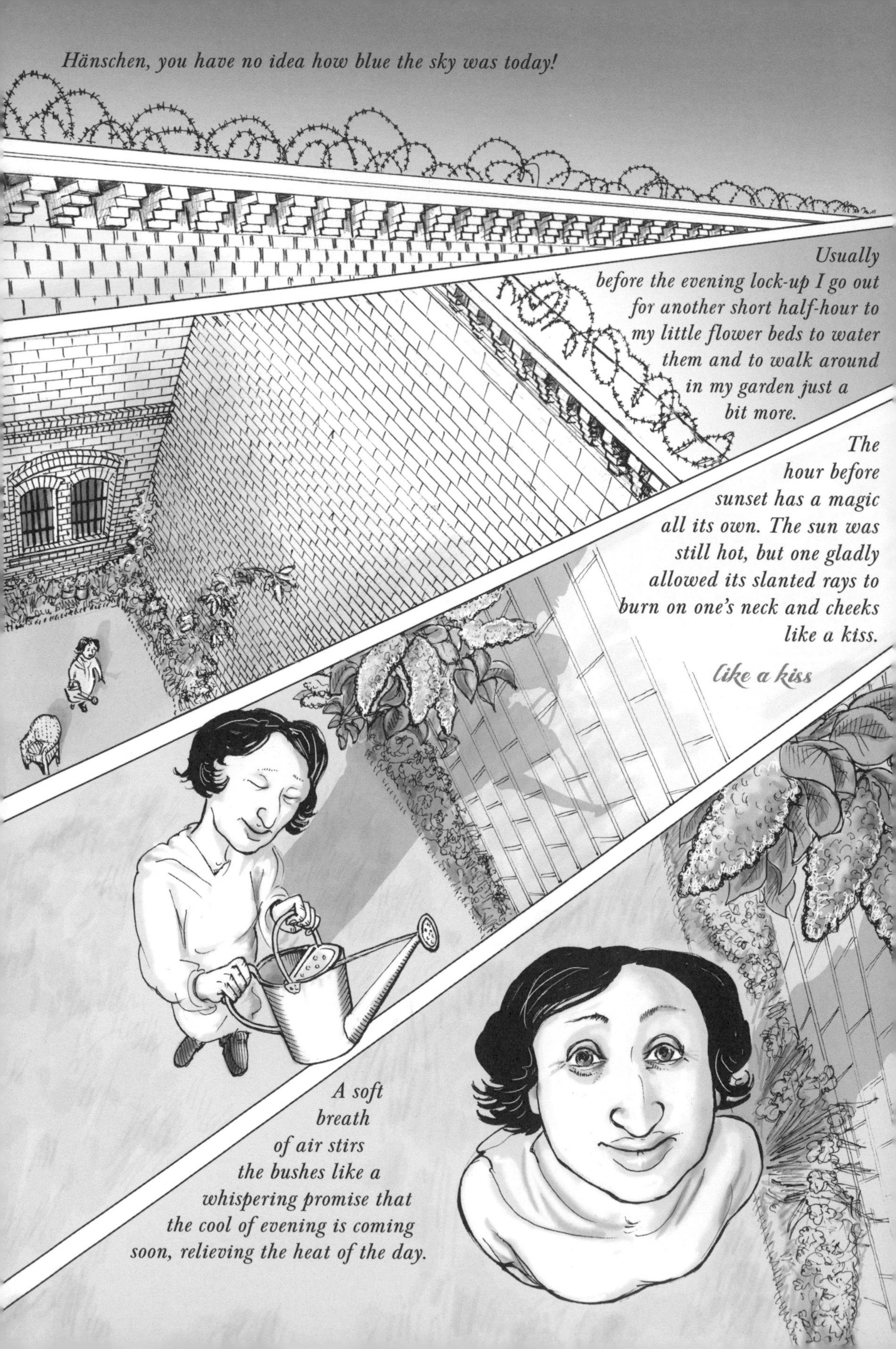
Hänschen, you have no idea how blue the sky was today!
Usually before the evening lock-up I go out for another short half-hour to my little flower beds to water them and to walk around in my garden just a bit more.
The hour before sunset has a magic all its own. The sun was still hot, but one gladly allowed its slanted rays to burn on one's neck and cheeks like a kiss.
like a kiss
A soft breath of air stirs the bushes like a whispering promise that the cool of evening is coming soon, relieving the heat of the day.

In the sky, which was of a trembling, shimmering blue, two towering white cloud formations were piled high, while a very pale half-moon swam between them as though in a dream.

The swallows had already begun their every-evening's flight in full company strength...

...and with their sharp, pointy wings snipped the blue silk of space into little bits...

...shot back and forth...

...overtaking one another with shrill cries...

...and disappearing into the dizzying heights.

I stood with my little watering can dripping in my hand and felt a tremendous yearning to dive up into that damp, shimmering blueness...

...to bathe in it...

...to splash around...

disappear

dissolve

damp shimmering blueness

...to let myself dissolve completely in that dew, and disappear.

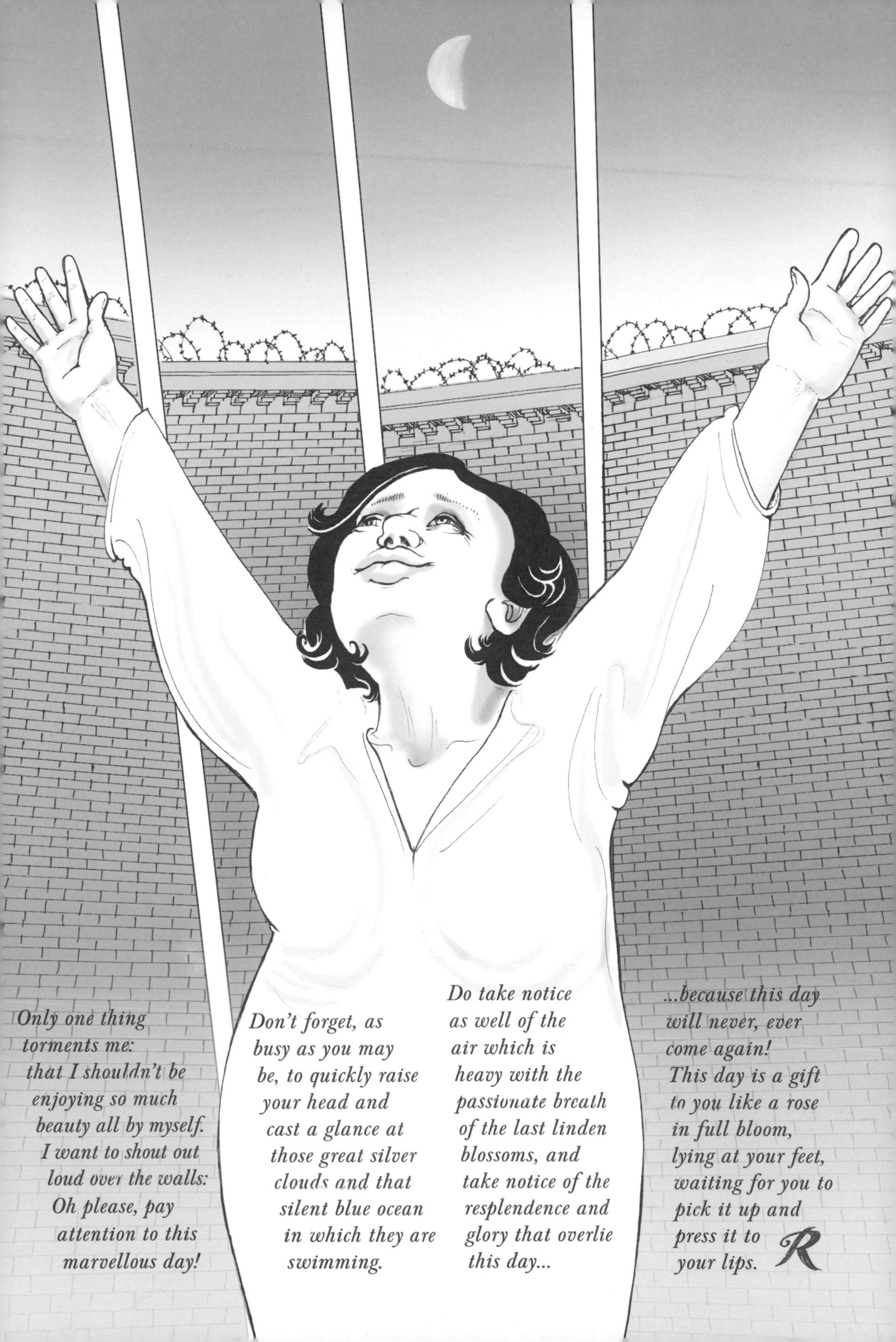
Only one thing torments me: that I shouldn't be enjoying so much beauty all by myself. I want to shout out loud over the walls: Oh please, pay attention to this marvellous day!
Don't forget, as busy as you may be, to quickly raise your head and cast a glance at those great silver clouds and that silent blue ocean in which they are swimming.
Do take notice as well of the air which is heavy with the passionate breath of the last linden blossoms, and take notice of the resplendence and glory that overlie this day...
...because this day will never, ever come again! This day is a gift to you like a rose in full bloom, lying at your feet, waiting for you to pick it up and press it to your lips.
R

Outside the walls of Wronke Fortress, World History plays on...

By January 1917 many millions of lives have been sacrificed to the incompetence of military commanders who fail to recognise that men cannot run through machine-gun fire.

The battle lines of the Eastern and Western fronts are essentially static. Casualty rates soar. The unimaginable horror of trench warfare continues.

In March (February by the Russian calendar), rallies for International Women's
Day spiral into mass strikes that engulf Petrograd (St Petersburg).

Soldiers refuse to fire on crowds of mainly women.

Tsar Nicholas abdicates and is placed under house arrest.

The Duma attempts to rule the country, but much
power now lies with workers' councils.

The Bolsheviks campaign for an end to the hated war.

By May, 54 divisions of the French army are
in open rebellion. They force the cessation of French offensive operations.

British engineering workers strike,
winning all their demands.

*I am making this statement as an act of wilful defiance of military authority because I believe that
the war is being deliberately prolonged by those who have the power to end it.*

30th July. British soldier
Siegfried Sassoon's letter is read out in the House of Commons.

In the Reichstag, resistance to the war grows.
The SPD splits: pacifist deputies leave to form the independent USPD.

2nd August. German sailors on the dreadnought *Prinzregent Luitpold* refuse to follow orders.
The ringleaders are executed by firing squad.

12th September. A thousand British soldiers mutiny for a week at Étaples.

On 25th October (by the Russian calendar) Lenin and the Bolsheviks storm the Winter Palace...

...disband the Provisional Government...

...and seize control of Russia.

Late on the night of 24th October, Hans Diefenbach is blown apart by a grenade.

So much of Rosa's life is expressed through letters. So poignant now, that this is the medium by which she learns of Hans Diefenbach's death.

I received the dreadful black envelope.

My hands and heart were already trembling when I saw the handwriting and the postmark, but I still hoped that the worst would not be true.

How can this be possible?

To me it is like a word cut short in mid-sentence,

like a musical chord broken off, although I still keep hearing it.

We had a thousand plans for life after the war. We wanted to enjoy life, travel, read good books, and gaze in wonder, as never before, at the coming of spring.

I cannot comprehend it. I dare not even think about it, otherwise I could not bear it. On the contrary, I live on with the dream that he is still here, I see his living form in front of me, chat with him in my thoughts about everything; in me he continues to live.

Yesterday my letter to him was returned; that's the second one already.

Letters that never reached him.

Waiting for you to pick it up and press it to your lips.

I've lived through something sharply, terribly painful here.

Into the prison courtyard there often come military supply wagons, filled with sacks or old army coats and shirts, often with bloodstains on them... They're unloaded here, distributed to the prison cells, patched or mended, then loaded up and turned over to the military again.

One of these wagons arrived with water buffaloes harnessed to it instead of horses. These animals have a stronger, broader build than our cattle, with flat heads and horns that curve back flatly; they are completely black, with large, soft, black eyes. They come from Romania, the spoils of war. It was a lot of trouble to catch these wild creatures and even more difficult to put them to work as draft animals, because they were accustomed to their freedom. They had to be beaten terribly before they grasped the concept that they had lost the war.

The load on the wagon was piled so high that they couldn't pull it over the threshold at the entrance gate. The soldier accompanying it, a brutal fellow, began flailing at the animals fiercely with the blunt end of his whip handle...

The animals finally started to pull again and got over the hump, but one of them was bleeding... the hide of a buffalo is proverbial for its thickness, but this tough skin had been broken.

The animals stood, quite still, exhausted, and that one stared into the empty space in front of him with an expression on his face and in his soft, black eyes like an abused child. It was precisely the expression of a child that has been punished and doesn't know why or what for, doesn't know how to get away from this torment and raw violence.

Tears were running down my face... they were his tears.

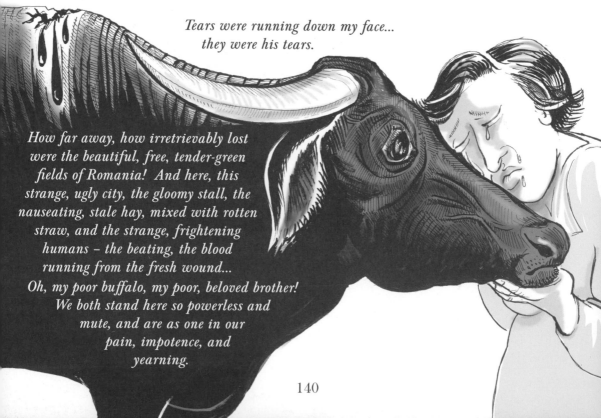

How far away, how irretrievably lost were the beautiful, free, tender-green fields of Romania! And here, this strange, ugly city, the gloomy stall, the nauseating, stale hay, mixed with rotten straw, and the strange, frightening humans – the beating, the blood running from the fresh wound...
Oh, my poor buffalo, my poor, beloved brother! We both stand here so powerless and mute, and are as one in our pain, impotence, and yearning.

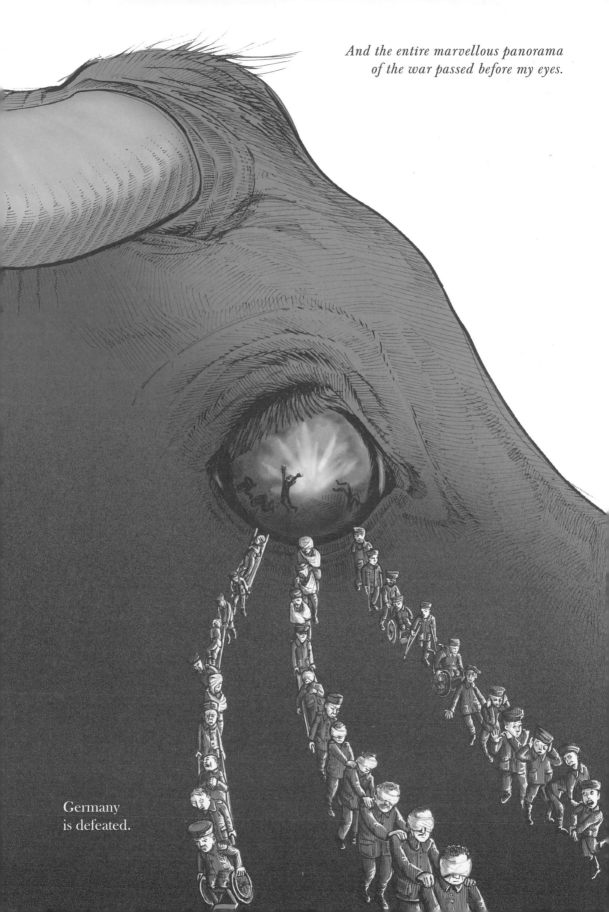

And the entire marvellous panorama of the war passed before my eyes.

Germany is defeated.

Having fought three major military powers to a standstill, Germany has no reserves to battle a fourth. In the summer of 1918, two million fresh US soldiers arrive at the Western front. Germany's defences collapse.

On October 3rd, Prince Max of Baden is appointed Chancellor, and a cross-party government is formed. A socialist, Philipp Scheidemann, becomes a Government minister. That night, a request for peace negotiations is issued. Too late. It isn't enough.

Throughout October, the war drags on. Since the British will make an armistice conditional on the destruction of the German Navy, the German Admiralty decide to engage their ships in a last desperate battle for death or glory.

The sailors have other ideas.

October 29th, 1918. Wilhemshaven naval base.

143

Only the Thüringen and the Markgrav have red flags. But no ship has sailed to make war.

Death or glory? Better to die right here.

The Admiralty abandon their battle plans. They manage to regain control of the fleet, return to the home port of Kiel and arrest 49 sailors for insurrection. Their attempt to contain the rebellion backfires.

In Kiel, the contagion spreads.

RETURN TO YOUR SHIPS IMMEDIATELY! BY NAVAL COMMAND!!!

They can't arrest us all!

Join us!

Save our brothers from the firing squad!

PEACE! BREAD! FREEDOM!

=RATATTATTA

That's gunfire son. We must

144

By nightfall, revolutionary soldiers' and workers' councils have seized control of the city. Infantry troops are sent to suppress the uprising but are immediately converted to the cause.

With the outcome of the world war, bourgeois class rule has forfeited its right to exist.
It is no longer able to lead society out of the catastrophic economic collapse which the imperialist orgy has left behind. *Rosa Luxemburg — What Does the Spartacus League Want?*

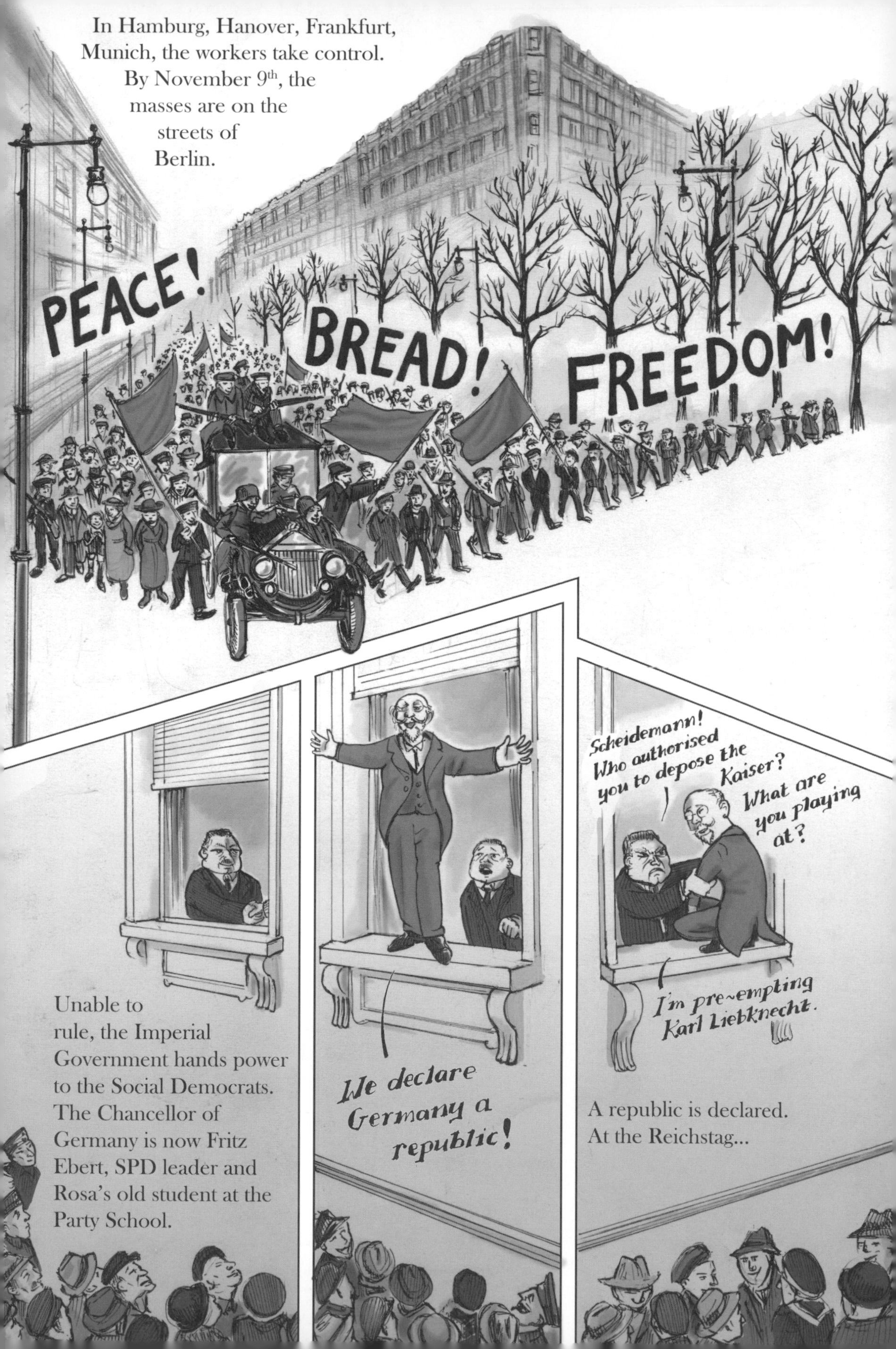
In Hamburg, Hanover, Frankfurt, Munich, the workers take control. By November 9th, the masses are on the streets of Berlin.
PEACE!
BREAD!
FREEDOM!
Unable to rule, the Imperial Government hands power to the Social Democrats. The Chancellor of Germany is now Fritz Ebert, SPD leader and Rosa's old student at the Party School.
We declare Germany a republic!
Scheidemann! Who authorised you to depose the Kaiser?
What are you playing at?
I'm pre-empting Karl Liebknecht.
A republic is declared. At the Reichstag...

We proclaim the Free Socialist Republic of Germany! The rule of capitalism is over! The day of liberty has begun!

...and at the City Palace.

ONG LIVE LIEBKNECHT!

PEACE!

BREAD!

The abdication of the Kaiser (who is absent) is a *fait accompli.*

The Reichstag is occupied by the Revolutionary Stewards, a grassroots workers' organisation. They propose an entirely new form of government. Every factory and every regiment is to elect a delegate to the Council of the People's Deputies.

The socialists are in charge! Direct rule by the workers is a reality!

The German Revolution is here!

Late that night, Rosa Luxemburg is released from gaol.

...Where great things are in the making... .
...where the wind roars about the ears...
...that's where I'll be...
...in the thick of it!

FREEDOM!

Berlin, 11th November 1918.

Paul! Karl! Leo! Darling Mathilde!

Rosa!

Our new paper: Die Rote Fahne

You will be editor?

Of course!

The armistice will be signed later today. Can you get us a lead article within the hour?

We found these soldiers and —cheers, mate— we stormed the offices of the Berliner Lokal paper. We printed the first edition yesterday.

How are you, Rosa?

I'm fine— I'm very well indeed!

We will not be printing your filthy rag.

Your soldiers were easily bought.

Soldiers! Printers! Brothers! Don't let the capitalists steal your labour and your soul! Can you not see that your interests lie with us? The true voice of the working people!

You're not my sister.

Herr Scherl pays us well.

I'm not sure that they can see that, Rosa. Nice try.

Let's go.

My God. What kind of revolution is this?

Nobody knows, yet.

Well, assuming we can get a paper printed...

...What are our demands? I've been giving this some thought.

I bet you have!

Firstly, secure the revolution. Impound food and distribute it to the starving. Confiscate weapons and arms. Create a workers' militia from the entire adult working population; choose the officers by election and make them subject to worker control.

Put Ludendorff and the generals on trial for war crimes.

Abolish the aristocracy. Confiscate all private wealth above a certain level. Use this to fund the overhaul of the food, housing, health and education systems.

The economy? Repudiate national debt and war loans ~ We need a clean slate. Nationalise the banks, mines and heavy industry. Take over the public transport system. Occupy large landed estates and farm them collectively. A six-hour working day.

How do we achieve this? The people elect workers' and soldiers' councils. The central council of these bodies meets every three months and this directs the work of the executive committee.

What else? Ah, yes, complete social and legal equality of the sexes.

Does anyone have anything to add?

What name do we sign it by?

The same name we used during the war.

The Spartacus League. If ever there were a need for a slave rebellion, it's now.

But the Spartacists' publication won't appear until November 18th. They are allotted a miserly ration of paper. Someone in power doesn't want their message to be heard...

The previous day, 10th November: the first day in office for the new leader of Germany.

We're offering the loyalty of the armed forces...

Thank you, sir. I mean, thank you, yes.

But enough of this soldier-worker-council nonsense. We won't have mob rule.

Tell him we're a law unto ourself.

We're a law unto ourself. That's the condition for our support.

There are radicals on every street corner. You won't last five minutes without us. Stamp out this Bolshevik madness.

I've said it before and I'll say it again. I hate revolution like a mortal sin.

Glad to hear it.

Preserve private property. SCOFF Appeal for calm. GOBBLE Get the masses off the streets.

MUNCH
SCOFF
CRUNCH

And ensure that every workers' council out there is packed with SPD men.

151

The radicals remain on the street corners, attempting to bring clarity to a confused populace.

In this hour, socialism is the only solution for humanity. In the words of the Communist Manifesto: 'Socialism or Barbarism!'

But we already chose socialism. The SPD's in charge.

The Kaiser's gone.

We got one man, one vote.

An eight-hour day. That's a bit better surely?

'A bit better'? Is that all you strive for? Imagine! In place of employers and their wage slaves, free working comrades! Labour as nobody's torture because everybody's duty! A human and honourable life for all!

To make socialism a truth and a fact we must destroy capitalism! Root and branch!

As ever, questions of national identity muddy the field of class politics.

She's a Russian agent! She want us to be part of socialist Russia!

No! I want to see a socialist Germany! Proletarians of all nations must unite and rise up!

Comrades...

You won't catch me uniting with bleedin' Russia!

A Russian agent?

Tough crowd.

I have reservations about events in Russia.

There's no ladder. Catch me, Paul.

Pray tell.

Oh, there's no time to go into it now. I'll write a book on it. Suffice to say I'm disappointed by my old friend Lenin's use of terror.

Why do the Bolsheviks outlaw freedom of the press and freedom of assembly? All that is instructive, wholesome and purifying in politics depends upon this: 'Freedom' can never be a special privilege.

Freedom only for the supporters of one party is no freedom at all.

Freedom is always and exclusively freedom for those who think differently.

I despise killing. The proletarian revolution requires no terror for its aims.

We do not need those weapons.

Ebert does need those weapons. The terror specialists are training their troops: the Freikorps.

The counter-revolutionary propaganda machine swings into action.

Have you seen the latest posters?

No.

Die rote Fahne

'Women of Germany! Under the Spartacists, women will be communal property! Any man will be able to use them with a permit from the Worker's Committee.'

Hey Leo, should we apply for permits?

Oh do stop talking tosh!

Rosa's response is to dedicate herself to *Die Rote Fahne*, day and night.

The gentlemen of the bourgeoise are quaking in their boots for their property, their privileges, their profits and prerogatives.

There is much to report. December 6th. Demonstrators shot on Chausseestrasse. Eighteen confirmed dead!

Oh! The filthy curs!

The next day. Karl has been arrested! No! He's released now. Thank God Police Chief Eichorn is a socialist. A real socialist.

20th December. It is as we feared. The first congress of the Workers' and Soldiers' Councils will be its last. The SPD members, stupid sheep, voted its powers away to a National Assembly. Parliamentary cretinism rules.

24th December. The People's Naval Division have repelled an attack by government troops! Brave women mingle with the attackers, exhorting them to lay down their arms! Hold the front page!

We must have unflagging spirits and iron concentration of... energy... ...in order to...

Don't wake her. She hasn't slept properly for weeks.

zzzzz

Muh! Wha-? Where was I? ...in order to continue the work. The abolition of capitalism can be born only of the conscious action of the masses.

Mathilde! How could you let me sleep? Awaken me at once in future!

'Time to inform our readers of our new party: The German Communist Party.'

I still think we should have stuck with 'socialist'.

I agree with you, Leo, but we were outvoted.

December 31st, 1918.

There are so many young hotheads around. They lack theoretical consistency.

Happy New Year, Rosa.

It's water. Sorry we have no champagne.

Your New Year's Resolution?

You know as well as I do, Leo. History is not making things easy for us. A bourgeois revolution could simply overthrow the official power and replace it with a couple of new men. But we must work from the bottom to the top.

CHINK!

We can only come to power with the clear and explicit will of the great majority of the proletarian masses.

Who knows how long that will take?

And what does that matter, so long as our lives are long enough to bring it about?

t doesn't take long for the explicit will of the people to be felt. Ebert's next move is to remove the radical Berlin police chief Emil Eichhorn from office. Eichhorn refuses to leave, and hundreds of thousands of working people come out onto the streets in his support. Suddenly, it seems very clear who the socialists really are...
Sunday, 5th January 1919.

TRUE PEACE!

TRUE FREEDOM!

DOWN WITH THE EBERT GOVERNMENT!

TO THE FIGHT!

No one knows who starts the shout

TO THE VORWÄRTS BUILDING!

but the crowd moves as one.

Vorwärts newspaper is a symbol of the SPD sell-out. When war broke out, the trusted socialist party paper became a propaganda sheet, praising first the Kaiser, and now the new emperor in his new clothes.

RIP EBERT

PEACE & ORDER

Who's in charge?

I don't know.

What shall we do now?

Let's have a meeting!

Can we have some dinner? Is there anything here to eat?

The Spartacists and other revolutionaries scramble to keep pace with events.

This is it, boys. We must seize the moment.

The troops of the People's Naval Division are with us?

I think so.

This government no longer has the support of the people.

We must arrest Ebert.

It must be done tonight.

We need action! We need soldiers!

Comrades! It's two o'clock in the morning. We need sleep.

But Rosa knows nothing of this meeting.

We'll go with 'Unemployment' for the lead article. There's a notice for another demonstration tomorrow — put that in half a column at the side.

The next edition of *Die Rote Fahne* carries no call to overthrow the government.

Monday morning, 6th January. Ebert has not been arrested in the night. Nobody has tried. But hundreds of thousands of Berliners pour onto the streets once again. This time some of them are armed.

Much of the day is taken up with speeches. Someone, somehow, takes the decision to storm major government buildings.

How should a revolution proceed? Do you know? Does anyone know?

The German revolution, it seems, only proceeds with the correct paperwork.

But it's late now, and our messenger is cold and hungry. He goes home.

And he does.

The revolution loses the support of the People's Naval Division.

But the uprising has already run out of steam, defeated by cold and hunger, confusion and indifference. The rebels are in possession of a handful of buildings of little strategic importance.

...while Noske lays a net around the rebel forces, and oh, so slowly, draws it in.

9th January. Troops take the *Rote Fahne* offices.

Oh! They're throwing the papers out on the street. The dogs!

But Mathilde! Did you see the look on those boys' faces?

'Those boys' are Government troops, Rosa.

Hunger must have driven them to this. Let me speak to them.

NO!

Rosa! They want to kill you!

You can't prevent me! The revolution needs me.

Listen. They captured a woman comrade last night because they thought she was you. Do you want me to tell you what they did to her?

The revolution needs you alive.

Back in the *Vorwärts'* building.

There are Government troops in the square outside!

That's not the item on the agenda.

Perhaps we should discuss the armed defence of the building?

No need. Germans won't fire on Germans. We saw that on November 9th.

We could knock down the walls in the basement, so we have an escape route. Just in case they do?

That option has been voted down. Back to the subject under discussion.

11th January 1919, 2 a.m.
Noske's Freikorps
attack.

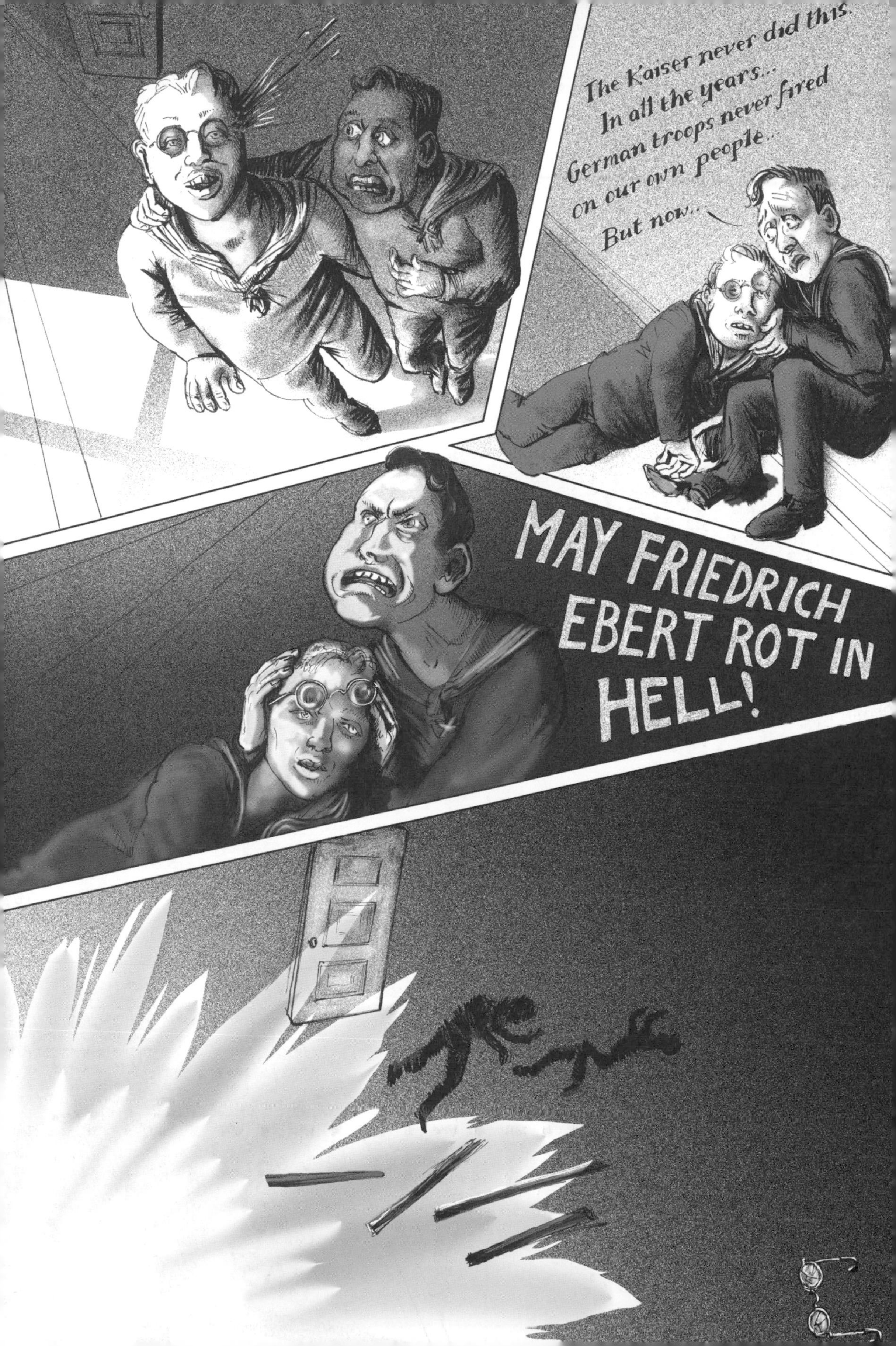
The Kaiser never did this.
In all the years...
German troops never fired
on our own people...
But now...
MAY FRIEDRICH EBERT ROT IN HELL!

Dawn.

Noske speaking. What?
Go ahead and shoot them.
No, I will not give you written authorisation. Just go ahead and do it.

You play with matches, you get burned.

13th January 1919.

We could get you a car. Get you away.

Switzerland?

Leo, I can't leave, like a rat from a sinking ship.

Have you seen today's edition of Vorwärts?

I have. Such poetry. 'Many hundred corpses in a row. Proletarians! But Rosa she is not there, she is not there. Proletarians!'

The SPD's Reichstag Regiment set a price of 100,000 marks on the heads of Karl Liebknecht and Rosa Luxemburg.

Oh Clara, Luise, When shall we three meet again? In thunder, lightning or in rain? When the hurlyburly's done...

When the battle's lost And won.

165

15th January 1919.

Do you think that
forty-seven is old enough to die?
If you do, you must be very young.

Rosa Luxemburg
lost half a
lifetime.

If she had lived,
what more could
she have achieved?

Maybe saying this does
her philosophy a
disservice...

*You see, I've learned
from history that
one should not
overestimate the
impact that one
individual can have.*

...and her death was only one moment
among many in the history of the
working people of the world.

166

But it was a very dark moment. With Germany poised between socialism and barbarism, the actions of the Freikorps foreshadowed far greater crimes against humanity to come.

Do you think she went calmly?

Eagerly embraced the mantle of the martyr?

No! She would have raged!

CLICK

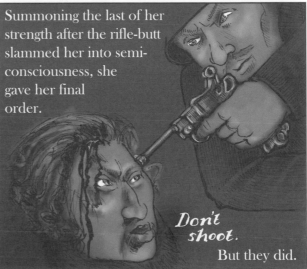

Summoning the last of her strength after the rifle-butt slammed her into semi-consciousness, she gave her final order.

Don't shoot.

But they did.

167

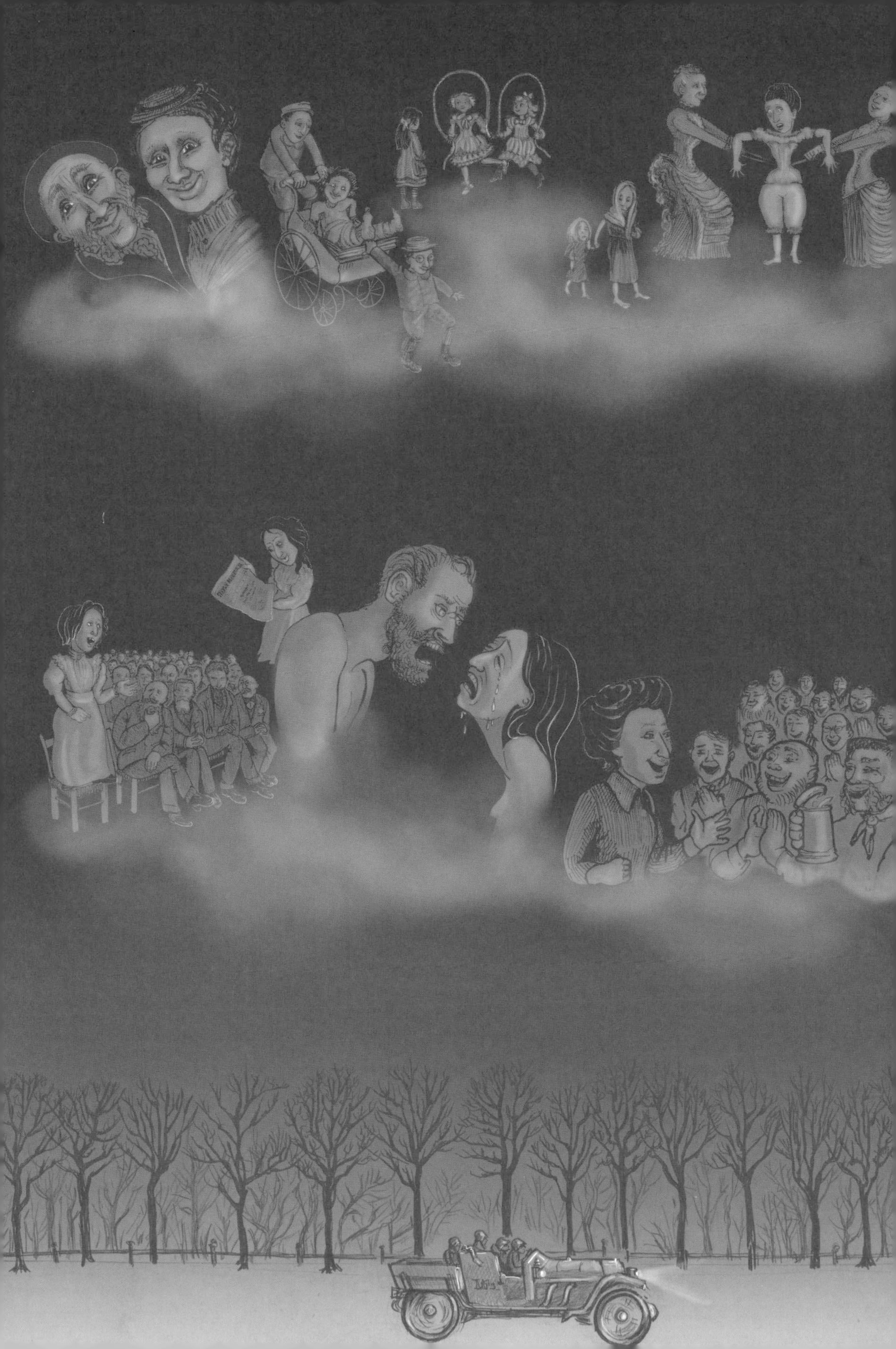

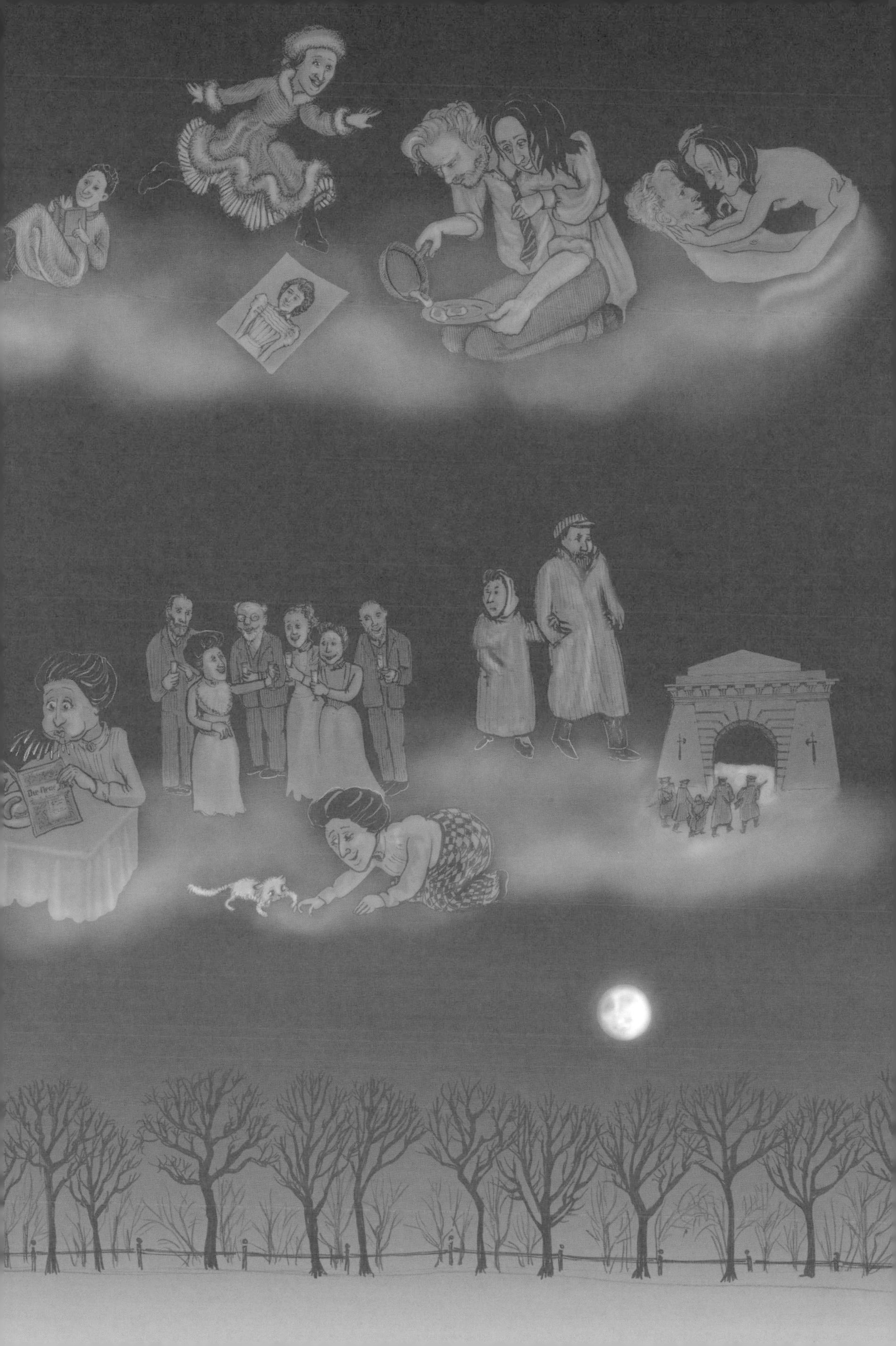
Die Neue

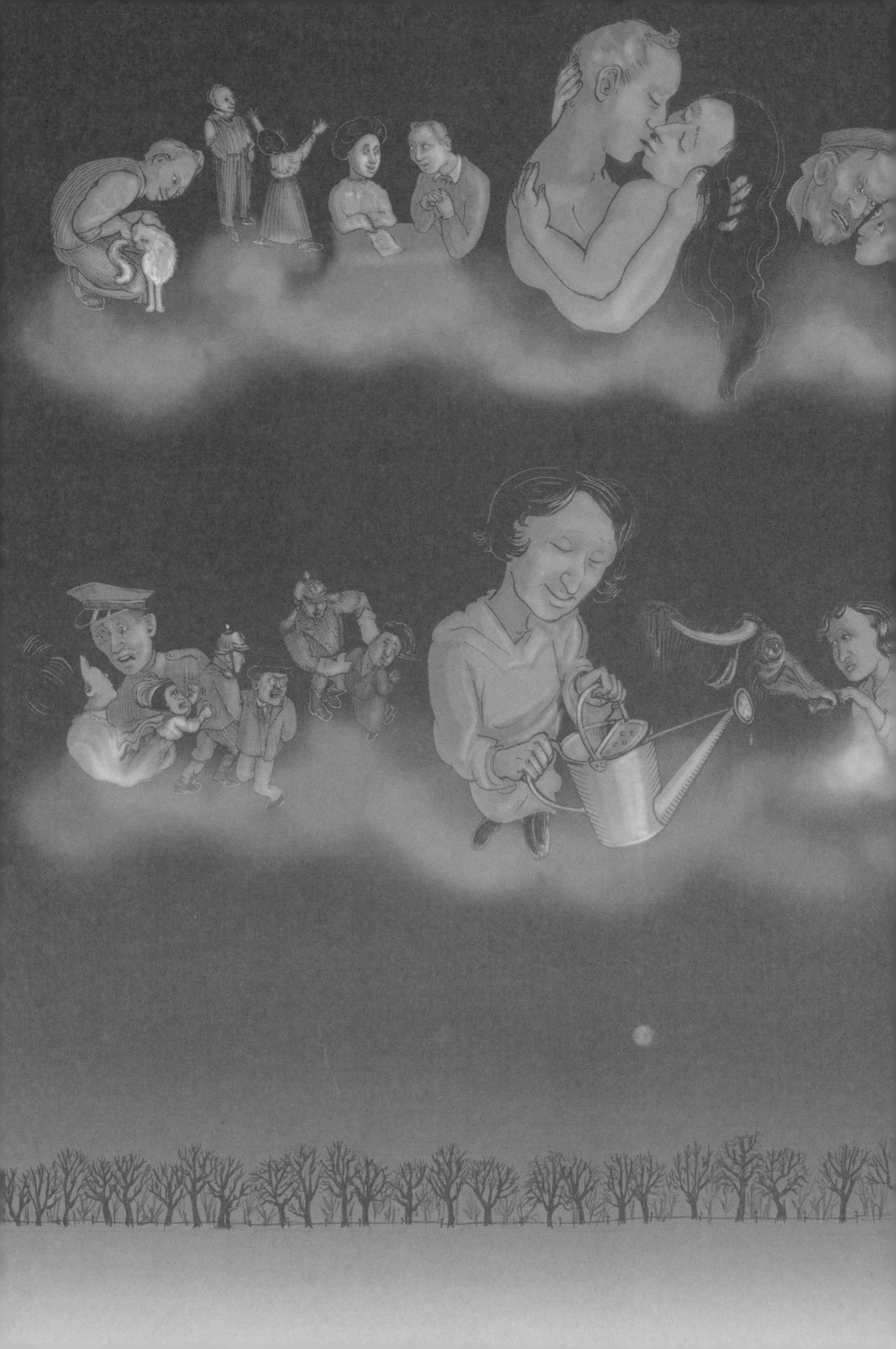

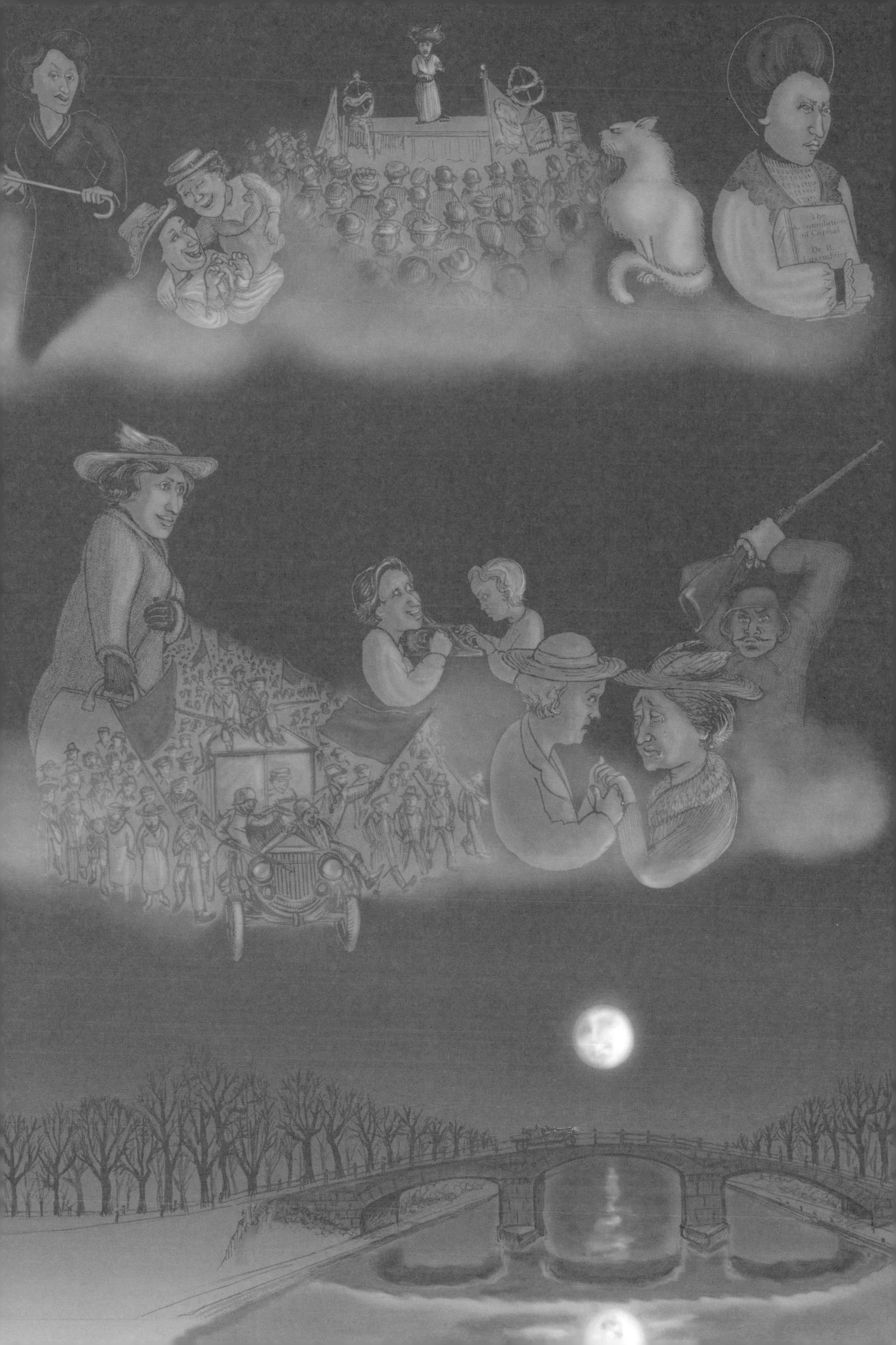
The Accumulation of Capital
Dr R. Luxemburg

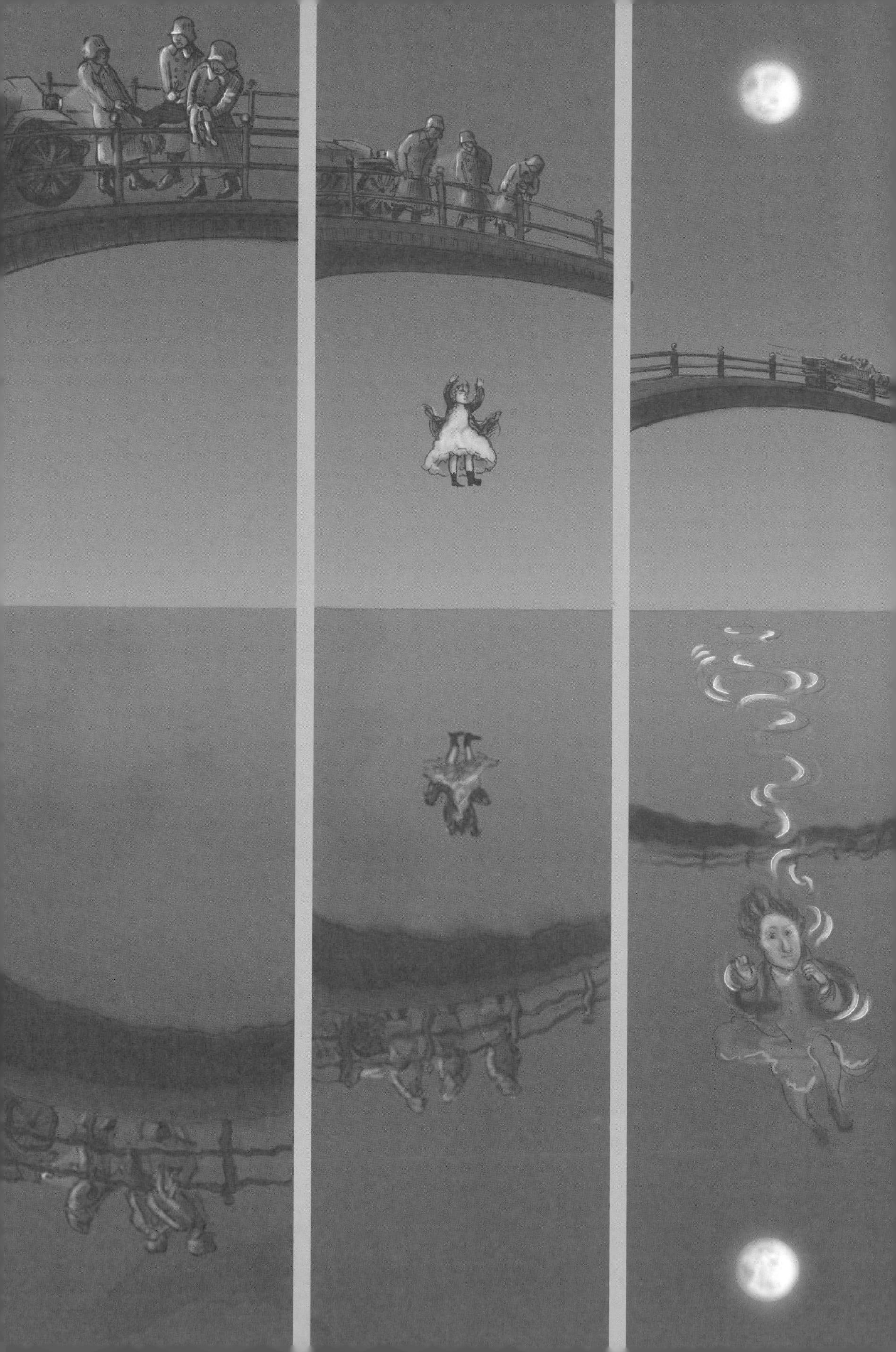

*...in the dark I smile at life, as if I knew some sort of magical secret that gives the
lie to everything evil and sad and changes it into pure light and happiness.
And all the while I'm searching within myself for some reason for this joy,
I find nothing and must smile to myself again – and laugh at myself.*

I believe that the secret is nothing other than life itself...

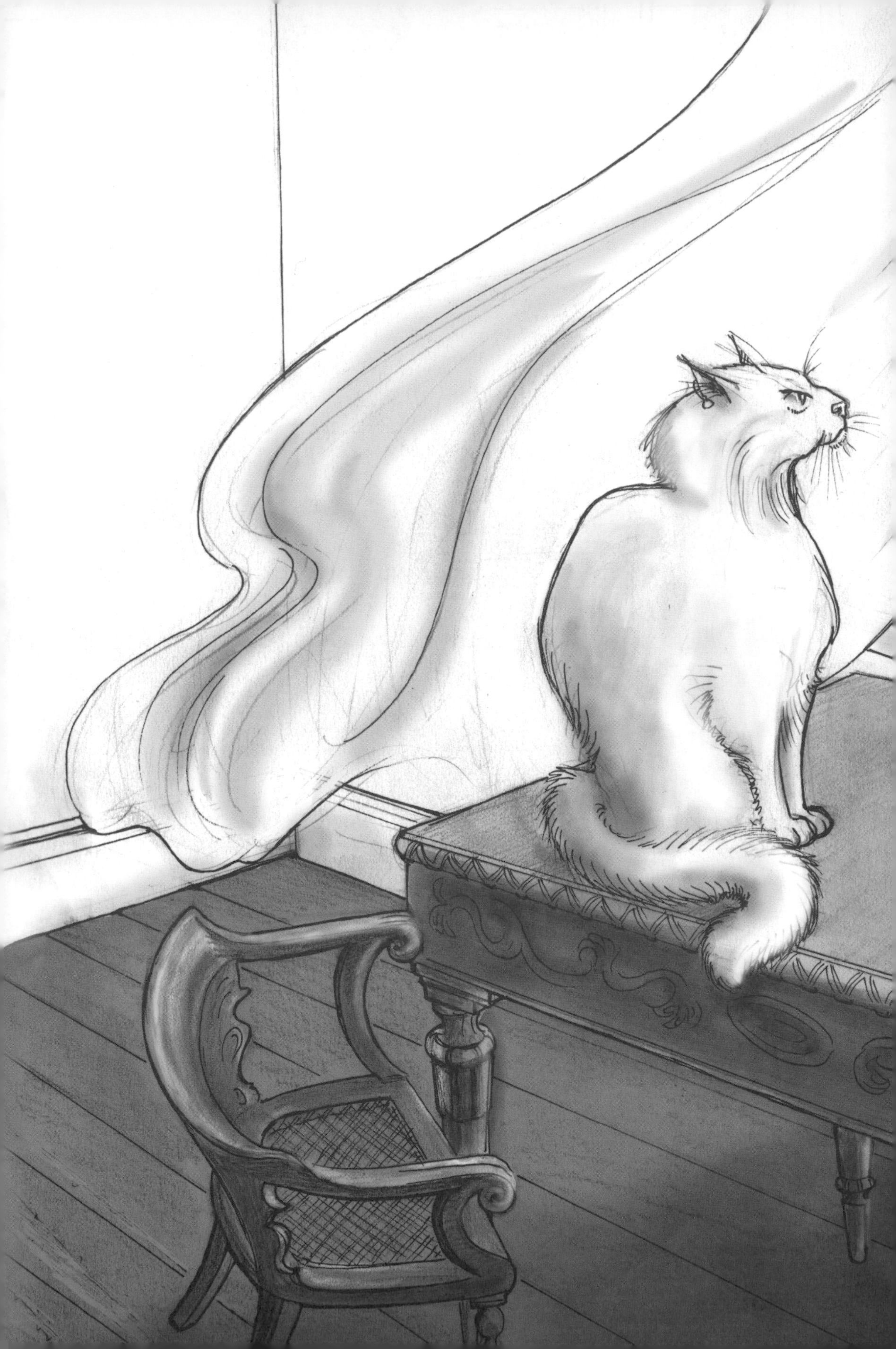

'Order prevails in Berlin!'
You foolish lackeys!
Your 'order' is built on sand.
Tomorrow the revolution will rise
up again, clashing its weapons, and
it will proclaim with trumpets blazing:

I was, I am, I shall be!

On my grave, as in my life,
there will be no pompous phrases.

Only two syllables will be allowed to
appear on my gravestone: 'Tsvee-tsvee.'
That is the call made by the large blue
titmouse, which I can imitate so well that
they all immediately come running.

And in this call, which is usually
quite clear and thin, sparkling like
a steel needle, in the last few days
there has been quite a low, little
trill, a tiny chesty sound.
And do you know
what that
means?

That is the
first soft stirring of
the coming spring.

ROSA LUXEMBURG
ERMORDET
15 JANUARY 1919

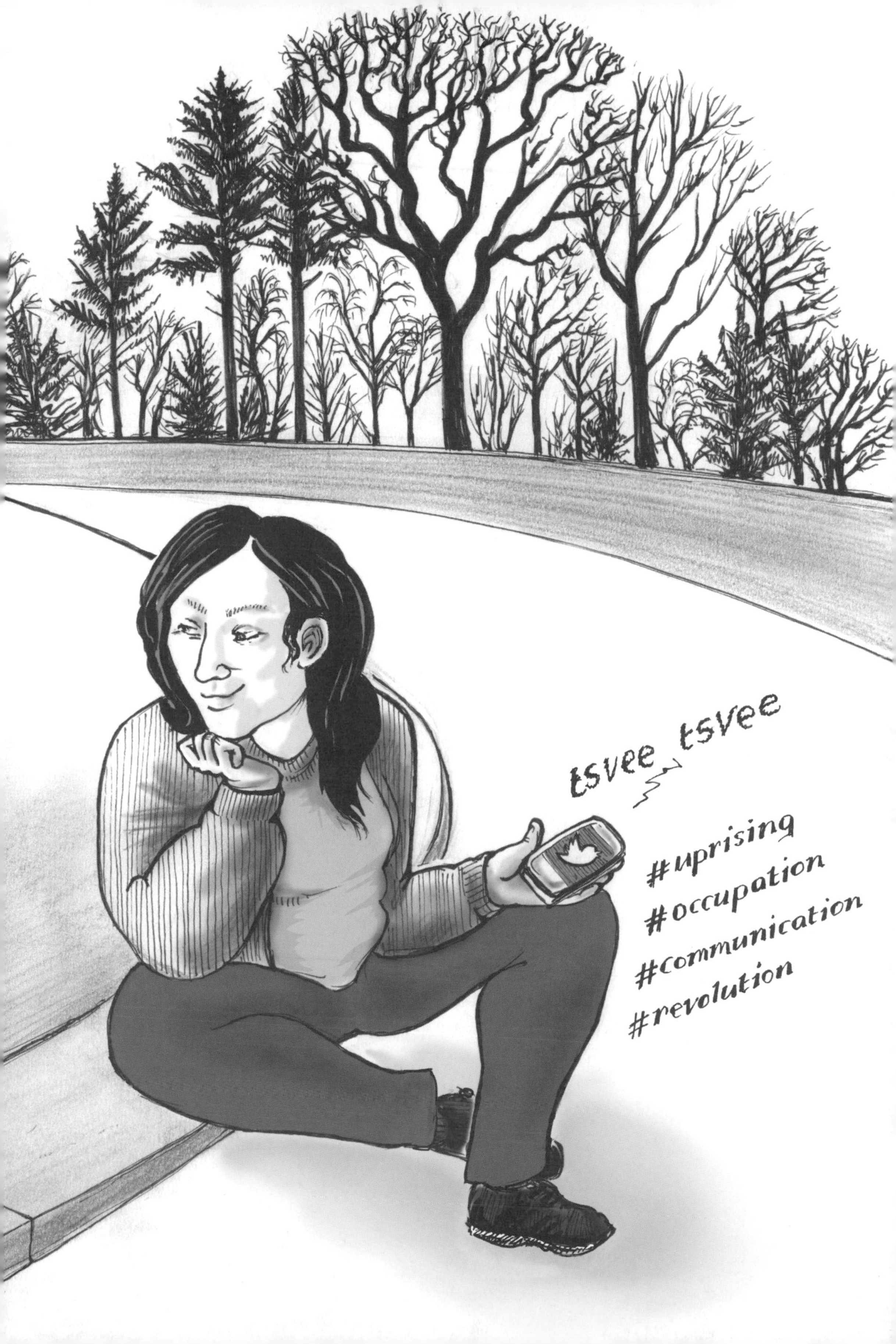
tsvee tsvee
#uprising
#occupation
#communication
#revolution

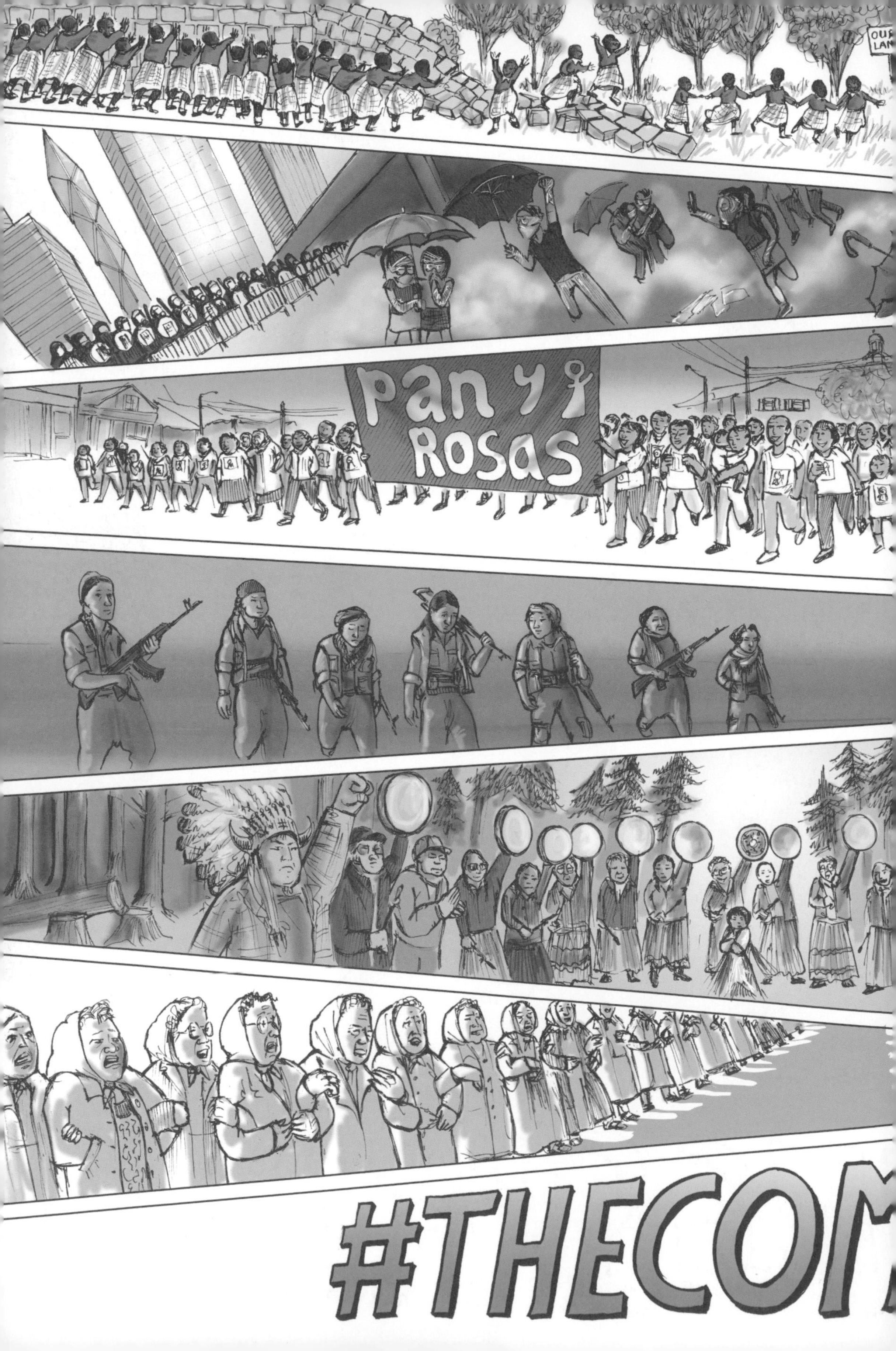
OUR
LAN
pan y
Rosas
#THECOM

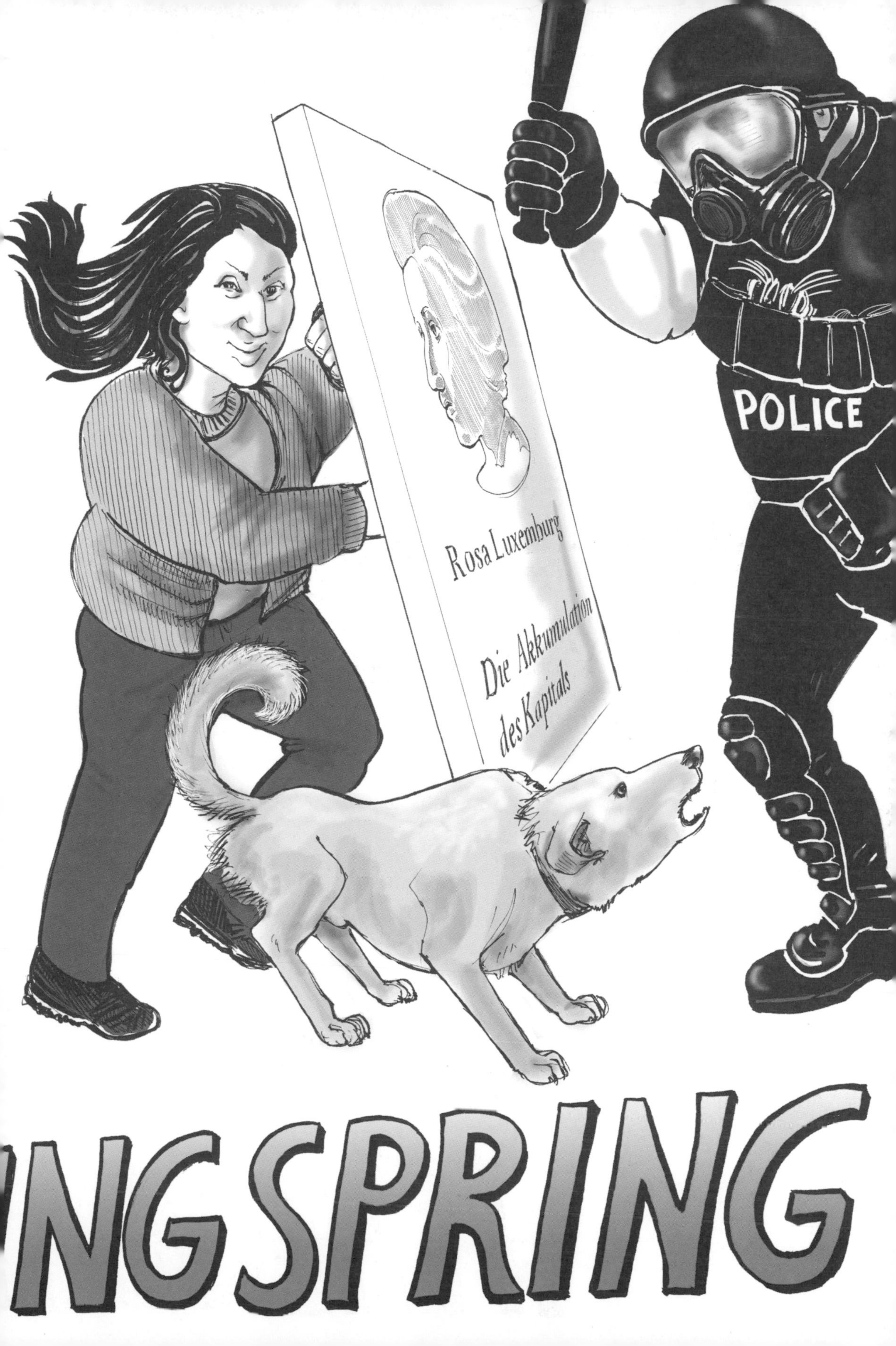
POLICE
Rosa Luxemburg
Die Akkumulation des Kapitals
NGSPRING

Notes

Page 5
Pan Tadeusz, trans. Kenneth MacKenzie. The poem is set in Lithuania, not Poland. This is a deliberate misquotation to emphasise Rosa's Polish national identity.

Page 6
For an insight into the kind of disability that results from uncorrected congenital hip dysplasia (CDH), see the YouTube video 'CDH in Saskatchewan Indians (1/2)'. At 2:16 we see a woman with a gait which would probably have resembled Rosa's: her limp would have been pronounced, but not necessarily disabling. CDH has a genetic component, and we know that Rosa's older sister, Anna, had the same condition. The condition is also associated with osteoarthritis, which Anna suffered from in later life.

Page 8
So we'll see you at last, mighty man of the West!
But don't go pretending that I'm coming to pay tribute, For I don't give a toss about getting honours from people like you.
On the other hand, I'm all too eager to find out what you talk about in your sort of circles. You should be on first name terms with the Tsar by now.
As to politics, I'm still wet behind the ears, so I won't waste time on a long speech
But there's one thing you shouldn't forget, my dear Wilhelm:
Tell that creeping toad von Bismark,
That he shouldn't wear a hole in the trousers of peace, and thereby shame them.
You do that for Europe, oh Kaiser of the West!
Translated from the German by Henry Holland.

Page 10
I want to burden the conscience of the affluent with all the suffering and all the hidden, bitter tears.
This is a quote from a poem Rosa wrote in Polish while still at school. *Rosa Luxemburg Exhibition pdf*, Rosa Luxemburg Siftung, 22 January 2009.

page 14
The Pale of Jewish Settlement was established in 1791. A major pogrom occurred in Warsaw in 1881, when Rosa was ten. Although it passed her house, neither she or her family ever mentioned it, so it is possible that they were not in Warsaw at the time. In 1882 the May Laws forbade new settlement and the issuing of mortgages, restricted the rights of Jewish people to hold stocks in corporations, and prohibited Sunday trading. The restriction of the educational quotas occurred in 1887. In 1891, 20,000 Jewish people were expelled from Moscow. The year 1892 saw the disenfranchisement of Jewish people in elections to town Dumas.

page 15
...the mist-enveloped regions of the religious world. In that world the productions of the human brain appear as independent beings endowed with life...
Karl Marx, ed. C.J. Arthur, *Marx's Capital, A Student Edition* (Lawrence & Wishart, 1992), p. 32. Marx's most famous quote on religion: "Religion... is the opium of the people" was made in an obscure journal of 1844 which Rosa is unlikely to have read as a teenager.
What do you want with this theme of the "special suffering of the Jews"? I am just as much concerned with the poor victims on the rubber plantations of Putumayo, the Blacks in Africa with whose corpses the Europeans play catch... so many cries of anguish have faded away unheard, they resound within me so strongly that I have no special place in my heart for the ghetto. I feel at home in the entire world, wherever there are clouds and birds and human tears.
R. Luxemburg, eds. G. Adler, P. Hudis, A. Laschitza, trans. George Shriver, *The Letters of Rosa Luxemburg* (Verso, 2011), p. 376.

Page 17
This page summarises the opening chapter of *Das Kapital*, 'Commodities. The Two Factors of a Commodity: Use-Value and Value (The Substance of Value and the Magnitude of Value).

As use-values, commodities are, above all, of different qualities, but as exchange-values they are merely different quantities, and consequently do not contain an atom of use-value. K. Marx, *Marx's Capital, A Student Edition*, p. 5.

Page 18

This page gives a simplified flavour of Chapters 2 and 3 of *Das Kapital*, 'Exchange' and 'Money, or the Circulation of Commodities'.

...a task is set us, the performance of which has never yet even been attempted by bourgeois economy, the task of tracing the genesis of this money-form, of developing the expression of value implied in the value-relation of commodities, from its simplest, almost imperceptible outline, to the dazzling money-form. Ibid., p. 13.

Page 19

The labour theory of value is Marx's incomparably original contribution to economic thought:

If we leave out of consideration the use-value of commodities, they have only one common property left, that of being products of labour... all are reduced to one and the same sort of labour, human labour in the abstract. Ibid., p. 5.

...this ultimate money-form of the world of commodities... [conceals] the social character of private labour, and the social relations between the individual producers. Ibid., p. 35.

...the exchange of commodities breaks through all local and personal bounds inseparable from direct barter... it develops a whole network of social relations spontanous in their growth and entirely beyond the control of the actors. Ibid., p. 61.

...the relations connecting the labour of one individual with that of the rest appear, not as direct social relations between individuals at work, but as... material relations between persons and social relations between things. Ibid., p. 33.

Page 20

The first of these interactions is described by Marx using the formula C–M–C, Commodity – Money – Commodity. The second follows the form M–C–M, or Money – Commodity – Money. It's clear that where the first exists, so can the second, but they represent very different human interactions.

...money itself is a commodity, an external object capable of becoming the private property of any individual. Thus social power becomes the private power of private persons. Ibid., p. 74.

The desire after hoarding is in its very nature

unsatiable. In its qualitative aspect, or formally considered, money has no bounds to its efficacy, i.e. it is the universal representative of material wealth, because it is directly convertible into any other commodity. But, at the same time, every actual sum of money is limited in amount, and, therefore, as a means of purchasing, has only a limited efficacy. This antagonism between the quantitative limits of money and its qualitative boundlessness, continually acts as a spur to the hoarder in his Sisyphus-like labour of accumulating. It is with him as it is with a conqueror who sees in every new country annexed only a new boundary. Ibid., p. 75.*

our friend, Moneybags, must be so lucky as to find, within the sphere of circulation, in the market, a commodity, whose use-value possesses the peculiar property of being a source of value, whose actual consumption, therefore, is itself an embodiment of labour, and consequently, a creation of value. The possessor of money does find on the market such a special commodity... labour power. Ibid., p. 98.

This concept is further explained in Chapter 7 ('The Labour-Process and the Process of Producing Surplus-Value') and Chapter 9 ('The Rate of Surplus-Value').

Page 21

The exploitation of workers and child labourers is explored in Chapter 10 ('The Working Day') and in Chapter 15 ('Machinery and Modern Industry: Section 3 a) Appropriation of Supplementary Labour-power by Capital. The Employment of Women and Children').

One thing, however, is clear – Nature does not produce on the one side owners of money or commodities, and on the other men possessing nothing but their own labour-power. This relation has no natural basis, neither is its social basis one that is common to all historical periods. Ibid., p. 100.

Page 22

The essential difference between... a society based on slave-labour and one based on wage-labour, lies only in the mode in which this surplus-labour is in each case extracted from the actual producer, the labourer. Ibid., p. 140.

Marx explores shift work, piece work and the deskilling of craftspeople in 'Machinery and Modern Industry', Chapter 15 of *Das Kapital*.

Rosa's words to the worker spoons echo the final lines of Karl Marx's *Communist Manifesto*: 'The proletarians have nothing to lose but their chains. They have a world to win. Working Men of All Countries, Unite!'

Life plays an eternal game of tag with me. It seems to me always that it's not inside me, not here where I am, but somewhere far off. Back then, at home, I used to sneak across to the window—it was strictly forbidden to get up before Father was up—I would open it quietly and peek out at the big courtyard. There was certainly not much to see there. Everything was still asleep, a cat crept by on its soft paws across the courtyard, a pair of sparrows were having a fight with a lot of cheeky chirping, and long, tall Antoni in his short sheepskin jacket, which he wore summer and winter, stood by the pump with both hands and chin resting on the handle of his broom, deep reflection etched on his sleepy, unwashed face…

And that was actually the loveliest moment, before the dreary, noisy, pounding, and hammering life of the big apartment building woke up. The solemn stillness of the morning hour spread above the triviality of the courtyard's paved surface; the window panes glittered with the early morning gold of the young sun, and way up high swam sweet-smelling clouds with a touch of pink, before dissolving into the grey sky over the metropolis. Back then I firmly believed that "life," that is, "real life," was somewhere far away, off beyond the rooftops. Ever since then I've been chasing after it. But it is still hiding behind some rooftop or other. In the end was it all some kind of wanton playing or frivolous toying with me? And has real life actually remained right there in that courtyard…? R. Luxemburg, *Letters*, pp. 176–7.

Page 26

You must never forget mother's words—that you alone will make our family's name famous.
Letter to Rosa from her sister Anna.
Quoted in Elzbieta Ettinger, *Rosa Luxemburg: A Life* (Beacon Press, 1986), p. 68.

Page 30

The photograph of Rosa with short hair is dated 1893, and she met Jogiches in 1889 or 1890. I have reversed the order of events for dramatic effect. Of course, 1893 may not have been the first time she cut her hair. I think it's reasonable to assume, from the photograph, that she cut it herself. It certainly wasn't done by a professional barber.

Page 32

The task of our revolutionary intelligentsia therefore comes, in the opinion of the Russian Social-Democrats, to the following: they must adopt the views of modern scientific socialism, spread them among the workers, and, with the help of the workers, storm the stronghold of autocracy.
Georgi Plekanhov, 'Speech at the International Workers' Socialist Congress in Paris, (14–21 July, 1889)', trans. D. Gaido, <https://www.marxists.org/archive/plekhanov/1889/07/speech.html.> [accessed December 2013].

'I warmly shake your hand.' (p. 470); 'I wish all of you much success in your undertaking, and I shake all of your hands.' (p. 287); 'Greetings and a clasp of the hand.' (p. 288); 'I send hearty handshakes to all.' (p. 23); R. Luxemburg, *Letters*. It seems that Luxemburg enthusiastically, heartily and warmly shook people by the hand.

'Jogiches went straight to Plekanhov and proposed collaboration: his money and technique, Plekhanov's prestige and copyrights. When Plekhanov frigidly asked what basis he had in mind, the young man coolly proposed fifty-fifty and was promptly shown the door. Their icy differences were confirmed by letter. Jogiches was unabashed.' J.P. Nettl, *Rosa Luxemburg* (abridged edition), (Oxford University Press 1969), p. 43.

Grosovski, Jan Tyszka, Leonie, Otto Engelmann, and K. Krysztalowicz are Jogiches' known pseudonyms, but there may have been more.

Page 33

'[Jogiches] had already been arrested and imprisoned twice and had each time got away before escaping finally to Switzerland.' J.P. Nettl, *Rosa Luxemburg* p. 43.

'he worked as a locksmith at the bench… in order to understand the workers better and influence them more strongly.' Paul Frölich, *Rosa Luxemburg: Ideas in Action*, trans. J. Hoornweg (Pluto Press, 1967), p. 13.

Leo smokes. 'What are you doing now? No doubt you're lying in bed, with the lamp on the table next to you, and you're reading or scribbling something and puffing clouds of smoke from your cigarette.' Luxemburg, *Letters*, p. 8.

Note the one-sided nature of this initial conversation. She is interested in his life history, but he doesn't have the emotional depth to learn about hers. Luxemburg complains that Jogiches' letters to her are exclusively focused on revolutionary theory and are devoid of emotional content.

Page 35

Leo, for example is totally incapable of writing in

spite of his extraordinary talent and intellectual sharpness; as soon as he tries to put his thoughts down in writing he becomes paralysed... he doesn't himself write a single line, but is none the less the very soul of our party publications. Letter from Rosa Luxemburg, July 1909, quoted in J.P. Nettl, *Rosa Luxemburg,* p. 259. The description indicates that Jogiches may have been dyslexic.

Page 36

...you arrived at 8:20 in the evening from Lugano with groceries. I ran downstairs with the lamp and we struggled together dragging those big packages upstairs and later we unloaded them on the table—oranges, cheese, salami, and a little cake in a paper wrapper. You know we probably never had a more fabulous supper than at that time on that little table in an empty room with the balcony door open and the sweet aroma coming up from the garden. You were cooking eggs in the frying pan with great skill, and from the distance in the darkness we could hear the train to Milan going over the bridge with a tremendous clatter...

Dziodzio, dear, I throw my arms around your neck and kiss you a thousand times. I want you to pick me up and carry me in your arms (but you always have the excuse that I'm too heavy). Luxemburg, *Letters,* pp. 115–6.

The textual authority for Luxemburg achieving orgasm is implied in a letter to Jogiches describing a moment of conflict between them: 'you didn't feel you wanted anything "physical"—in other words, [you thought] that's all I was concerned about at that moment.' (Luxemburg, *Letters* p. 34). If Luxemburg wasn't deriving physical pleasure from sexual relations, there would be no impetus for her to initiate sex, and therefore no possibility of Jogiches misinterpreting her need for affection as a desire for sex.

The question of exactly how Rosa Luxemburg managed to avoid becoming pregnant in her sexual relations with men will never be conclusively answered. It is worth noting that although she never discusses contraception or fertility awareness, there is a reference in her correspondence to the menstrual cycle:

I have a feeling similar to that which a forty-year-old woman certainly has, when the physical symptoms of sex life stop showing up. Luxemburg, *Letters,* p. 42.

Luxemburg uses the phrase 'wife' to denote the start of their sexual relationship. The analogy with marriage is hers, revealed in her command to Jogiches to, 'read this letter seriously and with your heart, with the same feeling that you read my letters back then—in Geneva—when I was not yet your wife.' Luxemburg, *Letters,* p. 34.

Page 38

It is an immanent law of the capitalist method of production that it strives to materially bind together the most distant places, little by little, to make them economically dependent on each other, and eventually transform the entire world into one firmly joined productive mechanism. From the conclusion of Luxemburg's dissertation, *The Industrial Development of Poland,* trans. Tessa DeCarlo, <https://www.marxists.org/archive/luxemburg/1898/industrial-poland/ch11.htm> [accessed December 2013].

Do you remember... when I was writing "Step by Step"? (I always think with pride of what a superb piece of writing that is.) I was sick, lying in bed and writing, and nervous about it, and you were so good and kind, you were calming me down, giving me a kiss, talking to me with your dear, kind voice, which I can still hear. "Now, now, Ciucka, don't worry, everything will be all right." I will never forget that. Luxemburg, *Letters,* p. 115.

Page 39

My only one, my Bobo! When will I see you? I miss you so much that my soul is simply thirsting! I saw the Trocadero, the Arc de Triomphe, the Eiffel Tower, and the Grand Opera. I'm deafened by the noise. And how many beautiful women there are here! Really, all of them are beautiful, or at least they seem to be. No, under no circumstances will you come here! You stay in Zurich! Ibid., p. 8.

There's a police agent who regularly visits the concierge. (Write to me with caution. If necessary, use a code, as with Karol [Brzezina]. Instead of my last name, put an x over an m.) Otherwise the concierge is ready to make a denunciation because she's just a simple-minded woman. Ibid., p. 31.

Page 40

I received the brassiere and the underclothes. Ibid., p.17. Luxemburg was not a strict adherent to the concept of rational dress. The photographic record indicates that she sometimes wore corsets on formal occasions such as for her wedding, and when she addressed the Stuttgart Socialist International in 1907.

I kiss you strongly, right on the kisser. Ibid., p. 119.

Page 41

The party actually adopted the 'and Lithuania' part of its title later, in 1900.

...it was just this concept of nations as one of the categories of bourgeois ideology that Marxist theory attacked most fiercely, pointing out that under slogans like 'national self-determination' – or 'freedom of the citizen', 'equality before the law' – there lurks all the time a twisted and limited meaning. In a society based on classes, the nation as a uniform social-political whole simply does not exist. Instead there exist within each nation, classes with antagonistic interests and 'rights'. There is literally no social arena – from the strongest material relationship to the most subtle moral one – in which the ruling class and the enlightened proletariat figure as one undifferentiated national whole.

These words are from Luxemburg's 1908 essay 'The question of nationality and autonomy' quoted in J.P. Nettl, *Rosa Luxemburg*, p. 507. We have no record of the text of her first speech to the Third Congress of the Second International in Zurich in August 1893, so I took the opportunity to substitute a later summary of her thoughts on the national question.

Rosa, 23 years old at the time, was quite unknown outside one or two Socialist groups in Germany and Poland... but her opponents had their hands full to hold their ground against her... She rose from the delegates at the back and stood on a chair to make herself better heard. Small and looking very frail in a summer dress... she advocated her cause with such magnetism and such appealing words that she won the majority of the Congress at once and they raised their hands in favour of the acceptance of her mandate. Emil Vandervelde's reminiscence of Luxemburg's speech, quoted in J.P. Nettl, *Rosa Luxemburg*, pp. 47–8. (He misremembers events. She didn't win the mandate.)

The men represented here are from the Socialist International in Amsterdam in 1913. I couldn't source a photo of the Zurich Congress.

Page 42

With all these articles plus the one by Krichevsky, if we use a double signature, seven columns would remain unfilled. They can be filled in as follows: one column on women; one or one-and-a-half columns on wages; and finally, I'll have to write another lead article, a political one. That one worries me the most because on that subject my head feels quite empty. Naturally, I'll write it anyhow. Luxemburg, *Letters*, p. 13.

I'm sending these to you because I'm already a little tired, the articles don't make a sufficiently fresh

impression on me, and I'm afraid I'll be reprimanded. Ibid., p. 11.

Except for the most necessary things, I've made no improvements in the article about the social patriots. That's because (1) I've already rewritten this article six times, though I don't know why; and (2) because the wise Adolf is having the issue set en pages. And so the typesetter has to break open and redo the whole article and the whole issue, and meanwhile the pages already had to be broken open previously. Reiff is typesetting very slowly. Ibid., p. 27.

Page 43

"...on 1 May 1897 she graduated 'magna cum laude' [with great honour] as doctor of law. Her professor indeed awarded her 'summa cum laude' [with the highest honour] but the faculty heads decided that this was too much for a woman." From Paul Levi's memorial speech at Luxemburg's funeral, quoted in Mathilde Jacob, *Rosa Luxemburg: An Intimate Portrait*, trans. Hans Fernbach (Lawrence & Wishart, 2000) p. 118.

Mother alternately laughed and wept... refusing to part with your letter for a single moment, eager for the whole world to know how proud and happy she was... Every morning mama and papa go through prolonged negotiations about who's going to keep your letter – mama at home, just in case someone drops by, or papa in his pocket to show it in the city. Anna Luxemburg writing to Rosa, May 1898, E. Ettinger, *Rosa Luxemburg: A Life*, pp. 66–7.

Duncker and Humblot did not publish Luxemburg's thesis until 1898. She was awarded her doctorate in May 1897, and wrote to tell her parents about it. I included the printed book in this scene to illustrate the fact that her thesis was published. Some conflation of events is essential telling a life story like Rosa's in 180 pages.

Page 44

My golden one, my only one, in my thoughts I embrace you and rest my head on your chest, with my eyes closed, to get some rest. I am so exhausted! Luxemburg, *Letters*, p. 28.

This particular passage is worth reading in full: *I've been letting it run through my head a little, the question of our relationship, and when I return I'm going to take you in my claws so sharply that it will make you squeal, you'll see. I will terrorize you completely. You will have to submit. You will have to give in and bow down. That is the condition for our living together further. I must break you, grind the sharp edges off your horns, or else I can't continue with you. You are a bad-tempered person, and now, within myself, I am as sure of that as that the sun is in the sky, after having thought about your entire spiritual physiognomy. And I'll smother this rage and fury that you have in yourself as sure as I'm alive. Such weeds can't be allowed to get in among the cabbages. I have the right to do this because I'm ten times better than you, and I quite consciously condemn this very salient aspect of your character. I am now going to terrorize you without any mercy until you become gentle, and begin to feel and conduct yourself toward other people as any ordinary good person would. At one and the same time I feel a boundless love for you and an implacable strictness toward the failings in your character. Therefore note well—get a hold of yourself! Because I'm already standing here with the carpet beater in my hand, and as soon as I arrive I'm going to start beating the dust out of you. Ibid., p. 32.*

Page 45

I believe that Leo Jogiches was on the high-functioning autistic spectrum. This explains the disparity between the unwavering nature of Leo's love for Rosa, and her complaints that he displayed very little affection and was bemused by her emotional needs. His single-minded fixation upon the revolutionary cause could also be seen as an autistic trait.

I feel it after every time we are together, when you shove me aside, and close yourself off in your work. Ibid., p. 34.

You little monkey, you have to imitate me in everything. You never have a mood of your own (except when you're furiously raging and unbearable)... What do you imitate me for? Sometimes it really seems to me that you're a piece of wood. It was said once, or it actually happened, that you loved me, and now you're trying to act as if that were so... Ibid., p. 28.

At this point you no doubt smile [and quote me] — 'You know nowadays I cry over the tiniest trifle'! ...My dear one, my love, I am not complaining, I am not asking for anything, all I want is that you not interpret any weeping on my part as "just the scenes that women put on".

...no doubt your eyes are already glancing around, impatiently searching: "What in the world does she want?"

...Oh my God, I'm turning to you and appealing to you so much that maybe, as a result, it's become true, what more and more often seems to me to be so, that perhaps—you don't love me so much anymore, do you? Truly, truly—I feel that so often. You now find

everything about me so bad and hateful. You scarcely feel the need to spend time with me!...

...Oh my God, what's the use of talking about it— it's pointless. Ibid., pp.34–6.

Page 46

I feel as though I have arrived here as a complete stranger and all alone, to "conquer Berlin," and having laid eyes on it, I now feel anxious in the face of its cold power, completely indifferent to me. At the same time I console myself with the thought that the whole of Berlin will arouse my interest. Ibid., p. 40.

In general, Berlin makes a most unfavorable impression on me: cold, massive, and lacking in taste—a true and proper barracks; and the dear Prussians with their arrogant demeanor, as if each one had swallowed the stick previously used for beating him! Ibid., p. 59.

Page 47

As for me, not only have I moved to Berlin, but have firmly established myself here and have even— (but this must remain strictly between you and me for now) obtained German citizenship. Two hours after I had moved here I really had had my fill of Berlin and the Germans, but what should we people without roofs over our heads do? A Johnny without a country, such as I am, must make do even with a German Fatherland. Ibid., p. 86.

Luxemburg lived in a succession of apartments in Berlin. She initially moved into a single small room at Cuxhavenstraße 2, an expensive central location. The illustration on page 45 shows Cranachstraße 58, in Friedenau, a larger apartment which she rented for almost ten years from 1902. Then in 1911 she moved to Lindenstraße 2, in the suburb of Südende. Jogiches refused to hand back his keys to her Cranachstraße apartment, so she had no choice but to move.

Page 49

The room corresponds more or less to all my requirements. It's on the first floor, is elegantly furnished, with a piano, sunny, with a small balcony overgrown with greenery, with a writing desk, a rocking chair, a mirror covering the whole length of the wall, the balcony and the window opening onto the garden, and all around one sees nothing but greenery. Ibid., p. 46.

Together with the books from you this will, all of a sudden, be an entire library, and the landlady will have to give me a new bookshelf, besides the two that I already have. Ibid., p. 112.

...a house owned by philistines who surely would have fainted if the police asked about me (they've never seen a "Frau Doktor" before). Ibid., p. 46.

...in this district for such a room, and with a balcony besides—the price is fabulously cheap. The lady actually wanted 40 but I talked her down. Ibid., p. 47.

Page 50

The marriage took place in Zurich in April, the month before Rosa left for Berlin.

Page 51

Rosa's initial meeting with Herr Auer at the SPD headquarters:

And then I explained: 'I would like to help all of you in your work, to this end I have obtained German citizenship, and I came in order to take an active part. I of course have my own action plan in this respect, but I would prefer not to start out on my own without reaching an understanding with the German party leadership.' At this point he uttered another 'Ah' ... The fellow was greatly impressed that I have German citizenship—he expressed surprise and immediately asked for my address, which he entered into the party address book, and after that we began to discuss quite frankly, a discussion that I cannot repeat to you word for word because it lasted for more than an hour. Luxemburg, Letters, p. 50.

A word spoken in Polish has quite a different effect than when spoken in that "foreign" tongue, German. Ibid., p. 121.

You have no inkling of what a good effect my attempts so far to speak at public meetings have had on me. I didn't have the slightest self-assurance in this respect, but had to take a chance and step out on the ice. Ibid., p. 68.

I want to affect people like a clap of thunder, to inflame their minds not by speechifying but with the breadth of my vision, the strength of my conviction, and the power of my expression. Letter from Luxemburg to Jogiches. R. Luxemburg, eds Peter Hudis & Kevin B. Anderson, The Rosa Luxemburg Reader (Monthly Review Press, 2004), p. 382.

The miners, some of them came directly from work, completely black with coal dust. Ibid., p. 121.

Page 52

I'm sure that in half a year's time I will be among the best of the party's speakers. The voice, the effortlessness, the language—everything comes out right for me, and what's most important, I step onto the speaker's stand as calmly as if I had been speaking in public for at least twenty years, I don't even feel the least bit of stage fright. Ibid., p. 68.

I gave my talk—exactly one hour. It went very well, and they interrupted me several times with applause, and at the end they "thunderously" shouted bravo and burst forth with cheers [Hochrufe] for me. An old mine worker came up to me after the meeting, patted me on the face, and said, "You did that real well." Ibid., p. 125.

...among other things I had to tell where and what I have studied, how old I am, how I make my living, how my family is, etc., etc. It is humorous and touching at the same time. Ibid., p. 121–2.

I had to promise the workers that I would come again and that at the latest it would be Whitsuntide. Ibid., p. 126.

The local comrades in their naïve way made the confession to me that they had imagined me quite differently: large and fat! Ibid., p.121.

Page 53

The series of articles 'The Problems with Socialism' first appeared in Neue Zeit in 1897–8. Luxemburg's response was formulated after the 1898 election.

The opportunist current in the Party, whose theory is formulated by Bernstein, is nothing but an unconscious attempt to assure the predominance of the petty bourgeois elements that have entered our Party, to change the policy and aims of our Party in their direction. Luxemburg, 'Social Reform or Revolution', trans. Dick Howard, The Rosa Luxemburg Reader, p. 130.

Legal reform and revolution are not different methods of historical progress that can be picked out at pleasure from the counter of history, just as one chooses hot or cold sausages. They are different moments in the development of class society which condition and complement each other, and at the same time exclude each other reciprocally as, e.g., the north and south poles, the bourgeoisie and the proletariat. [This last phrase is a good description of Marxist dialectic.] Ibid., p. 156.

Page 54

A note on Luxemburg and servants. She had them, once she could afford them. In 1905 she writes:

The maid is constantly absent. She was supposed to come yesterday but it seems she won't come until Sunday... it is with the greatest calmness of spirit that I put up with the disorder and the absence of the maid. Luxemburg, Letters, p. 196.

...my cares as a housewife don't end there. This maid has been wailing at me that she suffers from *headaches, that she can't climb stairs, that she can't lift anything. I definitely won't be able to put up with her for even a month, if that. I already have my eye on "something" as a replacement. Ibid., p. 198.*

It seems that nineteenth-century socialist intellectuals' sympathies with the trials of the working classes didn't extend to their personal lives. When Rosa Luxemburg writes about the proletariat, it is always as 'them', never as 'us'.

...as a result of its own inner contradictions, capitalism moves towards a point when it will be unbalanced, when it will simply become impossible. 'Social Reform or Revolution', *The Rosa Luxemburg Reader*, p. 132.

Page 55

...the scientific basis of socialism rests on three results of capitalist development. First, and most important, on the growing anarchy in the capitalist economy, leading inevitably to its ruin. Second, on the progressive socialization of the process of production, which creates the germ of the future social order. And third, on the growing organization and class consciousness of the proletariat, which constitutes the active factor in the coming revolution. ibid, p 132. [The substitution of the word 'chaos' where Luxemburg writes 'anarchy' is deliberate, as Luxemburg's writings have resonance for anarchists everywhere.]

...the market outlets begin to shrink because the world market has been extended to its limit and has been exhausted by the competition of the capitalist countries—and it cannot be denied that sooner or later this is bound to occur... Ibid., p. 137.

Luxemburg's analyses of financial crises as an expression of the contradictions inherent within capitalism are not fully explored in this book. Please see 'History of Crises' in *The Complete Works of Rosa Luxemburg, Volume 1, Economic Writings*.

Page 56

*For Social Democracy there exists an indissoluable tie between social reforms and revolution. The struggle for reforms is its **means**; the social revolution, its **goal**.* 'Social Reform or Revolution', *The Rosa Luxemburg Reader*, p. 129. The Bernstein quote— 'The final goal, whatever it may be, is nothing to me; the movement is everything'—is from the same source.

Credit has diverse functions in the capitalist economy. Its two most important functions, as is well known, are to increase the capacity to expand production and to facilitate exchange. ...when the inner tendency of capitalist production to expand limitlessly strikes against the barrier of private property (the limited size of private capital), credit appears as a means of surmounting these limits in a capitalist manner. Through stock companies, credit combines in one mass a large number of individual capitals. It makes available to each capitalist the use of other capitalists' money—in the form of industrial credit. Further, as commercial credit, it accelerates the exchange of commodities and therefore the return of capital into production, and thus aids the entire cycle of the process of production.

The effect of these two principal functions of credit on the formation of crises is quite obvious. If it is true that crises appear as a result of the contradiction between the capacity for expansion, the tendency of production to increase, and the restricted consumption capacity, then... credit is precisely the specific means of making this contradiction break out as often as possible. First of all, it immensely increases the capacity for the expansion of production, and thus constitutes an inner driving force that constantly pushes production to exceed the limits of the market. But credit strikes from two sides. After having (as a factor of the process of production), credit (as mediator of the process of exchange) destroys, during the crisis, the very productive forces it itself created. At the first symptom of the stagnation, credit melts away. It abandons the exchange process just when it is still indispensable, and where it still exists, it shows itself instead ineffective and useless, and thus during the crisis it reduces the consumption capacity of the market to a minimum.

Besides these two principal results, credit also influences the formation of crises in many other ways. It offers not only the technical means of making available to an entrepreneur the capital of other owners, but at the same time stimulates bold and unscrupulous utilisation of the property of others. That is, it leads to reckless speculation. Not only does credit aggravate the crisis in its capacity as a dissembled means of exchange; it also helps to bring on and extend the crisis by transforming all exchange into an extremely complex and artificial mechanism which, having a minimum of metallic money as a real base, is easily disarranged at the slightest occasion...

[Credit] introduces everywhere the greatest elasticity possible. It renders all capitalist forces extendable, relative, and sensitive to the highest degree. Doing this, it facilitates and aggravates crises, which are nothing but the periodic collisions of the contradictory forces of the capitalist economy. Ibid., pp. 134–5.

Page 57

*...since the final goal of socialism is the only decisive factor distinguishing the Social Democratic movement from bourgeois radicalism, the only factor transforming the entire labor movement from a vain attempt to repair the capitalist order into a class struggle **against** this order, for the suppression of this order – the question "Reform or Revolution" as it is posed by Bernstein is, for Social Democracy, the same as the question "To be or not to be?"*

*...everybody in the Party ought to understand clearly that it is not a question of this or that method of struggle, or the use of this or that **tactic**, but of the very **existence** of the Social Democratic movement* Ibid., p. 129.

What? Is that all you have to say? Not a shadow of an original thought! Not a single idea that was not refuted, crushed, ridiculed, and reduced to dust by Marxism decades ago! It was sufficient for opportunism to speak in order to prove that it had nothing to say. That is the only significance of Bernstein's book in the history of the Party. Ibid., p. 167.

Page 58

The day before yesterday [the Kautskys] invited me for dinner again, and he took the opportunity to ask if I'd help him work on Marx's fourth volume. It didn't take me long to find out what this "work" meant: he's transcribing the whole manuscript (terribly illegible) and intends to put in order later on. Obviously my "help" would consist in transcribing or in taking his dictation. He's anxious for me to do it because, he said, after Engel's death, except for E. B[ernstein], he's the only person left who can read Marx's handwriting. He wants to initiate me into Marx's hieroglyphs, so that if he were to die while working on the fourth volume, I'd continue the work (!...) He is much too honest and simple a man to have consciously tried to trick me into doing the copying, but unconsciously that naive story about his possible death had no other purpose. Knowing full well that neither our contemporaries nor posterity would learn about my silent contribution to Marxism, I told him straight out, I'm nobody's fool! Of course, I put it in elegant form, that is, poking fun at his fear and assuring him it would be pointless to teach me Marx's handwriting, since my chances of sudden death are the same as his. I also advised him to buy a Remington typewriter and to teach his wife to type. Luxemburg writing to Jogiches, quoted in *Comrade and Lover: Rosa Luxemburg's Letters to Leo Jogiches*, (MIT Press, 1979), pp. 101–2.

I have no intention whatever of limiting myself to criticism. *On the contrary, I have the intention and the desire to push in a positive direction, and not just to push individuals but the movement as a whole, to bring our entire positive effort under review, to demonstrate new ways of doing agitation and practical work (to the extent that such ways can be found, and I have no doubt they can), to fight against casualness, routinism [Schlendrian], etc. In a word, to be constantly giving new impetus to the movement… And then to put the spoken and written propaganda on a new track, because in the old forms it has become petrified and has almost no effect on anyone any more, and in general to bring new life to the press, the pamphlets, and the public meetings.* Luxemburg, *Letters*, pp. 117–8.

Rosa Luxemburg: champagne socialist?
I have a very heart-warming memory of our last "carousal" with champagne. It was in the last summer when I was in the Black Forest... it was a marvellous day and after eating, we sat out in the open around a small battery of bottles of Mumm, we rejoiced in the sun and were very merry. Luxemburg, *Letters*, p. 365.

Page 59

...people, when they're writing, forget for the most part to go deeper inside themselves and experience the full import and truth of what they're writing. I believe that people need to live in the subject matter fully and really experience it every time, every day, with every article they write, and then words will be found that are fresh, that come from the heart and go to the heart, instead of the old familiar phrases. Ibid., p. 65.

...Above the desk next to the bust of Voltaire in a pile of papers there is a large paper bag with my Russian manuscript in it... Ibid., p. 221.

The quotes from Luxemburg's writings here and on the next page are from 'Martinique', first published in May 1902, a scathing analysis of the international humanitarian response to the recent volcanic eruption in Martinique and subsequent loss of life. Luxemburg, *The Rosa Luxemburg Reader*, pp. 123–5.

Page 61

...the entire bourgeois press had sunk its teeth into this roast beef; there was even a lead article in Vossin! Everywhere this same 'r-r-revolutionary Rosa' is presented as a terrifying monster; a bugaboo. Luxemburg, *Letters*, p. 213.

The caricature source is <http://en.wikipedia. org/wiki/Stab-in-the-back_myth#mediaviewer/

File:Stab-in-the-back_postcard.jpg> [accessed May 2014].

And now I have work to do, as I do every summer: I have to climb up on a chair and, however far up it is, reach to the upper windowpane, take hold of the wasp ever so carefully, and deliver it once again to freedom, because otherwise it would torment itself against the glass until it was half dead. They don't do anything to me; out in the open they even land on my lips, and that's very ticklish; but I'm worried about doing harm to the wasp when I take hold of it. In the end it all worked out, and suddenly it's completely quiet here in the room. Luxemburg, *Letters*, p. 389.

...with every little fly that one carelessly swats and crushes, the entire world comes to an end, in the refracting eye of the little fly it is the same as if the end of the world had destroyed all life. Luxemburg, *Letters*, p. 449.

...the German people insofar as they do not paddle in the wake of the Socialists, are unable to understand why an end is not put to the impertinent behaviour of this female. Resolution of a National Liberal meeting in Würtemburg, 2 April 1914, quoted in J.P. Nettl, *Rosa Luxemburg*, p. 323.

Listen, if [the work at the] **Vorwärts** *brings in 200 marks, we'll be in a splendid position! I'll buy a frightfully large amount of underwear. That is my greatest wish.* Luxemburg, *Letters*, p. 197.

Page 62

Dziodziu, you know what happened to me yesterday while I was walking in the Tiergarten? Something totally unexpected, without any exaggeration. All of a sudden some little child (a little Bobo) three or four years old was at my feet, wearing a pretty dress and with long blond hair, and started to stare at me. Suddenly something came over me. I had the desire to pick up that child and quickly run home and keep it as mine. Oh, Dziodziu, will I never have a Bobo!? Ibid., p. 114.

Page 63

You write to me that you are suffering terribly from the loss of your mother; perhaps now you will also believe me that for me too that is a terrible pain... I don't suffer on my own account, but what makes me shudder every time is this one thought: what kind of life was that! What has this person lived through, what is the point of a life like that! Ibid., pp. 74–5.

...the Chaffinch Family comes here several times a day. The mother, who I have known intimately since her days as a bride, always brings a little daughter with her to my window. The "Little Darling," who is much larger and fatter than Mama, sits there with her feathers ruffled, throws open her huge beak with hoarse squawking, while shaking her bald head like an epileptic and letting herself be filled up by her emaciated, care-worn, and unkempt mama. Entire loads of my oats thus go down the throat of "Little Darling" while Mama barely swallows even one grain herself. All this despite the fact that the brat can fly quite well and peck food for herself, which she actually condescends to do now and then.... in my family it was regarded as an unbreakable law of nature, in exactly the same way, that mother existed in the world exclusively to fill our little beaks, which were forever opened wide (above all, the beak of the paterfamilias!) in every possible way.* Ibid., pp. 414–5.

Careful readers will note that Mimi is the world's longest-living cat in this fictionalised account of Rosa's life. In fact, Rosa had a succession of pets, including an unsuccessful attempt to keep a rabbit in her apartment. She actually found Mimi as a kitten when working at the Party School.

Page 64

...in the winter of 1901, the Radical Women's Union, "The Welfare of Women," sent in a petition to the Prussian Landtag asking that the right of voting for that body might be granted to women, but only to those who had qualified by living for one year in the constituency, and who paid a certain sum, however small, in direct taxation. The meaning of that is clear, that for this, as for other bodies, the franchise should only be granted to ladies and not to the working women, who are without property... Yet such a scheme is palpably absurd, for I would ask – do not the poor pay taxes? They do, and it is the ruling classes who receive them.

...These women's unions must declare their hostility to these tactics if they are really in favour of women's rights, and not of ladies' rights.
Clara Zetkin, Social-Democracy & Woman Suffrage (1906), trans. Jacques Bonhomme, <https://www.marxists.org/archive/zetkin/1906/xx/womansuffrage.htm> [accessed December 2013].

I have put Clara Zetkin's words into Rosa's mouth here. This is based on the representation of their friendship by biographers J.P. Nettl and Elzbieta Ettinger.

Nettl describes Clara Zetkin's acceptance of Rosa's primacy and her agreement with nearly every view propounded by Rosa. (J.P. Nettl, *Rosa Luxemburg*, p. 12). Ettinger goes further: 'Rosa thought that, intellectually, Clara was 'an empty hose,' easily filled by her latest interlocutor. Capable of assimilating but not of creating ideas, [Ettinger quotes Luxemburg as stating] "she never has her own opinon... her entire speech was a literal repetition of my last five articles, as though learned by rote."' (E. Ettinger, *Rosa Luxemburg: A Life*, p. 101).

Aside from the few who have jobs or professions, the women of the bourgeiosie do not take part in social production. They are nothing but co-consumers of the surplus value their men extort from the proletariat. They are parasites of the parasites of the social body. Luxemburg, 'Women's Suffrage and Class Struggle' (1912) trans. Rosemarie Waldrop, *The Rosa Luxemburg Reader*, p. 240.

Page 65

I would take my hat and go out into the fields... to gather fresh, juicy grass for Mimi. Luxemburg, *Letters*, p. 411.

In her letter to Sophie Liebnecht, 17 August 1917, Rosa refers to her fellow prisoners as people 'whose age, gender, or individual features have been blotted out under the stamp of the most profound human degradation' and refers to discovering 'a mass of stupidity, such a base mentality' in the other inmates. (Luxemburg, *Letters*, p. 430). She really wasn't that good at identifying with or connecting with 'the masses'.

Page 66

Dearest! Many thanks for the photo of Karl with the lovely dedication! The picture is marvelous, the first really good picture of him that I've seen. The eyes, the expression on the face—it's all superb. (Only the necktie, teeming with little white bean shapes, which really catch the eye!—Such a tie is grounds for divorce...) Luxemburg, *Letters*, p. 174.

I'm feeling terrific. I gave thanks from the fullness of my heart for the peace and solitude in which I was once again able to patch up my inner self...

Day before yesterday I was suddenly, and for me quite unexpectedly, released from prison, or much more accurately, I was thrown out, because I made some difficulties about accepting the blessings of amnesty from the Kingdom of Saxony... Luxemburg, *Letters*, pp. 178–9.

Page 67

...Tracking down instances of opportunist stupidity and repeating, parrot-like, our criticisms of them is for me not a satisfying form of labor; ...I feel that with this purely negative activity we are not making any steps forward. *And for a revolutionary movement not to go forward means—to fall back. The only means of fighting opportunism in a radical way is to keep going forward oneself, to develop tactics further, to intensify the revolutionary aspects of the movement. Generally speaking, opportunism is a plant that grows in swamps, spreading quickly and luxuriantly in the stagnant water of the movement; when the current flows swiftly and strongly it dies away by itself.* Ibid., p. 183.

Page 68

These, Your Majesty, are our chief wishes... if you do not grant or heed our supplications, we shall die here, on this very square before your palace... May the sacrifice of our lives be for Russia, who has suffered too much; we shall make it readily. Petition to the Tsar quoted in P. Frölich, *Rosa Luxemburg: Ideas in Action*, p. 79.

Page 69

...a struggle which caught on the one hand all the petit-bourgeois and liberal professions (commercial employees, technicians, actors and members of artistic professions), and on the other hand penetrated to the domestic servants, the minor police officials and even to the stratum of the lumpenproletariat, and simultaneously surged from the towns to the country districs and even knocked at the iron gates of the military barracks. Luxemburg, 'The Mass Strike, the Political Party, and the Trade Unions', trans. Patrick Lavan, *The Rosa Luxemburg Reader*, p. 180.

After every foaming wave of political action, a fructifying deposit remains behind from which a thousand stalks of economic struggle shoot forth. Ibid., p. 195.

Page 70

[Tsar Nicholas] felt 'sick with shame at this betrayal of the dynasty' Attributed to the Tsar, <http://en.wikipedia.org/wiki/Revolution_of_1905> [accessed December 2013]. I couldn't find a more reliable source.

Anyone listening here to the previous speeches in the debate on the question of the mass strike would really be inclined to clutch his head and ask: 'Are we really living in the year of the glorious Russian Revolution or are we in fact ten years previous to it?' (Quite right.) Day by day we are reading news of revolution in the papers, we are reading the despatches, but it seems that some of us don't have eyes to see or ears to hear. Luxemburg's speech to the Jena Congress, quoted in J.P. Nettl, *Rosa Luxemburg*, p. 212.

...the final words of *The Communist Manifesto* are not merely a pretty phrase to be used at public meetings... we are in deadly earnest when we shout out to the masses: "The workers have nothing to lose but their chains; they have a world to win." Luxemburg's speech to the Jena Congress, quoted in P. Frölich, *Rosa Luxemburg: Ideas in Action*, p. 98.

The debate has taken a somewhat unusual turn... I have attended every congress except during those years when I was the guest of the government but a debate with so much talk of blood and revolution I have never listened to. (Laughter.) Listening to all this I cannot help glancing occasionally at my boots to see if these are not already wading in blood. (Much laughter.) August Bebel's speech to the Jena Congress, quoted in J.P. Nettl, *Rosa Luxemburg*, p. 212.

The final part of this exchange between Luxemburg and Bebel took place a month after the Jena Congress while discussing the debate: *August accused me (though in a perfectly friendly manner) of ultra radicalism and shouted: 'Probably when the revolution in Germany comes Rosa will no doubt be on the Left and I no doubt on the Right,' to which he added jokingly, 'but we will hang her, we will not allow her to spit in our soup.' To which I replied calmly, 'It is too early to tell who will hang whom.' Typical!* J.P. Nettl, *Rosa Luxemburg*, p. 213.

Two years later, in 1907, Rosa was convicted of incitement to riot as a result of her speech at the Jena Congress and sentenced to two months in prison. Her speech in her defence was sublime: *...in conclusion I ask you to acquit me; not because I am afraid of the imprisonment to which you may treat me. If it is a question of enduring the punishment meted out to us by the ruling class for our convictions, every Socialist submits to it with the greatest indifference. But I ask you to acquit me, because my conviction would be an injustice.* Riot and Revolution: Speech by Rosa Luxemburg on Trial for Inciting to Riot. <https://www.marxists.org/archive/luxemburg/1906/misc/riot-revolution.htm> [accessed December 2013].

Page 71

Yesterday at 9 in the evening I arrived safely in a train that was unheated, had its lights out, and was escorted by the military; it crept along at "Granny's pace" for fear of surprises. The city is like a place of the dead, general strike, soldiers everywhere you turn. The work is going well, today I start in. Luxemburg, *Letters*, pp. 220–1.

Hopefully, in Warsaw I won't be met with Brownings! Many kisses, R. Ibid., p. 219.

Page 72

...there's a vacillating, wait-and-see attitude. The reason for all this is the simple circumstance that the general strike by itself, plain and simple, has played out its role. Only direct, universal fighting in the street can now bring a resolution, but for that there must be more preparation for the right moment. Ibid., p. 220.

'*...the printing of the paper was carried out by force, even at gunpoint. Sometimes, to keep up appearances, even those printers who were willing to do the work demanded that they, too should be raided and "coerced".*' P.Frölich, *Rosa Luxemburg: Ideas in Action*, pp. 101–2.

Page 73

Everywhere the workers are making certain arrangements on their own initiative so that, for example, the employed workers regularly take up a weekly collection for the unemployed. Or where employment has been reduced to four days a week, they arrange things so that no one is left out, but everyone works at least a few hours a day. All this is done so smoothly and self-reliantly ... in all the factories "on their own initiative" committees have been formed by the workers that make decisions about all conditions of work, the hiring and firing of workers, etc. The employer has literally ceased to be "master in his own home." Luxemburg, *Letters*, p. 228.

The history of the strikes and economic struggles in the Russian Empire before 1905 is outlined in Luxemburg's work 'The Mass Strike, the Political Party, and the Trade Unions.'

Page 74

The overthrow of absolutism is a long, continuous social process. Luxemburg, 'The Mass Strike' trans. Patrick Lavan, *The Rosa Luxemburg Reader*, p. 182.

It is absurd to think of the mass strike as one act, one isolated action. The mass strike is rather the indication, the rallying idea, of a whole period of the class struggle lasting for years. Ibid., p. 192.

Cause and effect here continually change places; and thus the economic and the political factor in the period of the mass strike, now widely removed, completely separated or even mutually exclusive, as the theoretical plan would have them, merely form the two interlacing sides of the proletarian class struggle in Russia. Ibid., p. 195.

...only in the period of the revolution, when the social foundations and the walls of the class society are shaken and subjected to a constant process of disarrangement, any political class action of the proletariat can arouse from their passive condition in a few hours whole sections of the working class who have hitherto remained unaffected, and this is immediately and naturally expressed in a stormy economic struggle. Ibid., p. 196.

The mass strike does not produce the revolution, but the revolution produces the mass strike. Ibid., p. 197.

It is clear that the mass strike cannot be called at will, even when the decision to do so may come from the highest committee of the strongest Social Democratic party. Ibid., p. 197.

...the mass strike is not artificially "made", not "decided" at random, not "propagated"... it is an historical phenomenon which, at a given moment, results from social conditions with historical inevitability. Ibid., p. 170.

The element of spontaneity, as we have seen, plays a great part... be it as a driving force or as a restraining influence... in every individual act of the struggle so very many political and social, general and local, material and psychical, factors react upon one another in such a way that no single act can be arranged and resolved as if it were a mathematical problem. Ibid., p. 198.

Page 75

...we see a bit of pulsating life of flesh and blood, which cannot be cut out of the large frame of the revolution, but is connected with all parts of the revolution by a thousand veins. Ibid., p. 191.

If the sophisticated theory purposes to make a clever dissection of the mass strike for the purpose of getting at the "purely political mass strike," it will by this dissection, as with any other, not perceive the phenomenon in its living essence, but kill it altogether. Ibid., p. 195.

Page 76

Rosa and Leo were in bed together when they were arrested: 'I was found in a rather awkward situation, but let's pass over that in silence.' Luxemburg, *Letters*, p. 229.

On the whole the case is a serious one, because, after all, we are living in turbulent times, when "all that exists deserves to perish."

Therefore, I don't believe at all in any long-term money changing and promissory notes. So be of good cheer and thumb your nose at everything. On the whole, for us here, during my lifetime things have gone superbly. I am proud of that...

The cell doors are being closed. I hug you both with all my heart. Ibid., pp. 230–1.

This letter was written from the City Hall prison. She was transferred to the Warsaw Citadel at some point after this.

Page 77

[Visitor facilities consisted of] a real cage consisting of two layers of wire mesh, or rather a small cage that stands inside a larger one, so that the prisoner can only look at visitors through this double trellis work...

It was just at the end of a six-day hunger strike in prison and I was so weak that the Commanding Officer of the fortress had more or less to carry me into the visitor's room. I had to hold on to the wires of the cage, and this must certainly have strengthened the resemblance of a wild beast in a zoo. The cage was standing in a rather dark corner of the room, and my brother pressed his face against the wires. 'Where are you?' he kept asking, continually wiping away the tears that clouded his spectacles.

Letter from Luxemburg quoted in J.P. Nettl, *Rosa Luxemburg*, p. 237.

Some news of Rosa as I promised... Matters are very bad. The threat of a court martial was real enough. We decided to force the issue with money.

Letter from Adolf Warszawski to Karl Kautsky, quoted in J.P. Nettl, *Rosa Luxemburg*, p. 237. Adolf Warszawski is shown here, talking to Jozéf Luxemburg.

Page 76

Rosa uses the phrase *sintemalen sie selbst zuallererst in die Hosen gemacht haben* in her correspondence, which translates as 'because they themselves were the first to soil their pants'. Luxemburg, *Letters*, p. 237.

Rosa on writer's block:

I feel poisoned when I have any kind of difficulty with my writing... I get into a bad mood and am incapable even of writing an ordinary letter. I feel as though I can't look anyone in the eye or be seen by anyone. Ibid., p. 198.

Page 82

August [Bebel], and the others even more so, have given themselves over entirely to parliamentarism and for parliamentarism. They will totally renounce any turn of events that goes beyond the limits of parliamentarism; indeed, they will go further, seeking to push and twist everything back into the parliamentary mold. Thus, they will fight furiously—as if against an "enemy of the people"— against everything and everyone wishing to go beyond that. The masses, and still more the great mass of comrades, in their heart of hearts have had their fill of parliamentarism. That's the feeling I get. They would welcome joyously any breath of fresh air in party tactics. Ibid., p. 237.

'At one meeting in Mannheim the crowd brushed aside the formal agenda with shouts of: "Tell us about Russia."' J.P. Nettl, *Rosa Luxemburg*, p. 249.

Page 83
I can assure you without exaggeration and in complete honesty that those months spent in Russia were the happiest of my life. Luxemburg's address to the Mannheim Congress, quoted in J.P. Nettl, *Rosa Luxemburg*, p. 250.

The revolution is everything, all else is bilge.
Letter by Luxemburg quoted in *The Rosa Luxemburg Reader*, p. 12.

'...an incident took place early in 1907. Rosa and Clara Zetkin had been for a walk on Saturday morning and were to meet Bebel for lunch at the Kautskys' house. They had lost count of the time and arrived late; when Bebel said jokingly that he had feared they were lost Rosa [replied] "Yes, you can write our epitaph: *Here lie the last two men of German Social Democracy!*"' J.P. Nettl, *Rosa Luxemburg*, p. 251.

Page 86
Oh, Dudu, if I only had two years to do nothing but paint—it would absorb me completely. I wouldn't go to any painter for lessons or instructions, nor would I ask anyone about anything, but just learn on my own by painting, and asking you! But those are crazy dreams. I can't let myself do it, because there isn't even a dog that needs my wretched paintings. However, people do need the articles I write.
Luxemburg, *Letters*, p. 264.

Page 88
...the memory of a soft pleading stammer: "Be true to me, be true to me," and a letter pleading: "Don't leave me, don't abandon me," held me like a chain of iron. Ibid., p. 286.

Pages 89–91
I'm sitting in the middle of the famous Whitechapel district. I'm sitting alone in a restaurant and have been waiting for an hour (it's after 10 pm)....
In a foul mood I traveled through the endless

stations of the dark Underground and emerged both depressed and lost in a strange and wild part of the city. It's dark and dirty here. A dim streetlight is flickering and is reflected in puddles and pools. (It's been raining the whole day.) To the left and right in the darkness the brightly colored restaurants and bars give off an eerie glow. Groups of drunken people stagger with wild noise and shouting down the middle of the street, newspaper boys are also shouting, flower girls on the street corners, looking frightfully ugly and even depraved, as though they had been drawn by Pascin, are screeching and squealing. Countless numbers of omnibuses creak past and crack their whips. It is chaos and also wild and strange...

Finally I found [the hotel—] "The Three Nuns." Why, the very name is suspicious as hell. A brightly lit dining room, but empty. I breathed a sigh of relief when I saw two women sitting at a little table. Unfortunately I then saw that all the guests were familiar with these women and without any formality and, still wearing their hats, were sitting down at the table to join them. On the other side of the wall some people are obviously putting on a variety show of an unambiguous sort. I can hear all the couplets being recited, and after each one comes a raucous round of applause with stamping of the feet as though a wild horde was loose...

But suddenly inside me now some gypsy blood has been awakened. The shrill chords of night in the big city, with its demonic magic, have touched certain strings in the soul of the children of the great city. Somewhere in the depths an indistinct desire is coming to light, a desire to plunge into this whirlpool...

What will the young man with the thick head and the deep dark eyes say about this? The young man whose face breathes of calm and stability, in whose soul the gray mist of morning is nevertheless beginning to stir and surge up at the sight of a marvelous mountain landscape at sunrise. This is all nonsense, dear boy, go get some sleep or take a walk. Adieu, R. L. Ibid., pp. 239–40.

Page 92
Jogiches escaped from prison in February 1907 and appeared in Berlin in April, where he would have made contact with Luxemburg before travelling to the London Congress in mid-May. Rosa was well aware that he was at the Congress and may have travelled there with him. However, in Luxemburg's correspondence, this letter of 23 May marks the point at which Leo Jogiches discovers her romance with Kostya Zetkin:

...your letter was intercepted by L. Yesterday things came to a brief and soft-spoken, but frightening confrontation—during a trip on an omnibus.

Without any mention of the letter, we were talking about my intention of leaving tomorrow. L won't let me go and declares that he would sooner kill me; I'll be staying here even if in a hospital ... We went directly into an elegant restaurant, where my brother was expecting me for dinner. A fine orchestra was playing, in the gallery, music from the last scene of Carmen, and while they were playing L softly whispered to me: I would sooner strike you dead.

... I feel a strange calm, and this quiet conflict, which perhaps will be the death of me; it makes my pulse beat in a lively way, almost joyfully. As stated, I know nothing. Only one thing I do know. I've become dreadfully anxious about you. Beloved little Bubi, be on your guard. You still have your whole life ahead of you. Ibid., p. 241.

Rosa met with her brother Mikolaj in London, not Max. Peripheral characters are condensed in this comic for clarity and brevity.

Page 93

Rosa writing to Kostya fourteen months later!
Yesterday Leo Jogiches was here, and this much is clear, that he wants to accompany me on my trip, in order to, in the event that I meet you, shoot you and himself... The state of mind he's in is no joke any longer, his inner self is shattered, he's become abnormal, and he lives only with this idea fixed in his sight. And so once again I'm beside myself... Ought I to place your life at risk?
Ibid., pp.261–2.

L rushed into the apartment and into my room and cried out that he had learned I was going to travel with K, but that a stop must be put to that, or else I would remain there on the spot, dead. An icy calm came over me, as always, while that was going on, I remained in my seat and said not one word in reply. That made him even more rabid, and he rushed off to try to find you, having demanded I give him your address (I answered nothing of course) and he made Gertrud [Zlottko] give him both keys. When I saw that, I went to K[arl] K[autsky]'s and remained there overnight. I cannot describe to you the way I felt, that night was frightening. On the next morning I went with the boys to my apartment to see about the letters, met him on the street, of course he didn't look at me, and I went upstairs. Up there my letters were lying around, having been opened...

And he took hold of something in his pocket. I remained calm and icy, not once did I turn my head,

and at that point he left. Inwardly, however, I was so frightfully upset and disturbed by this abuse...
Ibid., pp. 250–1.

'Rosa's purchase of a revolver mentioned by Luise Kautsky was no more than self-protection.' J.P. Nettl, *Rosa Luxemburg*, p. 258. The phrase 'I sleep with it under my pillow' is my addition, but if she has a gun to protect herself from a man who has the keys to her apartment, then she's not going to leave it in her desk drawer when she goes to sleep.

Page 94

'She began the course by dealing with the various economic systems, their characteristic features, their transformations and the causes thereof. In this connection the most important economic theories before and after Marx were examined. Finally, after long weeks spent in working out a total picture of the actual development of the relationships of production and exchange, and of their reflection in the bourgeois social sciences, the class worked its way through Marxist teachings, using *Capital* as the basic text.'
P. Frölich, *Rosa Luxemburg: ideas in action*, p. 147.

Luxemburg gave a speech to the Nuremburg SPD party conference on 14 September 1908, in which she defended the work of the Party School, and emphasised the importance of:
the materialist concept of history... the theory which gives us the possibility of systematizing the hard facts and forging them into a deadly weapon to use against our opponents.
Selected Political Writings of Rosa Luxemburg, 1971, edited by Dick Howard, trans. by John Heckman, <https://www.marxists.org/archive/luxemburg/1908/09/14.htm> [accessed December 2013].

Page 95

One cannot imagine anything simpler and more harmonious, than the economic system of the old Germanic mark... The immediate needs of everyday life and the equal fulfilment of everyone; this is the starting point and endpoint of the organisation. Everyone works for everyone else and collectively decides on everything. Whence does this spring, on what does it base itself, this organization, this power of the collective over the individual? It is nothing other than the communism of the land and the soil, that is to say, the common possession of the most important means of production on the part of those who work.

'The Dissolution of Primitive Communism' from *An Introduction to Political Economy*, trans. Ashley Passmore and Kevin B. Anderson, quoted in *The Rosa Luxemburg Reader*, p. 75.

A note on the 'so-called primitive'. Luxemburg uses the phrase 'so-called savage countries' in her *Introduction to Political Economy*. Although she clearly does view society as 'progressing' in defined stages, she is strongly critical of capitalist civilisation and draws direct parallels between 'primitive' and 'civilised' countries critiquing the distancing mechanisms of colonialism:

In every kind of culture... there are all kinds of objects that serve to improve life and satisfy intellectual and social needs, such as weapons for defense against enemies: among the so-called savages, dance masks, bows and arrows and idols; for us, luxury goods, churches, machine-guns and submarines. R. Luxemburg, *Introduction to Political Economy*, from *The Complete Works of Rosa Luxemburg: Vol 1, Economic Writings 1*, ed. Peter Hudis, trans. David Fernbach (Verso, 2013), p. 95.

[the] medicine man, or, as Europeans like to say in such cases, the magician or priest. Ibid., p. 182.

Page 96

A person earns 3,000 marks for a half-year course (October–March), with four lectures per week. These are actually rather glittering prospects... Entirely by chance it happens that for me I am quite prepared to teach this Berlin course, and I could use the existing teaching plan, only in more detail. Luxemburg, *Letters*, p. 246.

I let myself be roasted by the sun... Ibid., p. 253.

And the sight of you gives me such aesthetic pleasure. But Duduk shouldn't think that I love him only for his body, I cannot by any means separate that from the spiritual, to me they are one. Ibid., p. 269.

Page 97

...however, imagine that one fine day, in the communist community with this arrangement, common property ceases to exist, and along with it also common labor and the common will that regulates this. The highly developed division of labor that has been attained obviously remains. The shoemaker still sits at his last, the baker has nothing and knows nothing except his oven, the smith has only his smithy and only knows how to swing a hammer, etc. etc. But the chain that formerly connected all these special labors into a common labor, into the societal economy, is broken. Each person is now on his own: the farmer, the shoemaker, the baker, the locksmith, the weaver, etc. Each is completely free

and independent. The community no longer has anything to say to him, no one can order him to work for the whole, nor does anyone bother about his needs. The community that was previously a whole has been broken up into individual little particles or atoms, like a mirror shattered into a thousand splinters; each person now floats like a piece of dust in the air, as it were, and wonders how he will manage. R. Luxemburg, *Introduction to Political Economy*, from *The Complete Works of Rosa Luxemburg*, p. 235.

If today our shoemaker has been fortunate enough to make an exchange, and obtained means of subsistence in return, he can not only eat his fill and be properly clothed, but also pride himself on his way home that he has been recognized as a useful member of society, his labor recognized as necessary labor. If on the other hand he returns home with his boots, as no one wanted to relieve him of them, he has every reason to be melancholy, as he not only remains without soup, but on top of this it has more or less been explained to him, if only with a chilly silence: Society has no need of you, my friend, your labor was just not necessary, you are a superfluous person and can happily go and hang yourself. Ibid., p. 238.

Page 98

...the formal equality and freedom on which commodity production and exchange is based already breaks down, collapses into inequality and unfreedom, as soon as labor-power appears on the market as a commodity. Ibid., p. 273.

...of all humanity groaning with frightful suffering under the yoke of a blind social power, capital, that it has itself unconsciously created. The underlying purpose of every social form of production, the maintenance of society by labor, the satisfaction of its needs, is placed here completely on its head, with production not being for the sake of people, but production for the sake of profit becoming the law all over the earth, with the under-consumption, constant insecurity of consumption, and sometimes direct non-consumption of the immense majority of people becoming the rule. Ibid., p. 297.

Page 99

...anyone who thinks clearly, and has a genuine mastery of his subject matter, also expresses himself clearly and understandably. Someone who expresses himself in obscure and high-flown terms, if he is not a pure philosophical idea-constructor or a fantasist of religious mysticism, only shows that he is himself unclear about the matter, or has reason to avoid clarity... Ibid., p. 91.

Contradiction in the life of society, in other words, is always resolved by development, in new advances of culture. The great philosopher Hegel said: "Contradiction is the very moving principle of the world." And this movement in the thick of contradictions is precisely the actual mode of development of human society. Ibid., p. 251.

'In the course of 1910/11 a big debate was organized... to discover the opinions of the students on party policy... Mehring and Rosa were very shocked by the vigorous defence of the whole revisionist position from a section of the students. Surely the real value of education and agitation was to gain concrete concessions and as quickly as possible? Rosa Luxemburg said to Franz Mehring afterwards that "in that case I wonder whether the whole party school has any point?" None the less, she enjoyed working there...' J.P. Nettl, *Rosa Luxemburg*, p. 267.

Page 100

...only by sharpening the subject matter through teaching was I able to develop my ideas.
Luxemburg quoted in J.P. Nettl, *Rosa Luxemburg*, p. 265.

In volume 1 [of Das Kapital], in the very chapter on 'The Conversion of Surplus-Value into Capital' [Marx] says:
'In order to examine the object of our investigation, we must treat the whole world as one nation and assume that capitalist production is everywhere established and has possessed itself of every branch of industry'
Luxemburg, *The Accumulation of Capital*, trans. Agnes Schwarzchild (Routledge Classics, 2003), p. 311.

Page 101

...the movement of the total capital, 'as matters stand' depends in Marx's view on three categories of consumers only: the capitalists, the workers and the 'non productive classses' i.e. the hangers-on of the capitalist class (king, parson, professor, prostitute, mercenary), of whom he quite rightly disposes in volume ii as the mere representatives of a derivative purchasing power, and thus the parasitic joint consumers of the surplus value or of the wage of labour. Ibid., p. 312.

Page 102

I ask you for just one thing: If you no longer love me, say it to me openly, in just three words. I will certainly not utter the slightest reproach against you; after all, you can't do anything about it, and it must come out someday.

But be open. You owe it to the concept of "having truth in life"— and also out of consideration for me. I kiss you, and kiss you even if it's for the last time, my dear, sweet love. Luxemburg, *Letters*, p. 285.

...things have turned out as I said to you at the beginning: you forced me to love you because of your love, and if your love were to fade away into nothingness, that would happen with mine too. It pained me that I didn't relieve you of this burden earlier. I felt pained by the angry and tormented looks of a captured baby bird, but I never dared to say the emancipating word, because inwardly I regarded our relationship as a sacred and serious matter. You poor youngster, you felt you were trapped when at any moment the slightest little word could have freed you, as you now certainly see, and when in reality I was the trapped one, because the memory of a soft pleading stammer: "Be true to me, be true to me," and a letter pleading: "Don't leave me, don't abandon me," held me like a chain of iron...

I am going to work with pleasure and love and am determined to bring more strictness, clarity, and chasteness into my life. This conception of life for me has grown to maturity in dealing with you and therefore it is fitting for you to hear these words also Now you are free as a bird, and may you be happy.
Luxemburg, *Letters*, p. 491.

I cleave to the idea that a woman's character doesn't show itself when love begins, but when it ends.
Luxemburg's correspondence, quoted in *The Rosa Luxemburg Reader*, p. 9.

Page 103

The question of the right to vote in Prussia, which has remained in a condition of immutability for more than half a century, is today the focus of Germany's public life. A few weeks of energetic mass action by the proletariat have sufficed to stir up the old swamp of Prussian reaction and to blow a fresh breeze through the political life of all Germany. A reform of the Prussian electoral law cannot be achieved by parliamentary means; here only a direct mass action from without, in the country, can bring about change...
From Luxemburg, 'The Next Step', *Selected Political Writings*, trans. W.D. Graf <https://www.marxists.org/archive/luxemburg/1910/03/15.htm> [accessed December 2013].

The meeting was so full it could have knocked you out (about one and a half thousand), and the mood was terrific. Naturally I gave it everything I had, and the response was stormy applause. (Hannes [Diefenbach], Gerl[ach], Costia [i.e., Kostya Zetkin], and Eckst[ein] were there with me, and the latter has come over to my point of view since yesterday, as he told me.) Luxemburg, *Letters*, p. 290.

Dearest Lulu! All goes well, I have eight public meetings behind me and six more to go... Luxemburg, *Letters*, p. 290.

Page 104

'Karl never tells me anything' is a literary device. Luise was probably just as cognisant of current events as Karl. Their marriage was rocky, however. According to Nettl, Rosa was aware that Luise was in love with somebody else.

Under no circumstances could I print this... There is not one word in our program about a republic. Not out of oversight, not because of editorial caprice, but on well-considered grounds.
Kautsky's refusal, quoted by Luxemburg in 'Theory and Practice', *The Rosa Luxemburg Reader*, p. 209.

...a state which is nothing but a military despotism embellished with parliamentary forms, alloyed with a feudal admixture, obviously influenced by the bourgeoisie, shored up with a bureaucracy, and watched over by the police.
Marx's critique of the Gotha Programme, quoted in Luxemburg's 'Theory and Practice', Ibid., p. 213.

...in Germany we have the strongest party, the strongest unions, the best organization, the greatest discipline, the most enlightened proletariat, and the greatest influence of Marxism. By this method we would come, in fact, to the singular conclusion that the stronger Social Democracy is, the more powerless the proletariat. But I believe that to say mass strikes and demonstration strikes which were possible in various other lands are impossible today in Germany, is to fix a brand of incapacity on the German proletariat which it has as yet done nothing to deserve. Ibid., p. 231.

Tell [Karl] that I know well how to evaluate the loyalty and friendship in these little tricks, that he has put his foot in it badly by so bravely stabbing me in the back. Luxemburg, *Letters*, p. 291.

The use of the word 'invertebrate' echoes an insult that Rosa famously applied to the editors of *Vorwärts* in 1899:
There are two sorts of living organisms: namely those who have a backbone and therefore also walk, at times even run, and others who don't have one, and therefore only creep and cling. P. Frölich, *Rosa Luxemburg: Ideas in Action*, p. 42.

Page 105

Don't worry and be of good cheer, let yourself play Figaro and sing [the work] of the great master. Luxemburg, *Letters*, p. 254.

You know, once when we were coming home from an evening at Bebel's and around midnight in the middle of the street three of us were putting on a regular frog's concert, you said that when we two were together you always felt a little tipsy, as though we had been drinking bubbly. That's exactly what I love about you, that I can always put you in a champagne mood, with life making our fingers tingle and us ready for any kind of foolishness.
Ibid., p. 365.

I broke into cascades of laughter, the way you know I do. Ibid., p. 404.

Page 106

This line sounds like something from a Bond film, but it's a verbatim quote from Bebel to Victor Adler:
'Dear Rosa must not be allowed to spoil our plans for Madeburg... I shall see to it that the dispute will be relegated... to obscurity.'
[Victor Adler replied] *'It really is too bad—the poisonous bitch will yet do a lot of damage, all the more so because she is as clever as a monkey while on the other hand her sense of responsibility is totally lacking and her only motive is an almost perverse desire for self-justification. Imagine!... Clara already equipped with a mandate and sitting with Rosa in the Reichstag! That would give you something to laugh about, compared to which the goings on in Baden would look like a pleasure outing.'*
J.P. Nettl, *Rosa Luxemburg*, p. 291.

It's an odd thing about women. If their partialities or passions or vanities come into question, then even the most intelligent of them flies off the handle and becomes hostile to the point of absurdity. Love and hate lie side by side; a regulating reason does not exist.
Letter from August Bebel to Karl Kautsky, quoted in *The Rosa Luxemburg Reader*, p. 14.

I have libelled poor Dr Emanuel Wurm here by ascribing Victor Adler's lines to him, but in order to create a coherent narrative of Luxemburg's life story in fewer than 200 pages of graphics, I was forced to conflate some of the major characters.

Page 107

I recommend reading *The Accumulation of Capital — An Anti-Critique* before attempting *The Accumulation of Capital* itself, because it makes the same arguments more succinctly and entertainingly.

If we should ask why Marx's Capital *affords no solution to this important problem of the accumulation of capital, we must bear in mind above all that this second volume is not a finished whole but a manuscript that stops half way through.*
Luxemburg, *The Accumulation of Capital*, p. 139.

It is worth pointing out that Luxemburg's thinking on economics was far ahead of its time. Nobody was yet analysing national economies using terms such as gross domestic product or national income.

Perhaps we are acting like the rider who is desperately looking for the nag he is sitting on. Perhaps the capitalists are mutual customers for the remainder of the commodities — not to use them carelessly, but to use them for the extension of production, for accumulation. Then what else is accumulation but extension of capitalist production? Those goods which fulfil this purpose must not consist of luxurious articles for the private consumption of the capitalists, but must be composed of various means of production... and provisions for the workers.

All right, but such a solution only pushes the problem from this moment to the next. After we have assumed that accumulation has started and that the increased production throws an even bigger amount of commodities on to the market the following year, the same question arises again: where do we then find the consumers for this even greater amount of commodities? Will we answer: well this growing amount of goods will again be exchanged among the capitalists to extend production again, and so forth, year after year?

Then we have the roundabout that revolves in empty space. That is not capitalist accumulation, i.e. the amassing of money capital, but its contrary: producing commodities for the sake of it; from the standpoint of capital an utter absurdity. If the capitalists as a class are the only customers for the total amount of commodities... if they must always buy the commodities with their own money, and realize the surplus value, then amassing profit, accumulation for the capitalist class, cannot possibly take place...

You can twist and turn it as you wish but so long as we retain the assumption that there are no other classes but capitalists and workers, then there is no way that the capitalists as a class can get rid of the surplus goods in order to change the surplus value into money, and thus accumulate capital.
Luxemburg, 'Chapter 1: The Questions at Issue', *The Accumulation of Capital — An Anti-Critique*, trans. Rudolf Wichmann, <https://www.marxists.org/archive/luxemburg/1915/anti-critique/index.htm> [accessed December 2013].

Page 108

The time when I was writing the Accumulation of Capital *belongs to the happiest of my life. Really I was living as though in euphoria, "on a high," saw and heard nothing else, day or night, but this one question, which unfolded before me so beautifully, and I don't know what to say about which gave me the greater pleasure: the process of thinking, when I was turning a complicated problem over in my mind, pacing slowly back and forth through the room, under the close and attentive observation of Mimi, who lay on the red plush tablecloth with her little paws curled under her and kept turning her wise head back and forth to follow my movements; or the process of giving shape and literary form to my thoughts with pen in hand. Do you know, at that time I wrote the whole 30 signatures all at one go in four months' time—an unprecedented event!—and without rereading the brouillon, not even once, I sent it off to be printed.* Luxemburg, *Letters*, pp. 408–9.

Capitalism needs non-capitalist social strata as a market for its surplus value, as a source of supply for its means of production and as a resevoir of labour power for its wage system... Capitalism must therefore always and everywhere fight a battle of annihilation against every [other] economy that it encounters, whether this is slave economy, feudalism, primitive communism, or patriarchal peasant economy. The principal methods in this struggle are political force (revolution, war), oppressive taxation by the state, and cheap goods; they are partly applied simultaneously and partly they succeed and complement one another. In Europe, force assumed revolutionary forms in the fight against feudalism (this is the ultimate explanation of the bourgeois revolutions in the seventeenth, eighteenth and nineteenth centuries); in the non-European countries, where it fights more primitive social organisations, it assumes the form of colonial policy. These methods, together with the systems of taxation applied in such cases, and commercial relations also, particularly with primitive communities, form an alliance in which political power and economic factors go hand in hand.
Luxemburg, *The Accumulation of Capital*, pp. 348–9.

Luxemburg devotes a chapter of *The Accumulation of Capital* to the function of international loans as an agent of capitalist expansionism:

This business of paying for German goods with German capital in Asia is not the absurd circle it seems at first, with the kind Germans allowing the shrewd Turks merely the 'use' of their great works of civilisation — it is at bottom an exchange between German capital and Asiatic peasant economy, and exchange performed under state compulsion. On the one hand it makes for progressive accumulation and expanding 'spheres of interest' as a pretext for further political and economic expansion of German capital in Turkey. Railroad building and commodity exchange, on the other hand, are fostered by the state on the basis of a rapid disintegration, ruin and exploitation of the Asian peasant economy in the course of which the Turkish state becomes more and more dependent on European capital, politically as well as financially.

Luxemburg, *The Accumulation of Capital*, pp. 424–5.

The 'rampaging tiger' speech is not a quote from Luxemburg's writings. I put it in so I could continue to develop Mimi the cat as a visual metaphor.

The concept of 'primary accumulation' has been developed since Luxemburg's time to describe the process whereby capitalism moves into new markets within nations as well as between them. We now nominally live in a post-colonial world, where our governments are not as overtly dedicated to the maintenance of domination of other nations by force. Yet capitalist penetration of non-capitalist markets continues. It's the same process that privatises the provision of public services, and replaces the grocer on the High Street with a multinational supermarket chain, just as it razes the rainforest for cattle to make hamburgers, and continues to fuel 'military intervention' overseas. The enclosure of children's playing fields depicted in the first frame of page 178 is an example of primary accumulation.

Page 109

In the century and a half since modern industry was first established in England, the capitalist world economy has taken shape at the price of the pains and convulsions of the whole of humanity. It has seized one branch of production after another, taken hold of one country after another... [with] steam and electricity, fire and sword...

Luxemburg, *Introduction to Political Economy*, from *The Complete Works of Rosa Luxemburg*, p. 120.

Capitalism is the first mode of economy with the weapon of propaganda, a mode which tends to engulf the entire globe and to stamp out all other economies, tolerating no rival at its side. Yet at the same time it is also the first mode of economy which is unable to exist by itself, which needs other economic mediums as a medium and a soil. Although it strives to become universal, and, indeed, on account of this tendency, it must break down — because it is immanently incapable of becoming a universal mode of production. In its living history it is a contradiction in itself...

Luxemburg, *The Accumulation of Capital*, p. 447.

Page 110

Force is the only solution available to capitalism; the accumulation of capital, seen as a historical process, employs force as a permanent weapon.

Luxemburg, *The Accumulation of Capital*, p. 351.

All Europe will be called to arms, and sixteen to eighteen million men, the flower of the nations, armed with the best instruments of murder will make war upon each other. But I believe that behind this march there looms the final crash. Not we, but they themselves will bring it. They are driving things to the extreme, they are leading us straight into a catastrophe. They will harvest what they have sown.

August Bebel's speech to the Reichstag, 1912, quoted by Luxemburg in 'The Junius pamphlet'. Translation by the Socialist Publication Society. *The Rosa Luxemburg Reader*, p. 317.

German capitalism eagerly exports machines, iron, locomotives and textiles to Turkey, and does not collapse. **Rather, it is prepared to set the world on fire to monopolize this trade to an even greater extent** [original emphasis].

Luxemburg, *The Accumulation of Capital*.

Page 111

...it is the duty of the working classes and their parliamentary representatives in the countries taking part, fortified by the unifying activity of the International Bureau, to do everything to prevent the outbreak of war by whatever means seem to them the most effective...

Resolution of the Stuttgart Conference of the International, 24 August 1907, quoted in J.P. Nettl, *Rosa Luxemburg*, p. 270.

Victor Adler addressed the International Peace Conference in Basel, November 1912: *...oppose this crime of war, and if it should be accomplished, if*

we should really be able to prevent war, let this be the cornerstone of our coming victory.
Quoted in 'The Junius Pamphlet', *The Rosa Luxemburg Reader*, p. 318.

Will not a cry of horror, of fury and of indignation fill the country and lead the people to put an end to this murder? This is a quote from the 1911 official handbook for socialist voters. Ibid., p. 318.

We are fighting with all our might against a system that makes men the powerless tools of blind circumstance, against this capitalism that is preparing to change Europe, thirsty for peace, into a smoking battlefield. SPD Party press, 26 July 1914. Ibid., p. 319.

Page 112
'Rosa Luxemburg posed the question of whether the war should be accepted with impunity. When the answer came from the audience: "Never!", she continued: "If they expect us to murder our French or other foreign brothers, then let us tell them, 'No, under no circumstances!"' *Rosa Luxemburg Exhibition* pdf from the Rosa Luxemburg Siftung.

Page 113
...once the majority of working people come to the conclusion – and it is precisely the task of the Social Democracy to arouse this consciousness and to bring them to this conclusion – when, as I say, the majority of people come to the conclusion that wars are nothing but a barbaric, unsocial, reactionary phenomenon, entirely against the interests of the people, then wars will have become impossible...

'*Sir, I believe you, you would run away; a social democrat does not. He stands by his deeds and laughs at your judgements. And now sentence me.*'
Quoted in *Rosa Luxemburg Exhibition* pdf from the Rosa Luxemburg Siftung. These are both quotes from 'Militarism, War and the Working Class'.

Page 114
That there are comrades who can assume I would flee Germany because of the prison sentence – I could be quite amused by that if it were not, at the same time, rather saddening. Dear young friend, I assure you that I would not flee even if I were threatened by the gallows, and that is so for the simple reason that I consider it absolutely necessary to accustom our party to the idea that sacrifices are part of a socialists work in life, that they are simply a matter of course. You are right: "Long live the struggle!"
Luxemburg, *Letters*, pp. 329–30.

Leo and Rosa are friends again. They never stopped working together, even when he was stalking her, and Rosa invented some tortuous grammar in her letters to him to avoid using any personal pronouns. By this point, he has started an affair with his landlady and calmed down a lot.

Of all things, [Leo Jogiches] was here when your telegram arrived. But instinctively I was guarded about mentioning you, and when he asked me, later on, whether I was pleased with my attorney, I was quite reticent in my reply.
Luxemburg, *Letters*, p. 330.

Paul Levi was a bit of a playboy:
'He never married, and enjoyed the freedom of a bachelor existence, though at his funeral "alongside left-wing journalists and writers stood fur-clad young women, more than one of whom could have worn widow's weeds".'
Gruber, *International Communism*, pp. 391–2 quoted in David Fernbach, 'Rosa Luxemburg's Political Heir: An Appreciation of Paul Levi', *New Left Review*, Issue 238, November–December 1999 [accessed online, December 2013].

Page 115
'Luxemburg did not mince her words: drill and initiation rites were "torture", "inhumanity" was endemic in the armed forces.'
Henning Grunwald, 'The Rosa Luxemburg Trials of 1914 and the Emergence of the Ideal Type of the Weimar Party Lawyer: Courtroom to Revolutionary Stage Performance', *Oxford Scholarship Online*, January 2013, p. 1.

What do you think, darling, how fantastic! It's a prosecution from War Minister von Falkenhaym for insult to the officer corps and NCOs, because at the Freiburg meeting on 7 March I proposed proceedings against the abuse of conscripts and told how these "defenders of the fatherland" are kicked around.
Letter from Luxemburg to Levi, quoted in Fernbach, 'An Appreciation of Paul Levi'.

Page 116
'Underpinning this strategy was the "proof of allegation" defence for which German defamation law provided. Under the "Wahrheitsbeweis", Luxemburg could contest the charges by conceding that yes, she had insulted the armed forces but that substantially, her allegations were true. The real objective of this aggressive legal strategy would be "putting the Minister of War on the spot", as Paul Levi put it, by parading hundreds of

abused recruits through the witness stand. The rewards came at a price, though. Levi's strategy was only effective if the defendant was prepared to privilege the trial's propagandistic exploitation over arguments for an acquittal. The more aggressively Luxemburg repeated her allegations of army brutality during her defence, the less likely the court was to find any extenuating circumstances in her favour, as she well knew.' Grunwald, 'The Rosa Luxemburg Trials of 1914', p. 2.

Only in such rallies can we confront the Minister of War with his cowardice and thereby move him to behave differently, to turn and face us. If we produced pages and pages of written submissions for the court files, it would simply be a waste of paper... by mounting our rallies we prevent that which the Minister wants. He wants to drag the issue of military abuse into obscurity, we want it out in the open. It must be demonstrated to the Minister of War that in this respect, too, his 'victory' in court [meaning the suspension of proceedings] is of absolutely no use to him, on the contrary, that in this case we will present our material to the public by circumventing the courts. ...the propagandistic effect of any punishment, and especially of a harsh punishment, would be absolutely extraordinary.
Paul Levi, writing in response to an official report by Hugo Heinemann critical of Levi's use of judicial proceedings as material for mass rallies. Ibid., p. 12. (I was unable to find a picture of Hugo Heinemann – the lawyer pictured is Wolfgang Heine, another SPD lawyer who was publicly critical of Levi's methods.)

Page 117
The story of Gavrilo's sandwich has become a popular historical urban myth. See 'Past Imperfect: Gavrilo Princip's Sandwich' for a comprehensive debunking. <http://blogs.smithsonianmag.com/history/2011/09/gavrilo-princips-sandwich> [accessed December 2013].

Page 118
'The first 106 witnesses had been invited "as a sample", they could testify to 30.000 instances of abuse, in total, one could "easily" document "half a million" brutalities: "For the first time, the brutalities against recruits will be thoroughly examined in a monster trial before a bourgeois court, [...] perhaps a unique chance which has presented itself to Social Democracy in its struggle for human dignity."' Grunwald, 'The Rosa Luxemburg Trials of 1914', p. 18

The Minster of War represented here is Erich von Falkenhayn. The picture on page 140 is of Erich Ludendorff, but really, all these chiefs of staff look the same. They really do.

Page 119
This is fictionalised for dramatic effect. Rosa was actually sitting in her flat when the news reached her, although apparently she refused to believe it.

In contradiction to their previous teaching, the spokesman of the Social Democratic Party in the German Parliament on August 4, 1914, declared: 'In the hour of danger we shall stand by our fatherland.'
'The Wilhelmshaven Revolt' by Icarus, ed. and trans. Gabriel Kuhn. *All Power to the Councils! A Documentary History of the German Revolution of 1918-1919* (PM Press, 2012), p. 6.

Page 120
'Rosa Luxemburg... arrived later than the other representatives. Her face was pallid, and she was obviously trying to control a strong inner agitation. On the platform, where the members of the International Bureau were sitting, she remained standing for a long time and looked silently out at the crowds. She then sat down and hid her face in her hands. Members of the Bureau approached her twice, and spoke to her in pressing tones. She shook her head energetically and said only one word: "No!"... Although Rosa was again and again besieged by the crowd, she just sat there, motionless and lost in thought, deep sorrow written on her face.'
P. Frölich, *Rosa Luxemburg: Ideas in Action*, p. 202.

Page 121
It is a not an effective weapon in wartime; it is essentially an instrument of peace. Namely peace in a twofold sense; the struggle for peace and the class struggle in peacetime!
Kautsky, writing in *Neue Zeit*, October 1914, Ibid., p. 207.

In Kautsky's rendering, the world-historical appeal of The Communist Manifesto has been subjected to a substantial amendment, and now reads: "Proletarians of all countries, unite in peacetime, but slit one another's throats in war!" Thus today: "With every shot a Russian – with every blow a Frenchman!" And tomorrow, after the peace treaty: "Let's embrace all you millions and kiss the whole world!"
Luxemburg, quoted by Frölich, Ibid., p. 211.

Hannes actually left in August, months before Kautsky published his *Neue Zeit* article.

..the leave-taking on the balcony at my house on August 2, 1914, when Hannes, like a child with tears in his eyes, protested to us that he did not want to and could not go to war, he had the feeling he would not return, how I had to comfort him like a little child... I saw H[annes] once more...
Luxemburg, *Letters*, p. 445.

Page 122

Comrades Dr Südekum and Richard Fischer have made an attempt in the party press abroad to present the attitude of German Social Democracy during the present war in the light of their own conceptions. We therefore find it necessary to assure foreign comrades that we, and certainly many other German Social Democrats, regard the war, its origins, its character, as well as the role of Social Democracy in the present situation from an entirely different standpoint, and one which does not correspond to that of Comrades Südekum and Fischer. Martial law presently makes it impossible for us to enlarge upon our point of view publicly.
Signed—Karl Liebknecht, Dr Franz Mehring, Dr Rosa Luxemburg, Clara Zetkin.
J.P. Nettl, *Rosa Luxemburg*, p. 372.

From the minute Karl was arrested—it happened at 8:30 am, when we were promenading together with the crowd on Potsdamer Platz—I of course have not had a free moment, because it was necessary to find out where he had been taken and to force a way through to him. Indeed I tried with all the might of my fists to "free" him and I pulled at him and at the policemen all the way to the police station, from which I was unceremoniously expelled.
Luxemburg, *Letters*, p. 359.

Page 123

Luxemburg was imprisoned on two occasions during the war. In 1915 she served the sentence imposed on her in the trial recounted on page 113. On her release from prison in early 1916 she was greeted at the gates by thousands of women workers. Then on 10 July 1916 she was taken into 'military protective custody'. At first she was held in the police prison at Alexanderplatz in Berlin, then on 21 July, she was moved to the Berlin women's prison on Barnim Street. From 26 October 1916 to 22 July 1917 she was held in the Wronke fortress in the province of Poznan, where she had use of the little garden represented in this book. From there she was sent to the Breslau prison and was finally freed

by the German revolution on 8 November 1918.
Do you know, Hänschen, what Alexanderplatz is? The month-and-a-half stay that I had there left grey hairs on my head and rent my nerves in such a way that I will never get over it. Ibid., p. 424.

This is Mathilde Jacob, not Mathilde Wurm, who we met earlier, on page 57. (It's not easy to fit all of Luxemburg's circle of acquaintances into the book.) Jacob was vital to Luxemburg during the war, as she operated the stenograph machine upon which Luxemburg's pamphlets were printed. The two were close friends. Jacob visited her frequently in prison, smuggled out her manuscripts and facilitated their printing and distribution. Jacob's contribution to socialism has been consistently underestimated.

After about ten minutes, when she was in the middle of a sentence, the spy jumped up with a violent movement, and shouted at us in a sergeant-major tone: 'The visiting hour is finished.'
...'Oh no,' said Rosa Luxemburg calmly, 'I have to discuss a matter of great importance to me and I shall continue the conversation to its end. Please remain until then' ...he said sarcastically: 'Here you have to behave well and do what you're told.' At this she lost her temper and shouted: 'You dirty spy!' Most likely he had waited for such a remark, and immediately said to the supervisor, 'You heard that, I have been insulted.' 'Yes,' said Rosa Luxemburg, 'and rightly so.' He continued further with shameless insults and in rage Rosa Luxemburg threw into a corner a bar of chocolate which had been brought to her... and finally called out in agitation: 'One cannot expect better behaviour from a dirty spy.' M. Jacob, *Rosa Luxemburg: an Intimate Portrait*, pp. 54–5.

The accused is guilty of having insulted Constable Palm by word and deed, in Central Berlin on September 22, 1916, by shouting at him, 'You're just an ordinary police spy and a swine. Get out of here,' and at the same time throwing an inkpot at him ... The accused was under protective custody at the Berlin women's prison. On the day in question Constable Palm was present as overseer during her conversation with Mathilde Jacob. After the expiration of ten minutes he declared that the conversation was ended. The accused has now confessed to making the above-mentioned verbal insult. She denies having thrown anything at the police official.
Luxemburg, *Letters*, p. 655.

Pages 126–7

The scene has thoroughly changed. The six weeks' march to Paris has become world drama. Mass murder has become a monotonous task, and yet the final solution is not one step nearer. Capitalist rule is caught in its own trap, and cannot ban the spirit it has invoked.

Gone is the first mad delirium. Gone are the patriotic street demonstrations, the chase after suspicious looking automobiles, the false telegrams, the cholera-poisoned wells. Gone the mad stories of Russian students who had bombs from every bridge of Berlin, or Frenchmen flying over Nuremberg; gone the excesses of a spy-hunting populace, the singing throngs, the coffee shops with their patriotic songs; gone the violent mobs, ready to denounce, ready to persecute women, ready to whip themselves into a delirious frenzy over every wild rumour; gone the atmosphere of ritual murder, the Kishinev air that left the policeman at the corner as the only remaining representative of human dignity.

The show is over. The curtain has fallen on trains filled with reservists, as they pull out amid the joyous cries of enthusiastic maidens. We no longer see their laughing faces, smiling cheerily from the train windows upon a war-mad population. Quietly they trot through the streets, with their sacks upon their shoulders. And the public, with a fretful face, goes about its daily task.

Into the disillusioned atmosphere of pale daylight there rings a different chorus; the hoarse croak of the hawks and hyenas of the battlefield. Ten thousand tents, guaranteed according to specifications, 100,000 kilos of bacon, cocoa powder, coffee substitute—cash on immediate delivery. Shrapnel, drills, ammunition bags, marriage bureaus for war widows, leather belts, war orders —only serious propositions considered. And the cannon fodder that was loaded onto the trains in August and September is rotting on the battlefields of Belgium and the Vosges, while profits are springing, like weeds, from the fields of the dead. Business is flourishing upon the ruins. Cities are turned into shambles, whole countries into deserts, villages into cemeteries, whole nations into beggars, churches into stables; popular rights, treaties, alliances, the holiest words and the highest authorities have been torn into scraps; every sovereign by the grace of God is called a fool, an unfaithful wretch, by his cousin on the other side; every diplomat calls his colleague in the enemy's country a desperate criminal; each government looks upon the other as the evil genius of its people, worthy only of the contempt of the world. Hunger revolts in Venetia, in Lisbon, in Moscow, in Singapore; pestilence in Russia, misery and desperation is everywhere.

Shamed, dishonoured, wading in blood and dripping with filth, thus capitalist society stands. Not as we usually see it, playing the roles of peace and righteousness, of order, of philosophy, of ethics—but as a roaring beast, as an orgy of anarchy, as a pestilential breath, devastating culture and humanity—so it appears in all its hideous nakedness.

The opening words of Luxemburg's 'The Junius Pamplet: The Crisis in German Social Democracy'. *The Rosa Luxemburg Reader*, pp. 312–3.

Pages 128–9

Hänschen, are you sleeping? I'm coming with a long piece of straw to tickle your ear.

I need company, I'm sad, and I want to make a confession. The last few days I've been angry and therefore unhappy and therefore sick. Or was the order reversed: was I sick and therefore unhappy and hence angry?—I don't know anymore. Now I'm well again, and I vow never, ever again to lend an ear to my inner demons. Can you blame me that I'm sometimes unhappy because I always have to see and hear from a distance those things that for me mean life and happiness? But yes, go ahead and scold me, I swear that from now on I will be patience and gentleness and gratitude itself. Good lord, don't I have reason enough to be grateful and joyful, since the sun is shining down on me so and the birds are singing their age-old song, whose meaning I have grasped so well...

The one who has done the most to restore me to reason is a small friend whose image I am sending you enclosed. This comrade with the jauntily held beak, steeply rising forehead, and eye of a know-it-all is called *Hypolais hypolais*, or in everyday language the arbour bird or also the garden mocker. You have surely heard him somewhere because he likes to nest in the thickets of gardens or parks everywhere, you simply haven't noticed him, just as people for the most part pass by the loveliest things in life without paying attention.

This bird is quite an oddball. He doesn't sing just one song or one melody, like other birds, but he is a public speaker by the grace of God, he holds forth, making his speeches to the garden, and does so with a very loud voice full of dramatic excitement, leaping transitions, and passages of heightened pathos. He brings up the most impossible questions, then hurries to answer them himself, with nonsense, makes the most daring assertions, heatedly refuting views that no one has stated, charges through wide open doors, then suddenly exclaims in triumph: "Didn't I say so? Didn't I say so?" Immediately after that he solemnly warns everyone who's willing or not willing to listen: "You'll see! You'll see!" (He has the clever habit of repeating each witty remark twice.) And among other things it means nothing to him to suddenly squeak like a mouse whose tail has been caught or to break out in laughter that is supposed to be satanic but which comes out, given that his throat is so tiny, as unbelievably comical. In short, he never grows tired of filling the garden with the most blatant nonsense, and during the stillness that reigns while he's giving his speeches, one can almost see the other birds exchanging glances and shrugging their shoulders. But I don't shrug mine. I'm the only one who doesn't shrug; instead, I laugh every time with joy and call to him out loud: "Sweet dumbhead!" You see, I know that his foolish chatter is actually the deepest wisdom and that he's right about everything.

Luxemburg, *Letters*, p. 426.

This is probably a description of an Icterine Warbler. If you wish to hear the delights of his public speaking skill for yourself, go to http://www.xeno-canto.org.

Pages 130–2

Hänschen, you have no idea how blue the sky was today! Or was it just as blue where you are in Lissa? Usually before the evening lock-up I go out for another short half hour to my little flower bed (pansies, forget-me-nots, and phlox, planted by myself) to water them with my own little watering can and to walk around in my garden just a bit more. The hour before sunset has a magic all its own. The sun was still hot, but one gladly allowed its slanted rays to burn on one's neck and cheeks like a kiss. A soft breath of air stirs the bushes like a whispering promise that the cool of evening is coming soon, relieving the heat of the day. In the sky, which was of a trembling, shimmering blue, two towering white cloud formations were piled high, while a very pale half-moon swam between them as though in a dream. The swallows had already begun their every-evening's flight in full company strength, and with their sharp, pointy wings snipped the blue silk of space into little bits, shot back and forth, overtaking one another with shrill cries, and disappearing into the dizzying heights. I stood with my little watering can dripping in my hand with my head tilted back and felt a tremendous yearning to dive up into that damp, shimmering blueness, to bathe in it, to splash around, to let myself dissolve completely in that dew, and disappear...

Luxemburg, *Letters*, p. 425.

Page 133

Only one thing torments me: that I shouldn't be enjoying so much beauty **all by myself**. I want to shout out loud over the walls: Oh please, pay attention to this marvelous day! Don't forget, as busy as you may be, as you're hurrying across the courtyard in pursuit of the day's pressing tasks, do not forget to quickly raise your head and cast a glance at those great silver clouds and that silent blue ocean in which they are swimming. Do take notice as well of the air which is heavy with the passionate breath of the last linden blossoms, and take notice of the resplendence and glory that overlie this day, because this day will never, ever come again! This day is a gift to you like a rose in full bloom, lying at your feet, waiting for you to pick it up and press it to your lips. R.

Luxemburg, *Letters*, p. 429.

Page 134

I am ready at my post at all times and at the first opportunity will begin striking the keys of World History's piano with all ten fingers so that it will really boom. But since right now I happen to be "on leave" from World History, not through any fault of my own but because of external compulsion, I just laugh to myself and rejoice that things are moving ahead without me. Luxemburg, *Letters*, p. 392.

Page 136

Lt. Siegfried Sassoon.
3rd Batt: Royal Welsh Fusiliers.
July, 1917.

I am making this statement as an act of wilful defiance of military authority because I believe that the war is being deliberately prolonged by those who have the power to end it. I am a soldier, convinced that I am acting on behalf of soldiers. I believe that the war upon which I entered as a war of defence and liberation has now become a war of aggression and conquest. I believe that the purposes for which I and my fellow soldiers entered upon this war should have been so clearly stated as to have made it impossible to change them and that had this been done the objects which actuated us would now be attainable by negotiation.

I have seen and endured the sufferings of the troops and I can no longer be a party to prolong these sufferings for ends which I believe to be evil and unjust. I am not protesting against the conduct of the war, but against the political errors and insincerities for which the fighting men are being sacrificed.

On behalf of those who are suffering now, I make this protest against the deception which is being practised upon them; also I believe it may help to destroy the callous complacency with which the majority of those at home regard the continuance of agonies which they do not share and which they have not enough imagination to realise.

The executed sailor from the *Prinzregent Luitpold* is Albin Köbis.

Page 138

I just received via Breslau the dreadful black envelope. My hands and heart were already trembling when I saw the handwriting and the postmark, but I still hoped that the worst would not be true.
Letter of condolence to Marie and Adolf Geck on the death of their son, Luxemburg, *Letters*, p. 478.

I still fail to come out of the deep shock. How can this be possible? To me it is like a word cut short in mid-sentence, like a musical chord broken off, although I still keep hearing it.

We had a thousand plans for life after the war. We wanted to "enjoy life," travel, read good books, and gaze in wonder, as never before, at the coming of spring. ... I cannot comprehend it: How can this be possible? Like a blossom torn off and trampled underfoot.
Luxemburg, *Letters*, pp. 441–2.

I dare not even think about it, otherwise I could not bear it. On the contrary, I live on with the dream that he is still here, I see his living form in front of me, chat with him in my thoughts about everything, in **me** *he continues to live.*

Yesterday my letter to him of October 21 was returned, that's the second one already. Letters that never reached him.
Luxemburg, *Letters*, p. 451.

Page 139

Oh, Sonyichka, I've lived through something sharply, terribly painful here. Into the courtyard where I take my walks there often come military supply wagons, filled with sacks or old army coats and shirts, often with bloodstains on them ... They're unloaded here and distributed to the prison cells, patched or mended, then loaded up and turned over to the military again. Recently one of these wagons arrived with water buffaloes harnessed to it instead of horses. This was the first time I had seen these animals up close. They have a stronger, broader build than our cattle, with flat heads and horns that curve back flatly, the shape of the head being similar to that of our sheep, completely black, with large, soft, black eyes. They come from Romania, the spoils of war... The soldiers who serve as drivers of these supply wagons tell the story that it was a lot of trouble to catch these wild animals and even more difficult to put them to work

as draft animals, because they were accustomed to their freedom. They had to be beaten terribly before they grasped the concept that they had lost the war and that the motto now applying to them was "woe unto the vanquished" [vae victis]... There are said to be as many as a hundred of these animals in Breslau alone, and on top of that these creatures, who lived in the verdant fields of Romania, are given meager and wretched feed. They are ruthlessly exploited, forced to haul every possible kind of wagonload, and they quickly perish in the process. —And so, a few days ago, a wagon like this arrived at the courtyard. The load was piled so high that the buffaloes couldn't pull the wagon over the threshold at the entrance gate. The soldier accompanying the wagon, a brutal fellow, began flailing at the animals so fiercely with the blunt end of his whip handle that the attendant on duty indignantly took him to task, asking him: Had he no pity for the animals? "No one has pity for us humans," he answered with an evil smile, and started in again, beating them harder than ever. ...

Page 140

The animals finally started to pull again and got over the hump, but one of them was bleeding ... Sonyichka, the hide of a buffalo is proverbial for its toughness and thickness, but this tough skin had been broken. During the unloading, all the animals stood there, quite still, exhausted, and the one that was bleeding kept staring into the empty space in front of him with an expression on his black face and in his soft, black eyes like an abused child. It was precisely the expression of a child that has been punished and doesn't know why or what for, doesn't know how to get away from this torment and raw violence... I stood before it, and the beast looked at me; tears were running down my face—they were his tears. No one can flinch more painfully on behalf of a beloved brother than I flinched in my helplessness over this mute suffering. How far away, how irretrievably lost were the beautiful, free, tender-green fields of Romania! How differently the sun used to shine and the wind blow there, how different was the lovely song of the birds that could be heard there, or the melodious call of the herdsman. And here—this strange, ugly city, the gloomy stall, the nauseating, stale hay, mixed with rotten straw, and the strange, frightening humans—the beating, the blood running from the fresh wound. ... Oh, my poor buffalo, my poor, beloved brother! We both stand here so powerless and mute, and are as one in our pain, impotence, and yearning. —All this time the prisoners had hurriedly busied themselves around the wagon, unloading the heavy sacks and dragging them off into the building;

but the soldier stuck both hands in his trouser pockets, paced around the courtyard with long strides, and kept smiling and softly whistling some popular tune to himself. And the entire marvellous panorama of the war passed before my eyes.
Luxemburg, *Letters*, pp. 456–8.

Page 142

Groener is actually a Major-General, not a Lieutenant, by this point in the war. He is Ludendorff's second-in-command.

'After August 8 Ludendorff had been in a highly nervous state... Too proud to admit mistakes, let alone defeat... he insisted on the holding of forward positions, thereby tremendously increasing the risk of an eventual rupture of the German lines...

'On September 29 he surprised the government with the statement that "the condition of the army demands an immediate armistice in order to avoid a catastrophe"...'

[NB: This statement was made by a staff officer to the Reichstag; my representation assumes that Ludendorff must have communicated the same information to Kaiser Wilhelm.]

'[Ludendorff] made the democratic parties responsible for the defeat. "Let them conclude the peace that will now have to be concluded," he told William II, who agreed.'
Hajo Holborn, *A History of Modern Germany: 1840-1945*, Volume 3 (Princeton University Press, 1982), pp. 502–3.

Page 143

The sailors of the fleet had their own views on the "glory of the fatherland." When they met, they saluted one another with a "Long live Liebknecht." ...the Committee passed the message: "Guarded meeting after dark at the New Soldier's Cemetary. Send delegates from every unit."

According to the rules of the secret organisation, delegates had to proceed to the meeting alone or at most in pairs, and at suitable distances so as not to attract attention. The meeting took place and showed how general was the response to the call of the Committee. The meeting place was guarded by sailors. Those present stood, knelt, or sat between the graves. There was not time for discussion or speeches. The names of the ships moored in the harbour and river were called, and out of the dark the almost invisible delegates just answered, "Here."

One comrade spoke, briefly but firmly: "The time has come. It's now or never. Act carefully but resolutely. Seize officers and occupants. Occupy

the signalling stations first. When control has been gained, hoist the red flag in the maintop or gaff. Up for the red dawn of a new day!"
'The Wilhemshaven Revolt' by Icarus, *All Power to the Councils*, p. 9.

Page 144

On Sunday morning, thousands of sailors left their ships. The soldiers' and workers' bitterness was enormous and it only needed a small spark for an explosion.

The commander's office seemed prepared. Hornists and alarm patrols marched through the streets of Kiel and demanded all sailors to return to their troops. No one did. We even used the messengers of the commander's office for our own purposes by following right after them, encouraging the soldiers to join us at the meeting. Many came, along with a big number of ordinary citizens...

In front of the Kaiser-Cafe we suddenly received MG-fire. Our demonstration stopped. When we realized that nobody was hit, we moved on. After that the MG-shooters fired directly into our demonstration. Forty to fifty demonstrators, among them also women and children, collapsed under the bullets. Eight of them were killed and 29 injured severely...

The people screamed in indignation and protest. After the murderers, who were under the command of Leutnant Steinhäuser... were not ready to stop shooting, a marine jumped in front and hit Lieutnant Steinhäuser with the butt... Young marines and workers charged the position of the machine gunners and put them to flight.
Recollection of Karl Artelt, 1958, <http://www.kurkuhl.de/en/novrev/artelt_recollection.html> [accessed December 2013].

We carried our shot brothers and sisters to the Café Kaiser where we put the wounded on couches and the dead on the floor. We held hands and pledged to act with unrelenting determination against the perpetrators of this heinous crime, and against the warmongers in general. We would not rest until they were forced to stop their dirty work. The hour for a decisive confrontation had come. We had witnessed the spark that made the powder keg explode.
'With the Red Flag to Vice-Admiral Souchon' by Karl Artelt, *All Power to the Councils*, pp. 20–21.

Page 147

In this very hour we proclaim the Free Socialist Republic of Germany... The day of liberty has begun... The rule of capitalism, which has turned Europe into a cemetery, is broken...

Karl Liebknecht, Spartacists Proclamation of the Republic, 9 November 1918 < https://www.facinghistory.org/weimar-republic-fragility-democracy/politics/spartacists-proclamation-republic-november-9-1918-politics> [accessed December 2014].

...no more meetings, no more conventicles. Where great things are in the making, where the wind roars about the ears, that's where I'll be in the thick of it, but not the daily treadmill.
Letter from Luxemburg, quoted in J.P. Nettl, *Rosa Luxemburg*, p. 417.

Luxemburg was technically released at 10 p.m. on 9 November, but stayed overnight in prison as she had nowhere else to go. She addressed triumphant crowds in Breslau then hastened to Berlin by train.

Page 148

One of our friends had picked up ten soldiers somewhere on the street, and impelled to heroic deeds — 'a lieutenant and ten men' — he occupied the Berliner Lokal-Anzeiger... this was on the Sunday... This conquest of ours seemed secured by those ten men, who stood at the door armed to the teeth and let no one through unless they at least maintained that they were with us. On Monday morning [the 11th] we came back... We were all gathered — Rosa Luxemburg, Karl Leibknecht, ten or twelve other comrades — when suddenly the door opened, the publishing director appeared and declared that there would be no further edition. That's a bit cheeky, we thought... When one of us tried to leave in order to go to the Workers' and Soldiers' Council, he found rifles pointed at him at the door of the building. The Scherl company had bought over our guard, who now declared that none of us would leave the building alive unless the company agreed... And so we sat, a dozen prisoners of our own military force, on the third day of the revolution, and wondered how a revolution was to proceed if the 'revolutionary soldiers' could be so speedily snapped up by any capitalist at will between first and second breakfast.

That was only an episode. But there is no episode that does not contain part of the whole event. It was almost a symbol of the revolution.
Paul Levi, quoted in M. Jacob, *Rosa Luxemburg: An Intimate Portrait*, p. 92.

Page 149

Very approximately summarised from 'What does the Spartacus League Want?' This was first published in *Die Rote Fahne*, 14 December 1918.

Pages 150–1

At this point, Ebert was Chancellor of Germany and Minister President of Prussia. He was officially sworn in as president on 21 August 1919.

Ludendorff had resigned at this point and Wilhelm Groener had replaced him as Quartermaster General of the Army. I retained Ludendorff in the comic as a central character because he was instrumental in the invention of the stab-in-the-back myth, which motivated returning soldiers to attack the socialists.

'According to notes taken by Prince Max, Ebert declared on 7 November: "If the Kaiser does not abdicate, the social revolution is unavoidable. But I do not want it, indeed I hate it like sin." (Wenn der Kaiser nicht abdankt, dann ist die soziale Revolution unvermeidlich. Ich aber will sie nicht, ja, ich hasse sie wie die Sünde.)' Source: v. Baden: Erinnerungen und Dokumente p. 599 f. via Wikipedia, 'The German Revolution'.

This conversation actually took place in the evening, after Ebert had managed to assert control over the Council of the People's Deputies.

'Late on the evening of November 10, Groener called Ebert at the Reichskanzlei over a secret line the existence of which had been unknown to Ebert until that time. Groener was at Spa, Belgium at the headquarters of the OHL. Ebert never talked about what was said, so the only information on what was discussed has come from Groener. According to him, he offered Ebert the loyalty and cooperation of the armed forces in return for some demands: fight against Bolshevism, a speedy end to the soldiers' councils and restoration of the sole authority of the officers corps, a national assembly and a return to law and order. Ebert seemed still unsettled from the stormy meeting he had just attended and at the end of the conversation he thanked Groener.'
Wikipedia, 'Ebert–Groener pact'. Quotes from Haffner, Sebastian (2002). Die deutsche Revolution 1918/19 (German). Kindler. pp. 120–1

Page 152

In place of the employers and their wage slaves, free working comrades! Labor as nobody's torture, because everybody's duty! A human and honorable life for all who do their social duty...

In this hour, socialism is the only salvation for

humanity. *The words of the Communist Manifesto flare like a fiery menetekel above the crumbling bastions of capitalist society: Socialism or barbarism!*
'What does the Spartacus League Want?' first published *Die Rote Fahne*, 14 December 1918. Trans. Peggy Fallen Wright, *The Rosa Luxemburg Reader*, p. 350.

Incidentally, the Communist Manifesto doesn't contain the phrase 'Socialism or Barbarism'. Luxumburg also misattributed the phrase to Friedrich Engels, in her Junius Pamphlet, but Engels never wrote it either. The phrase comes from Karl Kautsky's discussion of the basics of German Socialism, the Efurt programme, in his book *Das Erfurter Programm in seinem grundsätzlichen Teil erläutert (The Erfurt Program: A Discussion of Fundamentals),1891*: '…we must either move forward into socialism or fall back into barbarism [es heißt entweder vorwärts zum Sozialismus oder rückwärts in die Barbarei]. These days, this prophetic phrase 'Socialism or Barbarism' is credited as Luxemburg's original invention, but she was simply rephrasing concepts with which her peers would have been familiar. See Angus, 'The Origin of Rosa Luxemburg's Slogan "Socialism or Barbarism"', *Monthly Review Magazine*, October 2014.

The eight-hour working day was the concession won by the Trades Unions in the Stinnes-Legien Agreement with the corporations, which has been regarded as another betrayal of the fundamental principles of socialism.

…we declare in our program that the immediate task of the proletariat is none other than – in a word – to make socialism a truth and a fact, and to destroy capitalism root and branch…
'Our Program and the Political Situation', Luxemburg's speech to the founding congress of the German Communist   Party on 31 December 1918. <https://www.marxists.org/archive/luxemburg/1918/12/31.htm> [accessed December 2013].

Page 153
…without a free and untrammelled press, without the unlimited right of association and assemblage, the rule of the broad mass of people is utterly unthinkable…
Freedom only for the supporters of the government, only for the members of one party — however numerous they may be — is no freedom at all. Freedom is always and exclusively freedom for the one who thinks differently. Not because of any fanatical concept of "justice" but because all that is instructive, wholesome and purifying in political freedom depends upon this essential characteristic, and its effectiveness vanishes when "freedom" becomes a special privilege.
Luxemburg, 'The Russian Revolution', trans. Bertram D. Wolfe, *The Rosa Luxemburg Reader*, p. 305.

Rosa wrote a detailed critique of the Russian Revolution in September 1918, which was published as a pamphlet posthumously by Paul Levi in 1922. Frölich states that:
'Leo Jogiches was against the publication of the work because he knew that in certain fundamental points Rosa had subsequently changed her views, and that she was thinking of writing a whole book on the Russian Revolution.' P. Frölich, *Rosa Luxemburg: Ideas in Action*, p. 214.

The proletarian revolution requires no terror for its aims; it hates and despises killing. It does not need these weapons because it does not combat individuals but institutions, because it does not enter the arena with naïve illusions whose disappointment it would seek to revenge. It is not the desperate attempt of a minority to mold the world forcibly according to its ideal, but the action of the great massive millions of the people, destined to fulfill a historic mission and to transform historical necessity into reality.
Luxemburg, 'What does the Spartacus League Want?' *The Rosa Luxemburg Reader*, p. 349.

Page 154
'The official birth of the term "stab-in-the-back" itself possibly can be dated to the autumn of 1919, when Ludendorff was dining with the head of the British Military Mission in Berlin, British general Sir Neill Malcolm. Malcolm asked Ludendorff why it was that he thought Germany lost the war. Ludendorff replied with his list of excuses, including that the home front failed the army.
'Malcolm asked him: "Do you mean, General, that you were stabbed in the back?" Ludendorff's eyes lit up and he leapt upon the phrase like a dog on a bone. "Stabbed in the back?" he repeated. "Yes, that's it, exactly, we were stabbed in the back". And thus was born a legend…'
John W Wheeler-Bennett, 'Ludendorff: The Soldier and the Politician', *Virginia Quarterly Review* 14 (2), 1938, pp. 187–202.

'In [Ludendorff's] world view, Jews, Freemasons and Jesuits formed a secret alliance. The Jews and the Jesuit Order both were the masters of the world's finances and Freemasonry was a Jewish invention with its higher degrees controlled by the Jesuits.'
'The anti-Masonic writings of General Erich Ludendorff', Jimmy Koppen, Interdisciplinary Research Group Freemasonry, Free University Brussels, paper presented at the 12th annual conference of the Canonbury Masonic Research Center, London, 30 October 2010, [accessed online, December 2013].

Noske wasn't actually officially appointed to the War Ministry until late December 1919.
'When the so-called Christmas Clashes of 1918 made it clear that the SPD did not hesitate to collaborate with the bourgeoisie and reactionary military forces to suppress radical workers' uprisings, the USPD [independent SPD] people's delegates resigned and two more SPD members entered the Council of People's Delegates, one of them being Gustav Noske who was appointed minister of the Reichswehr. Upon his appointment, Noske allegedly said, "One has to be the bloodhound—I am ready."'
All Power to the Councils, p. 28.

Page 155

The Danger of Bolshevism!... German Women! Do you know what Bolshevism and Spartacism threaten? ...women will become the property of the people... any man who wants to use that communal property needs a permit from the Workers' committee... everyone is duty-bound to report on women who refuse.
Poster by the Union to Combat Bolshevism, reported in E. Ettinger, *Rosa Luxemburg: A Life*, p. 232.

...the gentlemen of the bourgeoisie and all the parasites of the capitalist economy who are quaking in their boots for their property, their privileges, their profits and their ruling prerogatives... From our historical vantage point we can look upon the spectacle with a cool smile. We can see through their game—the actors, their managers and their roles.
Die Rote Fahne, 24 November 1918. P. Frölich, *Rosa Luxemburg: Ideas in Action*, p. 278.

This representation of 'Rosa in the *Rote Fahne* offices' is a narrative device which I used to compress multiple events onto a single page. In real life, troops occupied the *Rote Fahne* office on 6 December and Karl Leibknecht was also arrested there the following day.

Page 156

What is called for now is... the strictest self-criticism and iron concentration of energy in order to continue the work we have begun...

The abolition of the rule of capitalism... is a huge work which cannot be completed in the twinkling of an eye by a few decrees from above; it can be born only of the conscious action by the mass of workers in the city and in the country, and brought successfully through the maze of difficulties only by the highest intellectual maturity and unflagging idealism of the masses of the people.
Luxemburg, 'The Beginning' first published in *Die Rote Fahne*, 18 November 1918. *The Rosa Luxemburg Reader*, p. 343.

History is not making things as easy for us as it did for bourgeois revolutions; then it was sufficient to overthrow the official power and replace it by a couple or a couple of dozen new men. But we must work from the bottom to the top, and that is in accordance with the mass character of our revolution and its aims...

...I shall not venture to prophesy how long the whole process will take. But who expects that from us, to whom does it matter, so long as our lives are long enough to bring it about?
Speech to the founding congress of the German Communist Party, 31 December 1918, quoted in P. Frölich, *Rosa Luxemburg: Ideas in Action*, pp. 282–3.

The Spartakusbund will never take over governmental power except with the clear and explicit will of the great majority of the proletarian masses throughout Germany, except in accordance with their conscious approval of its views, aims and fighting methods.
Ibid., p. 270.

Page 157

'To the fight!' 'echoes the phrase 'Auf! Auf! Zum Kampf, zum Kampf!' the wartime patriotic song that was rewritten by Bertold Brecht in 1919 to become a left-wing revolutionary anthem.

No one will ever know who started the "Go to the Vorwärts!" calls. There have been many theories about possible agents provocateurs. It is a possibility. But it might as well have been a protestor excited by the moment and the enormous crowd. This is how spontaneous mass actions emerge: someone puts a sentiment into words that everyone is feeling. This is what happens in agitated times.
Karl Retzlaw, 'Noske and the Beginning of the Comrades' Murders', *All Power to the Councils*, p. 130.

Page 158

To Karl Leibknecht's right is Wilhelm Pieck, who survived the Freikorp's massacres and eventually became president of East Germany, becoming complicit in Stalinist rule.

The meeting of the Revolutionary Committee took place in the Imperial Stables, the current residence of the potentially revolutionary troops, the People's Naval Division, not the *Vorwärts'* building, as could be assumed from this illustration.

'According to Pieck's report, this "Revolutionary Committee", sitting from midnight, decided "to arrest the members of the cabinet during the night, to occupy the militarily most important buildings on Monday", to arm the workers and set up commissariats. However, the uprising's leadership no longer had the energy to put this decision into practice, and, in spite of Pieck's protests, the committee broke up just before 2am.' Ottokar Luban, 'Rosa at a Loss. The KPD Leadership and the Berlin Uprising of January 1919: Legend and Reality', *Revolutionary History*, Volume 8, no 4, p. 23.

Page 159

'...some armed troops were dispatched to occupy government buildings, and, for their legitimisation, obtained a typed declaration from the "Revolutionary Committee" declaring the dismissal of the Ebert–Scheidemann Government and the provisional seizing of power by the revolutionary body. The old garrison at the Ministry of War would only hand over the building to the armed revolutionaries if the signatures of the chairmen could be shown on the declaration that they produced, but it bore merely the typed names of the chairmen, Ledebour, Liebknecht and Scholze. Wilhelm Lemmgen, the sailor in charge of the revolutionary squad and responsible for the occupation, returned with the declaration for signing, and Liebknecht also signed for the absent Ledebour. Liebknecht, who was engaged for a large part of his time in giving speeches to the demonstrators, most likely had nothing to do with the composition of the declaration, as Lemmgen's statement of 22 January 1919 indicated: "Liebknecht studied the declaration for a long time. I had the impression that it was new to him." Instead of returning to his armed squad outside the Ministry of War, Lemmgen, who was beginning to have misgivings, went

home with the signed document and later handed it over to a representative of the SPD government.' Ibid., pp. 24–5.

Since Lemmgen, the man in possession of Liebknecht's 'pustch document', was a leader of a troop of sailors, he probably didn't have a wife and family in Berlin. This exchange is fictional. It is included to illustrate the conflicting economic and social pressures on the working poor.

'...on late Monday afternoon [the People's Naval Division] reneged on the promise of support given by their leader Dorrenbach — who was then deposed — and very forcefully ejected the rebels from the building. The revolutionary shop stewards were "expelled from the Marstall with the coarsest words of abuse", as Pieck put it in his 1920 manuscript.' Ibid., p. 26.

Page 160

This interchange occurred later, after the recapture of the *Vorwärts'* building. Luxemburg wasn't aware of Liebknecht's signature on the 'putsch' document until the SPD regained control of *Vorwärts* and published it in the next edition.

None of those present will forget the scene, as Rosa Luxemburg held the document up to Karl Liebknecht, which was signed: "The provisional government, Ledebour, Liebknecht, Scholze". She just asked him: "Karl, is that our programme?" The rest was silence. Recollection of Paul Levi, quoted by Ottokar Luban, ibid., p. 45.

...there is no time to lose. Sweeping measures must be undertaken immediately. Clear and speedy directives must be given to the masses, to the soldiers faithful to the revolution. Their energy, their bellicosity must be directed towards the right goals. The wavering elements among the troops can be won for the sacred cause of the people by means of resolute and clear actions taken by the revolutionary bodies.

Act! Act! Courageously, resolutely, consistently – that is the 'accursed' duty and obligation of the revolutionary chairmen and the sincerely socialist party leaders. Disarm the counterrevolution, arm the masses, occupy all positions of power. Act quickly! Luxemburg, 'What are the Leaders Doing?' *Die Rote Fahne*, 7 January 1919, translation by W.D. Graf, Marxist Internet Archive, marxists.org [accessed December 2013].

Page 161

'...on 9 January the [Rote Fahne] offices were evacuated. A patrol of government troops were

already before the door. As usual, Rosa seemed to ignore the danger completely. As she left the house, she took one scrutinising look at the men, and, having decided that only hunger could have driven them into the enemy camp, she immediately began to show them how they were letting themselves be misused against their own real interests. It was only with difficulty that her woman companion managed to whisk her away from an imminently dangerous situation. Soon afterwards Hugo Eberlein found her involved in heated discussion amid a crowd right in the heart of the fighting area, and had to drag her away almost by force. Rosa was contemptuous of danger, and, in fact, she was rather inclined to seek it from a romantic sense of responsibility, a feeling that she simply had to share every danger with the ordinary fighters of the revolution.'
P. Frölich, *Rosa Luxemburg: Ideas in Action*, p. 294.

The capture of the woman comrade occurred later, after the assault on the *Vorwärts* building: 'After the recapture of *Vorwärts*... a woman comrade, sent out to discover what was happening in the Rote Fahne offices, was seized on the street by the soldiery, who mistook her for Rosa Luxemburg and subjected her to long hours of frightful treatment before she finally managed to escape. It left no doubt as to Rosa's fate if she were caught. But when her "double" described the death threats and warned her to flee, she emphatically rejected the idea, explaining that she and Karl had to remain in Berlin to prevent the defeat of the workers from leading to their demoralisation.' Ibid., p. 295.

The Spartacists had actually been defending the building militarily for weeks, using rolls of paper erected as barricades around the entrance. This misrepresentation, for comic effect, is based upon the following account:
As bloodless as the occupation of the Vorwärts had been, as fatal was the following confusion and weakness. Karl Grubusch tried hard to coordinate the defense of the Vorwärts but he had little authority and the tiniest measure was discussed for hours in a randomly formed board of twenty to thirty people. ... when someone suggested pushing through the basement walls to create escape ways in case of an artillery attack, the proposal was voted down. Some of the most naïve among the occupiers refused to believe in an artillery attack until bullets started hitting the building...

By Thursday, the entire quarter around the Vorwärts was sealed off, although traffic was still allowed through. On the street corners, the troops had built pyramids of rifles and machine guns. Passersby were searched for weapons. All this happened under the eyes of Berlin's one million inhabitants, almost all of whom remained passive. Had larger segments of the population been truly revolutionary-minded, the troops could have been disarmed easily...
Karl Retzlaw, 'Noske and the Beginning of the Comrades' Murders', *All Power to the Councils*, pp. 131–2.

Pages 162–3
In the early morning, the unequal fight began. It ended after a few hours with our surrender. The government troops had advanced on the building from all sides in the cover of darkness. They had brought heavy machine guns, cannons, and mortars in position at a distance of about three to four hundred meters. Snipers lay on the roofs and behind the chimneys of the neighboring buildings. The snipers had clear sight into the Vorwärts building, which had large windows, and into the surrounding yards. Anyone defending the Vorwärts was an easy target....
We were still hoping that the workers of Berlin would come to our rescue. For days, rumors had been circulating among the occupants that hundreds of thousands of workers would attack the Noske troops from behind. We were eager to believe it. ...we were told that the workers of the Schwarzkopf factories and a thousand armed men from Spandau were coming to help. Repeatedly, we believed we heard signals behind the Noske troops. But those were all illusions. With this account, I do not want to discredit any of the men who were in the Vorwärts that day. Most of them had probably been social democrats before the occupation. They had no experience in revolutionary struggle and were obviously stunned that their party comrades in government mercilessly attacked them by means not used in Germany since 1848. Kaiser Wilhelm II had talked about soldiers possibly having to shoot their fathers and mothers, but he never ordered them to do so. The social democrats Ebert and Noske did.
Only a few brave men answered the fire of the government troops. They fought with such heart and determination that the government troops did not dare a direct assault. I carried water and ammunition from room to room. The only weapons and bullets we had were the ones found in the building...
With heavy machine guns, the Noske troops shattered all the windows and front walls of the Vorwärts and the neighboring buildings. When we

refused to surrender two hours into the fight, they continued with artillery fire. Grenades came through the walls, tore down jutties, and covered the building in dust. At times, the dust became so thick that we could no longer see. In some rooms, the gas lines were damaged and fires broke out. This caused panic among the occupiers who were ready to surrender. They ran through the hallways yelling, "Gas! Gas!" Ibid., pp. 132–3

It is worth contextualising this account with the fact that a considerable amount of weaponry, including machine guns and ammunition, had been found in the *Vorwärts* building. It was an ominous sign that the SPD government were planning brutal military repression.

Page 164

If any military weapons experts wish to point out that this picture shows a British, not a German tank, yes, it does. It was a captured British tank, painted up in German colours, which was actually used on the streets of Berlin in 1918–9 against the Spartacists.

People crowded into the room where Grubusch and others still tried to coordinate the defense, pleading with them to hand over the building.

Karl Grubusch and the poet Werner Möller offered to lead a delegation to negotiate. They left the building with five other men, waving white sheets. None of them ever returned. We saw their mutilated corpses two hours later in the courtyard of the Dragoner barracks in Belle Alliance Street. Shot, stabbed, and beaten, their corpses lay openly among laughing Noske troops, many of whom were covered in blood...

...they told us to put down our weapons and to leave the building one by one with the hands above our heads. We were about three hundred people, among them a number of women wearing Red Cross armbands...

We were ordered to line up in rows of four. Then we were escorted to the Dragoner barracks, our arms still up in the air. All the while, the Noske soldiers whipped us and beat us with their rifle butts...

When we arrived at the Dragoner barracks, we were led into the yard with the massacred envoys. Heavy machine guns were put in place, the barrels pointing at us, ready to shoot. I stood in the front row. I was not afraid. I quickly took off my coat and laid it down in front of me. I guess I irrationally assumed it would be returned to my mother... But nothing happened. We stood there for several hours. As I got to learn later, the officers were on the phone with the Ebert government, demanding written approval

for the shooting of three hundred prisoners. Noske apparently encouraged them to shoot us, but refused to give a written order. Ibid., p. 134.

According to Karl Retzlaw's account, Noske said of the mass killings of radicals by Freikorps during March 1919: 'You play with matches, you get burned!' Ibid., p. 140.

Page 165

'...the incitement against Spartakus, which had begun in the very first days of the revolution amid the ecstatic declarations of brotherhood, had become by January the chorus of raving sadists... The heights of unabashed shamelessness, never mind of brutal frankness, were scaled by *Vorwärts* on 13 January with its publication of a poem by Artur Zickler, a regular contributor—he later wrote an apology in the paper—which ended with the verse:
Many hundred corpses in a row—
Proletarians!
Karl, Radek, Rosa and Co.—
Not one of them is there, not one of them is there!
Proletarians!'
P. Frölich, *Rosa Luxemburg: Ideas in Action*, p. 298.

'...the so-called Reichstag Regiment, founded by the SPD. The true colours of this institution, officially known as the "Auxiliary Service of the SPD, Section 14", were later exposed in the libel proceedings conducted against a certain Herr Prinz. According to the findings of the court, [the Reichstag Regiment], in the names of Philipp Scheidemann and the regiment's financial backer, Georg Skarz (an evil grafter and speculator), set a price of 100,000 Marks on the heads of Karl Liebknecht and Rosa Luxemburg. Hesel, the officer in charge of Section 14... declared under oath that Fritz Henk, Scheidemann's son-in-law, had expressly confirmed... that the offer of the reward was serious and that money was available for such a purpose. A host of other members of the regiment confirmed this testimony, reiterating that an order to murder Liebknecht and Luxemburg had been given though it had never been put into writing.' Ibid., p. 297.

Page 166

'Pieck heard one of the maids say, "I shall never forget how they knocked the poor woman down and dragged her around."' J.P. Nettl, *Rosa Luxemburg*, p. 489.

You see, I've just learned from the history of the past

few years, and looking farther back, from history as a whole, that one should not overestimate the impact or effect that one individual can have. Fundamentally the powerful, unseen, plutonic forces in the depths are at work, and they are decisive, and in the end everything straightens itself out, so to speak, "of its own accord." Luxemburg, *Letters*, p. 392.

Page 173

I lie there quietly, alone, wrapped in these many-layered black veils of darkness, boredom, lack of freedom, and winter—and at the same time my heart is racing with an incomprehensible, unfamiliar inner joy as though I were walking across a flowering meadow in radiant sunshine. And in the dark I smile at life, as if I knew some sort of magical secret that gives the lie to everything evil and sad and changes it into pure light and happiness. And all the while I'm searching within myself for some reason for this joy, I find nothing and must smile to myself again—and laugh at myself. I believe that the secret is nothing other than life itself; the deep darkness of night is so beautiful and as soft as velvet, if one only looks at it the right way; and in the crunching of the damp sand beneath the slow, heavy steps of the sentries a beautiful small song of life is being sung—if one only knows how to listen properly. At such moments I think of you and I would like so much to pass on this magical key to you, so that always and in all situations you would be aware of the beautiful and the joyful, so that you too would live in a joyful euphoria as though you were walking across a multi-colored meadow. Luxemburg, *Letters*, p.455.

Page 174

These are Rosa Luxemburg's last written words, 'Order reigns in Berlin' written the night before her death and published in *Die Rote Fahne*, 14 January 1919. Translation by Peggy Wright. From *The Rosa Luxemburg Reader*, p. 378:

The leadership failed. But the leadership can and must be created anew by the masses and out of the masses. The masses are the crucial factor; they are the rock on which the ultimate victory of the revolution will be built. The masses were up to the task. They fashioned this "defeat" into part of those historical defeats which constitute the pride and power of international socialism. And that is why this "defeat" is the seed of future triumph.

"Order reigns in Berlin!" You stupid lackeys! Your "order" is built on sand. The revolution will "rise up again clashing", and to your horror it will proclaim to the sound of trumpets: I was, I am, I shall be.

Page 176

*Actually, right now, today, I want to recite a poem to you out of my head, it came back to me last night— God knows why. It's by Conrad Ferdinand Meyer, the dear Swiss author who also wrote **Jürg Jenatsch**. Sit down now, take Mimi in your lap, and put that dear reverent, sheepish look on your face, as you are accustomed to do when I read something out loud to you. Now then. Silentium!*

Hutten's Confession

Here now I step across a grave, my own.
Now, Hutten, won't you your confession make?
Good Christian custom. I will beat my breast.
What person has no consciousness of guilt?
How I regret my late-come sense of duty,
Regret my heart did not burn hot enough,
Regret I did not enter into battle
With sharper blows and with far greater zeal,
Regret that only one time I was banished,
Regret that often I knew human fears,
Regret the day I struck no wounding blow,
Regret the hour when I no armor wore,
And, overcome now with remorse, regret
That I was not three times more keen and bold.

You can have the closing part of this poem placed over my grave... Did you take that seriously Mathilde? Hey, laugh at it. On my grave, as in my life, there will be no pompous phrases. Only two syllables will be allowed to appear on my gravestone: "Tsvee-tsvee." That is the call made by the large blue titmouse, which I can imitate so well that they all immediately come running. And just think, in this call, which is usually quite clear and thin, sparkling like a steel needle, in the last few days there has been quite a low, little trill, a tiny chesty sound. And do you know what that means, Miss Jacob? That is the first soft stirring of the coming spring.
Luxemburg, *Letters*, pp. 372–3.

Afterword

The reader of this comic will naturally want to know what happened next, in other words, how Rosa Luxemburg's legacy became intertwined with the history of socialists and associated radicals in what has been almost a century since her death. The second volume of J. P. Nettl's monumental biographical work provides within its last pages a narrative, by no means exhaustive, of how she fared in posterity over thirty years or so after her assassination. Readers can turn to those pages for many arresting details. But it should be noted here that two astonishing events followed Luxemburg's death within a year or so, and together set the pattern for the collective memory of her life and work almost up to the present.

On the one hand, the 1920 publication of *Brief an Freunde* (Letters to Friends), a small book of twenty-two letters and postcards, had an outsize impact. Not only communists but socialists and many liberals embraced and exalted this historic figure and brilliant literary personage within German culture—a status denied her in life. The publishers noted in the introduction that her readers and supporters "have the right to see how this woman, rising above all her own sufferings, embraced all the products of creation with understanding love and truly poetic power, how her heart leapt up at the song of a bird, how vibrant and exalted lines of verse echoed in her soul, how she kept the secrets of both fateful events and everyday doings in the lives of her friends."

On the other hand, a destructive political struggle within the Left itself over her legacy began almost from the day of her murder. Entirely contrary to her insistence that no "Luxemburgites" existed or needed to exist, her supposed authority rapidly became a political football. The underground KPD (the German Communist Party), trying to organize itself secretly, hailed Luxemburg as an authority on nearly all subjects of theory, as well as an inspiration to revolutionary struggle. The overwhelming influence of Moscow drove this effort, and twisted it to suit an assortment of aims.

Her most ardent followers, Paul Levi first of all, understandably fell out of favour when they arranged for the reprinting of Luxemburg's criticisms of Leninism. Lenin himself had famously recited her "errors" but praised her as an "eagle" of revolution. The tortured official Comintern position became something different: she had "changed her mind" and, since she supported the Russian Revolution, would have supported the Dictatorship of the Proletariat. Clara Zetkin's capitulation to this view seemed

214

to many of their mutual friends both a personal and political betrayal.

It is fair to say that Luxemburg, the real Luxemburg, her life and writings, were no longer seen as central, except as appeals to sentiment and no less to a constructed historical narrative. After repeated further tussles over her legacy within the German Left, and as Trotsky and Trotskyism became the enemies of the emerging leaders in the Comintern, she became an ideological enemy. Even in Germany she became the heretic of Bolshevik theory and practice. Explicitly denounced as a deviationist, with her supposed belief in "spontaneity" substituting for the creation of Communist parties' discipline and styles of organization, she would become, after Lenin's death, a useful ghost for Stalin. Leninism had already been acclaimed the only valid Marxism, in Lenin's time. Therefore, Luxemburg's activities and ideas, "historical" at best, now became suspect from start to finish. Stalin himself completed the process in 1931 by explaining that German Bolsheviks had forced an unwilling Luxemburg to fight against the conservative, pro-war German socialists. Luxemburgism, not only but especially in Germany, represented the road back to the Yellow International of traitorous Social Democrats.

Nor was Stalinism alone in transforming Rosa Luxemburg into a creature of the political imagination. More kindly by far, the followers of Leon Trotsky, in parts of Europe but especially in the US (where for long periods the densest population of them was to be found) took up her cause. Their journals published many essays hailing her as the great leader who, if she had lived, would surely have agreed with Trotsky and supported his strategies. Trotsky himself took on the polemical task of cursing the "spontaneists," young socialist enthusiasts in France who called themselves followers of Luxemburg but declined to believe in the Vanguard Party. These quasi-anarchists needed to be unmasked as deviationists, distorters of her legacy. Indeed, she would become all the more valuable to Trotskyists because Stalin and Stalinism had turned against her. Reform-minded socialists as well as left-socialists (usually the youth movement) nevertheless continued to share their martyr with the followers of Trotsky. The overlapping categories of Rosa's devotees tended to merge over time, with the general decline of the old-time Left movements.

That said, the most frequent reprintings of Luxemburg's essays, again through small editions of various parts of her literary oeuvre, appeared in the journals and pamphlets of the Trotskyist movement in many parts of the world. Come the 1950s and early 1960s, disillusionment with Stalinism was spreading. Rumours circulated about institutional anti-Semitism and slave labour camps. With the crushing of the Hungarian Rebellion and Russian leader Nikita Khruschev's own repudiation of Stalin at the Soviet Congress of 1956, her reputation was bound to revive. Among the odd corners of such enthusiasm in the world, one of the oddest became a chief outlet, for a little while, of Luxemburg's pamphlets in the English language. In Ceylon, the colonial British island destined to become Sri Lanka, a leading leftwing independence party considered itself part of a barely existent Fourth International—the international body of Trotskyist parties—and proudly reprinted her pamphlets for popular education. This literature, sent from

Ceylon to the Socialist Workers Party headquarters in New York, was thence distributed in North America and presumably beyond, mostly to youthful enthusiasts.

New Leftists of Europe, the US and Canada, no doubt inspired in part by the appearance of the Nettl volumes, began even in the middle of the 1960s to treat Luxemburg as a female, then feminist, archetype, the revolutionary heroine who is fearless in politics, life and love. In the US, she could be placed alongside anarchist icon Emma Goldman, a pairing that would no doubt have made both of them uncomfortable in real life, especially considering the conflicts between anarchists and socialists of the 1910s. In Germany and some other parts of Europe, New Left parades and demonstrations held up banners of Luxemburg's name and face, the first time since the early 1920s. A handful of professors, especially in the US where new campuses sprung up like mushrooms, and with them the paperback market for classroom texts, meanwhile took a related but not entirely similar tack. In the hands of some prominent scholars, Rosa Luxemburg became what Stalin's distortions had tried to make her: a social democrat whose faith in "democracy" now included modern, reformed capitalism, someone who would have rejected not only Communism Russian-style but also Third World revolutionary movements with their direct-action agendas.

These views had broadened and changed, even by the early 1970s, in interesting ways. Sections of the New Left found in her writings on the general strike an invigorating, quasi-syndicalist formulation. There had also been an intriguing, under-documented parallel adoption or adaptation in South Africa under Apartheid. During the struggles of the African National Congress against the repressive South African state of the 1950s–'80s, experienced activists report that her writings were widely consulted during repeated waves of mass strikes. They found that the very act of striking was perforce an assault on the State, much as Luxemburg had suggested more than a half-century earlier. Her critique of Leninism itself was recovered, most notably by South African Communist Party leader Joe Slovo, but only after the fall of the Eastern Bloc.

Meanwhile, the generation of New Leftists had graduated into scholarship, and anthologies of her writings in fresh translations began to appear in numbers, not only in German and English languages, accompanied by scores and then hundreds of articles. Her following could properly be described as generically Left, the possession of no group or particular set of ideas, a milieu broadened by the "art film" audience of the 1986 German film *Die Geduld der Rosa Luxemburg,* directed by Margarethe von Trotta and widely seen elsewhere (titled in English: *Rosa Luxemburg*) with subtitles.

This process of popular recognition has continued with the emergence of still younger generations into the twenty-first century, perhaps tied most of all to the anti-austerity movements sweeping many parts of the globe. Her insistence that the expansion of Empire is at once the salvation of capitalism and doom for the planet is an ecological insight of ever-greater value for radicals drawn to her ideas and example. Marxist economists from Paul Sweezy to Samir Amin found in her studies, notably *The Accumulation of Capital,* much fruitful insight for an increasingly perilous situation. David

Harvey, perhaps the most admired popular interpreter of Marxism today, has recently made a special case for Luxemburg's grasp of the connections between ecology, class and empire.

The German case for her memory is, of course, a special one. On the West German side, Rosa Luxemburg's political heritage was claimed in particular by the left wing of the Social Democratic Party, of which Luxemburg had been a member most of her political life, and in particular by the Socialist Youth of Germany (SJD—Die Falken) which is loosely affiliated with the SPD. For decades, this organization has held up Rosa Luxemburg and Karl Liebknecht as two of the leading representatives of "a socialism that is inspired by the ideals of internationalism, anti-militarism, justice, and radical democracy."

The founding of the East German state or DDR inevitably rendered Luxemburg a favourite martyr, a source for street names and more than occasional official declarations. The enthusiasm displayed by the state was more than a little ironic. The yearly parades for Luxemburg and Liebknecht, in January, the month of their murder, took on a new significance when a small contingent in 1988 carried signs with her statement "Freedom Is the Right to Disagree" (Freiheit für Andersdenkende); other posters read "Freie Wahlen" (Free Elections) and "Luxemburg im DDR-Gefängnis" (Luxemburg in GDR Prison). They were hustled away by police, of course. But the end was near for Stalinism. The turn had been made in Luxemburg's memory, already, with the founding of the Rosa Luxemburg Stiftung in 1990. The creation of Die Linke, the Left Party, whose electoral status eventually allowed the Stiftung to become a modest global force for change, thus both inspired our volume and made it possible.

The fuller story has not yet been told, and will require much additional work in published sources and through oral histories of activists. It is a story without easy generalizations. Our own work, as artist and editor, is itself part of that continuing saga, as is the larger project of the Rosa Luxemburg Stiftung and Verso, publisher of the many volumes of her writings and letters, much of which is still forthcoming.

Acknowledgments

From the editor: Thanks go to Pallo Jordan, for information and insights about the reception of Rosa Luxemburg. Likewise to Luxemburg scholars Peter Hudis and Kevin Anderson for encouragement and scholarly assistance along the way. Most of all, our thanks go to Andrew Hsiao, our Verso editor, and to Albert Scharenberg and Stefanie Ehmsen, co-directors of the New York office of the Rosa Luxemburg Stiftung.

From the author and artist: It has been an honour and a pleasure to immerse myself in Rosa Luxemburg's life, and I hope my representation of her does her justice. I would like to thank Albert Scharenberg and Stefanie Ehmsen from the Rosa Luxemburg Stiftung as well as Andrew Hsiao at Verso for making this book happen. Seth Tobocman first suggested me for the job, for which I definitely owe him a drink. Rory Castle has been my touchstone for all things Rosa, and the academic and practical assistance of Till Bender, Henry Holland, Jörn Schütrumpf and Holger Politt is much appreciated. I am indebted to the staff at Die Falken for showing me the Kautskys' house, and Herr Kramer at the Deutsches Technikmuseum for his demonstration of nineteenth-century printing techniques. Linda McQueen's eagle eyes stripped the manuscript of errors. Hamie Wilkinson helped with the birdlife, Pippa with the wildlife, and Rachel Dredd and Lynne Vitale with the homelife. For my friends, including but not limited to Joy, Cai, Nadine, Gaeton, Denny, Jenny, Ellie and Chesh, thanks a million. My children made so many sacrifices and so many distractions, my sisters kept me sane, and my husband, Donach McKenna, thank you, because your unfailing love and enthusiasm carried me through.

Brief Bibliography

Inasmuch as *Red Rosa* is a comic, and inasmuch as the Luxemburg scholarship is growing significantly, we mention here only currently available English-language works. It is valuable to note, however, how thin the body of scholarship has been until recent times, given that Luxemburg is a major figure in twentieth-century socialist movements. The biography written by an intimate and political comrade, Paul Frölich, doubtless conveyed her to the life. Whatever the scholarly limitations of Frölich's work may be, it will remain mandatory.

So, one presumes, would the seemingly definitive—at least for its time—two-volume biography by distinguished scholar J. P. Nettl. This 900-plus-page tome was to a large extent about the Second International setting of Luxemburg, with no claim to penetrate her inner life or, in certain ways, her personal or political development, especially regarding her younger years. A reason for this limitation is obvious and has long remained a daunting prospect for Luxemburg scholars: the Polish background, her early essays and her efforts in the Polish leftwing press, a world connected with German social democracy but also a world of its own.

The political turmoil of the 1950s–60s and no less the rise of the Women's Liberation Movement all contributed heavily to the new scholarly interest in her work and life. Elizbieta Ettinger's *Rosa Luxemburg: A Life* seeks to penetrate a secret existence but in the process fills in the blanks with what can only be called biographer's inventions. One of the current key scholars of Luxemburg's work, Peter Hudis, comments that to go much further would require not only an in-depth knowledge of Polish- and Russian-language materials as well as of the German left politics of her lifetime, but also an intimate familiarity with economics in general, not only Marxist theories of economics. To go that far would surely take a team of authors.

Much of the literature with Luxemburg's name in the title or subtitle has historically been of the tendentious type, which is not necessarily to say inaccurate or uninteresting, but written at a substantial distance to primary sources. To speak only of the English-language material: the 1970s, more or less, brought this writing into existence, including some fresh translations in Dick Howard's 1971 anthology; Raya Dunayevskaya's somewhat rambling view of Luxemburg's contribution; Norman Geras' effort to place her beyond the limits of Bolshevism; and Italian Left (but not Communist) leader Lelio Basso's "reappraisal," published in London in the mid seventies. British Trotskyist leader Tony Cliff's work on Luxemburg, appearing in his group's journal back in 1959—spurred in part by the Hungarian uprising of three years earlier—was later published as a book that went through editions.

With the fading of the hopes set loose by the movements of the 1960s, discussion of Luxemburg seemed to fall into abeyance, or was left to group discussion again. Perhaps Annelise Laschitza's 1990s volume, never translated into English, was the first taste of yet another, this time post-Eastern Bloc, version of Luxemburg. Unpolemical, Laschitza's work set a new standard for another reason: she had access to letters previously unattainable, and became an editor of one of the volumes of Luxemburg's correspondence. What later scholars, including Peter Hudis and Kevin B. Anderson, have added is the outreach for essays not previously circulating in English, and a fresh approach to her life and work for its own sake, not as the subject of a political spin that would vindicate the scholar.

Select Titles

Major Biographies
Lelio Basso, *Rosa Luxemburg: A Reappraisal.* 1984.
Tony Cliff, *Rosa Luxemburg.* 1959, 1968, 1969, 1980.
Raya Dunayevskaya, *Rosa Luxemburg, Women's Liberation and Marx's Philosophy of Revolution.* 1982.
Elzbieta Ettinger, *Rosa Luxemburg: A Life,* 1988.
Paul Froelich, *Rosa Luxemburg: Her Life and Work,* 1939.
Norman Geras, *The Legacy of Rosa Luxemburg.* 1976.
David Harvey, *The New Imperialism.* 2003.
Annelise Laschitz, *Rosa Luxemburg: Im Lebensrauch, trotz alledem: Eine Biographie.* 2000.

Major Anthologies
Dick Howard, ed., *Rosa Luxemburg: Selected Political Writings.* 1971.
Peter Hudis, ed., *Rosa Luxemburg, Complete Works, Vol.I–II.* 2014. Ongoing.
Rosa Luxemburg, *Complete Works, Letters.* Forthcoming (Verso).

The Web
The Rosa Luxemburg Internet Archive
rosaluxemburgblog.wordpress.com